ARCHAEOLOGY OF BET DWARKA ISLAND

An Excavation Report

ARCHAEOLOGY OF BET DWARKA ISLAND
An Excavation Report

A.S. Gaur, Sundaresh & K.H. Vora

ARYAN BOOKS INTERNATIONAL
NEW DELHI

in association with

NATIONAL INSTITUTE OF OCEANOGRAPHY
GOA

ARCHAEOLOGY OF BET DWARKA ISLAND

ISBN-81-7305-298-0

First Published in **2005** by:
ARYAN BOOKS INTERNATIONAL
Pooja Apartments, 4B, Ansari Road, New Delhi-110 002 (India)
Tel.: 23287589, 23255799; Fax: 91-11-23270385, E-mail: aryanbooks@vsnl.com

in association with

NATIONAL INSTITUTE OF OCEANOGRAPHY
Dona Paula, Goa-403 004

Computer Typeset and Printed in India at
ABI Prints & Publishing Co., New Delhi

Dedicated

to

Dwarkadhish Temple of Bet Dwarka

Foreword

Marine archaeology deals with the study of ancient human settlement along the coasts of the world. Since 1981 the National Institute of Oceanography (NIO), a constituent laboratory of Council of Scientific Industrial Research (CSIR), is actively pursuing research in the field of Marine Archaeology of the Indian coasts. This research has led to important discoveries of ancient port-towns and shipwrecks. The areas explored include Dwarka, Bet Dwarka, Somnath, Sindhudurg, Vijaydurg, Goa, Poompuhar, and Lakshadweep. The findings from these explorations have been reported in national and international scientific and archaeological journals.

This report elucidates findings of an onshore excavation that was conducted at Bet Dwarka island in 2001. The excavation yielded a long cultural sequence beginning from the proto-historic period (1800 BC) to the medieval period. The artifacts like potsherds, beads, bones and shells, that have been recovered, provide new insights on the earlier civilizations of the region.

This book gives details of the onshore excavation and offshore exploration, and of scientific studies that have been carried out on the samples and artifacts that were recovered. It is hoped that the book will fulfill the need of scholars and students of history and archaeology of the Okhamandal region in general, and Bet Dwarka island, in particular.

S.R. Shetye
Director
National Institute of Oceanography

Preface

Strategically, Bet Dwarka island has played an important role in the maritime history of Okhamandal region of Gujarat State. This region has been the attraction for mariners since the Harappan times, as evident from the discovery of a Harappan site at Nageshwar, which is also one of the 12 *Jyotirlingas* of the *Saivism* cult. The primary objective of the early settler was to exploit the marine resources available in the Gulf region, particularly shells. Bet Dwarka island has been under habitation since the late Harappan times as evidenced by a late Indus-type seal which was discovered in 1986, and a large number of late Harappan pottery collected from the island. However, the habitation extended to many folds during the early historical period. The southeastern coast was habitated during the early historical period. Boats from the Mediterranean countries also visited the island as a large number of amphorae were recovered during offshore exploration near the present passenger jetty of the island. Further, the presence of different varieties of stone anchors in large number near the Bet Dwarka jetty suggest that this place has been serving as an anchoring point since historical times. Archaeological findings suggest that during the medieval period, the population of the island had increased significantly. The main occupation of the population was maritime activities and ceramic industry. Perhaps, a pond located in middle of the island, which has deposits of very fine clay for manufacturing pottery, was able to supply the required raw material. As per local information, till the early 70s, pottery from Bet Dwarka was exported to Saurashtra, Kachchh and Sind areas through coastal sea routes.

During the last two decades, the marine archaeological explorations around Bet Dwarka island necessitated the verification of the findings from offshore and inter-tidal zones with the huge archaeological deposit on the shore. The project review committee comprised of Dr. A.G. Untawale, then deputy director of NIO, Shri R.S. Bisht, then director of ASI, Prof. V.H. Sonawane, then Head, Department of Archaeology, MS University, Baroda, and Prof. S.N. Rajaguru, (Retired)

Deccan College, Pune. They suggested that a few trenches in the onshore region of the island should be excavated to understand the cultural sequence of the island and also the relation between the sea and man. With the above recommendations, the authors applied for a formal license to excavate a few trenches in the Bet Dwarka island, to the Archaeological Survey of India. The excavation was undertaken in December-January in the field season of 2001-2002. Six trenches were laid in different parts of the island, generally close to the shore, and excavated till virgin soil appeared in each trench. The results of the excavations at Bet Dwarka have been in the agreement of the earlier offshore and inter-tidal zones findings, although it has provided a few additional data on the settlement pattern, ancient industry, ancient tectonic disturbance and sea level changes around the Bet Dwarka island. The primary concern of the early man on the island was the exploitation of marine sources – particularly shells available around the island. Unlike the Okhamandal region, Bet Dwarka had an active cultural influence of Saurashtra and Kachchh, as most of the protohistoric and the historical period antiquities are found similar to above regions. The archaeological site has been dated by various scientific methods such as Accelerator Mass Spectroscopy (AMS), conventional carbon^{14} and thermoluminescence. The report consists of all scientific analysis undertaken by various scientific groups in the form of annexures such as tectonic activities, palaeobotanical study, zoological study, palaeo sea level variations around the island, besides the regular archaeological findings. The entire report has been presented in the seven segments of the book such as introduction, which consists of introduction to the report, geological and geographical background of the area, local and traditional information, archaeological background, besides environmental background of the region. The second chapter is dedicated to chronology, dealing with cultural and scientific dates obtained from the site. Planning and layout of trenches and structural findings, and identification of layers have been described in Chapter Three. Chapter Four deals with the antiquities discovered during the excavations, which include beads of terracotta, shell, glass, stone and fish bone, copper objects, coins, shell bangles and iron objects. The Fifth Chapter comprises of the detailed description of pottery of the protohistoric and historical period, and the last chapter deals with the shell remains from the island of Bet Dwarka. Besides the above chapters, there are seven annexures which include a late Harappan copper fishhook, signatures of earthquake during the early historical times, shoreline changes around the Bet Dwarka island, pollen analysis, animal bones, underwater investigations around Bet Dwarka island and conservation of antiquities. It is hoped that this report will help in understanding the maritime activities of the Okhamandal region and the cultural sequence of the Bet Dwarka island.

A.S. Gaur
Sundaresh
K.H. Vora

Contents

ANNEXURES

Acknowledgements

We are grateful to the Director General of the Archaeological Survey of India, New Delhi, for granting license to undertake excavations in Bet Dwarka island. Our thanks are also due to the Director, National Institute of Oceanography, Goa, for the support and permission to undertake onshore excavations towards the cause of permanent settlement of the archaeological problem of the Bet Dwarka island. Dr. Y.S. Rawat, Director, Department of Archaeology, Government of Gujarat, Ahmedabad, extended his support in this excavation by forwarding our proposal to the Archaeological Survey of India. He examined antiquities of the excavation and important pottery and also helped in identifying the antiquities and their archaeological context.

We are thankful to Dr. S.R. Rao, Father of Marine Archaeology in India for his valuable guidance in conducting underwater research in Okhamandal region. We thank members of the Marine Archaeology Project review committee, which include Dr. A.G. Untawale, Shri R.S. Bisht, Prof. V.H. Sonawane, and Prof. S.N. Rajaguru for recommending the excavation in Bet Dwarka to understand the cultural sequence and their relations with underwater findings. We are thankful to Prof. A.K. Singhvi, Physical Research Laboratory, Ahmedabad for Thermoluminescence dates of potsherds. We also thank Dr. C.P. Rajendran and Dr. Kushala Rajendran of the Centre for Earth Science Studies, Akkulam, Thiruvananthapuram, who inspected our excavated trenches for any possible signature of tectonic activities and they could trace some features in trench BDK-II which is located on the southeastern coast of the island. They were also helpful in obtaining two radiocarbon dates with Accelerator Mass Spectroscopy (AMS) method. Our thanks are also due to the Director, Birbal Sahani Institute of Palaeobotany, Lucknow, for providing conventional radiocarbon dates. Prof. Shiela Mishra visited the site during the excavation and suggested various points for better interpretation of the artifacts. Shri Pushkarbhai Gokani, a well-known historian of the Okhamandal region, encouraged us by discussing various archaeological problems of the region.

Dr. Anjum Farooqui of BSIP, Lucknow, analysed the palaeobotanical remains of the site. Dr. P.P. Joglekar of Deccan College, Pune, identified the animal bones from the excavated region. Shri Vardhan Patankar, a student of the Marine Science Department of Goa University, identified the remains of the shells found during the excavation. Dr. Rahul Mohan went through a few initial chapters and suggested some corrections. We thank them all.

Our sincere thanks go to Dr. Sila Tripati and Shri S.N. Bandodkar who helped us with the initial stages of the excavation; Shri Bandodkar also assisted us in the photography of shells and other artifacts in the lab; Shri Satish B. Chitari, who helped in laying down the trenches, and in preparing all the section drawings at the site and in the lab and also all the drawings of pottery and antiquity. Without his support, this massive work would not have been completed. We are also thankful to Shri Sham Akerkar, Shri R. Uchil, Shri Pramod Pawasker and Shri Arun Mahale, who helped in preparing the line drawings for this report; Shri Umesh Sirsat who took all the photographs at the site and in the lab; Shri Shaikh Ali Karim, who helped in the photography of antiquities; Shri G.R. Desai, who helped in various activities in the laboratory. We thank them all.

Last but not the least, we thank some local residents of the island without whose cooperation and support this work would not have been possible. For smooth conduct of the excavation, we remain thankful to Shri Hemat Vadher, resident of Bet Dwarka, who provided us with hotel accommodation and allowed us to lay down a few trenches in his agricultural land. Shri Suleman Abbas and Shri Rajjaq helped us by arranging the labourers and other requirements in the field. Shri Munna Bhai provided us with good food and a homely environment, which made our stay in the remote island very comfortable. We thank all the residents of the Bet Dwarka island who helped us with their support and coordination during the excavations. We are also indebted to Shri Vikas Arya of Aryan Books International for doing an excellent job in the production of the book.

Acronyms

AA - American Anthropology
AI - Ancient India
AJA - American Journal of Archaeology
AMS - Accelerator Mass Spectroscopy
ASI - Archaeological Survey of India
BAIMA - Bulletin of the Australian Institute of Maritime Archaeology
BC - Before Christ
BDCPRI - Bulletin of the Deccan College Post-Graduate and Research Institute
BDK - Bet Dwarka Island
BSIP - Birbal Sahni Institute of Palaeobotany, Lucknow
CS - Current Science
IAR - Indian Archaeology – A Review
IJES - Indian Journal of Earth Science
IJMS - Indian Journal of Marine Sciences
IJNA - International Journal of Nautical Archaeology
JGSI - Journal of Geological Society of India
JMA - Journal of Marine Archaeology
JOIB - Journal of Oriental Institute of Baroda
MAC - Marine Archaeology Centre
MAIOC - Marine Archaeology of Indian Ocean Countries
MASI - Memoir of Archaeological Survey of India

ME - Man and Environment
MM - Mariner's Mirror
NBP - Northern Black Polished Ware
NIO - National Institute of Oceanography
PRL - Physical Research Laboratory, Ahmedabad
RAMA - Recent Advances in Marine Archaeology
RURIMA - The Role of Universities and Research Institutes in Marine Archaeology
TL - Thermoluminescence Dates
WA - World Archaeology

List of Illustrations

FIGURES

PLATES

43. A. Opaque, black unidentified debris are less in number followed by amorphous organic matter. Few gelified tissues, filamentous debris and fungal fruiting body. Large size particles. B & C. Black unidentified debris increase in percentage. Amorphous debris decrease in size. Poorly sorted debris with round edges. D. Small size particles. Black unidentified opaque particles, more in number. Few elongated lath-shaped debris also present. Algal bodies present. E. Brown to black organic matter. Amorphous debris, low in number. Photomicrographs of palynomorphs and zooplanktons from Bet Dwarka island recovered mostly from surface (10 cm) and below 100 cm in BDK-I and at 95 cm in BDK-VI sedimentary soil sequence.
44. *Rhizophoraceae* 1 to 3; *Aegiceras* 4; *Excoecaria* 5; *Duranta* 6; *Aegiceras* 7; *Meliaceae* 8; *Anacardeaceae* 9; *Heritiera* 10; *Schefflera* 11; *Chenopodiaceae* 12; *Euphorbiaceae* 13; *Pinus* 14; *Aquatic pollen* 15; *Casuarina* 16; *Acacia* 17; *Hopea* 18; *Myrtaceae* 19; *Heritiera* 20; *Oleaceae* 21; *Chrozophora* 22; *Poaceae* 23; *Cyperaceae* 24; *Caryophyllaceae* 25; *Umbelliferae* 26; *Urticaceae* 27; *Asteraceae* 28; *Elaeocarpus* 29, 30; *Polyalthia* 31; *Aquatic pollen* 32; *Poaceae* 33-35.
45. Photomicrographs of monolete/trilete, marine acritarchs and unidentified palynomorphs.
46. Wholly marine multicellular/multinucleate vescicles or segments of Siphonocladales in *Dictyospharia* (Benthic green algae) 1-3; Algal fruiting bodies 4-10; Algal filament of *Rhizoclonium ?* 11; *Celyphus rallus* grows in an intermediate mildly saline environment 12; *Oocystis* 13.
47. *Cystopus cadidus* 3; *Gleocapsomorpa* 7; Multicellular thalloid body 9; *Tetraploa* 10; Rest Fungal fruiting body 1, 2, 4-6, 8. Insect wing 11; Protozoan cyst 12; Marine zooplankton 13; Marine chitinous exo-skeleton. Crustacean remain?
48. Photomicrographs of different types of phytoclasts. Upper leaf epidermal surface of *Avicennia* showing salt gland in the centre 1; Biostructured phytoclast (trachieds) 2; Opaque structured phytoclast 3; Lath-shaped opaque black unidentifiable organic debris 4; Outer cellular margin identifiable but inner portion gelified 5; Transparent cellular structure 6; Amorphous organic matter 7; Filamentous identifiable cellular brown phytoclast with irregular margins 8; Resinous particle 9.
49. Copper fishhook from BDK-VI.
50. A. Composite plate showing the ancient sand blow on the northern wall, formed over the oldest occupation level at site BDK-II. B. Sketch of the northern trench wall showing level 11 and the overlying sand blow deposit.
51. Sand vent (dashed line) exposed on the southern wall at BDK-II.
52. Schematic model showing stages of earthquake-induced sand blow at Bet Dwarka.
53. Measurement present shoreline and the oldest habitation at BDK-I.
54. Section facing to the sea near BDK-I.
55. Composite stone anchor from Bet Dwarka.
56. Composite stone anchor with four holes from Bet Dwarka.
57. Grapnel stone anchor lying off Bet Dwarka.
58. Circular lead anchor from Bet Dwarka waters.
59. Circular lead anchor from Bet Dwarka waters.
60. Lead ingot from Bet Dwarka waters.
61. Unidentified stone artifact from Bet Dwarka.
62. Upper portion of an amphora from Bet Dwarka waters.

Chapter I
Introduction

Indian sub-continent has been the focal point of human activity since the earliest times, and all phases of human development have been recorded in history. When the major rivers of the world witnessed the rise of well-developed civilizations, Indus-Saraswati valleys also did not remain unaffected in the 3rd millennium BC. Alternatively known as Harappan civilization, it was spread in the widest area (among the contemporary civilizations), encompassing what is presently known as Pakistan, Southern Afghanistan, Jammu-Kashmir, Punjab, Haryana, Rajasthan, Uttar Pradesh, Gujarat and Maharashtra. The town-planning, internal trade network, uniformity in pottery, script and many other aspects in day-today life, defer the Indus civilization from the rest of the contemporary civilizations of the world. Mesopotamian texts have mentioned the import of several items from the Indian Territory (Ratnagar, 1981). Mention has been made that boats of *Meluhha* (identified with western parts of Indian sub-continent) are anchored in Agade harbour (Kramer, 1964). The excavations in the several Mesopotamian sites and other Gulf countries have provided evidence of the active presence of Indians in their region (Frankfort, 1933; Rao, 1973; and Cleuziou, 1992). Now, it is popularly believed that climatic conditions (Singh, 1971 and Naidu, 1996) and other natural factors (Sahni, 1956; Raikes, 1964) were responsible for the collapse of the Indus civilization. However, maritime activities initiated in that period continued in many parts adjacent to coastal areas of India, even after the decline of the Harappans. During the Mauryan Period, maritime activities again gained momentum and led to the establishment of a department whose chief was called *Navadhyksha*. Subsequently, navigators of the Mediterranean Sea also arrived on the Indian coast in search of spice and silk. They traded for nearly seven centuries and left several legacies in social and cultural aspects. Next came the Arab traders, who took over the control of trade network in the Indian Ocean and continued for a long period until the arrival of the Europeans in the beginning of the 16th century AD (Hourani, 1975).

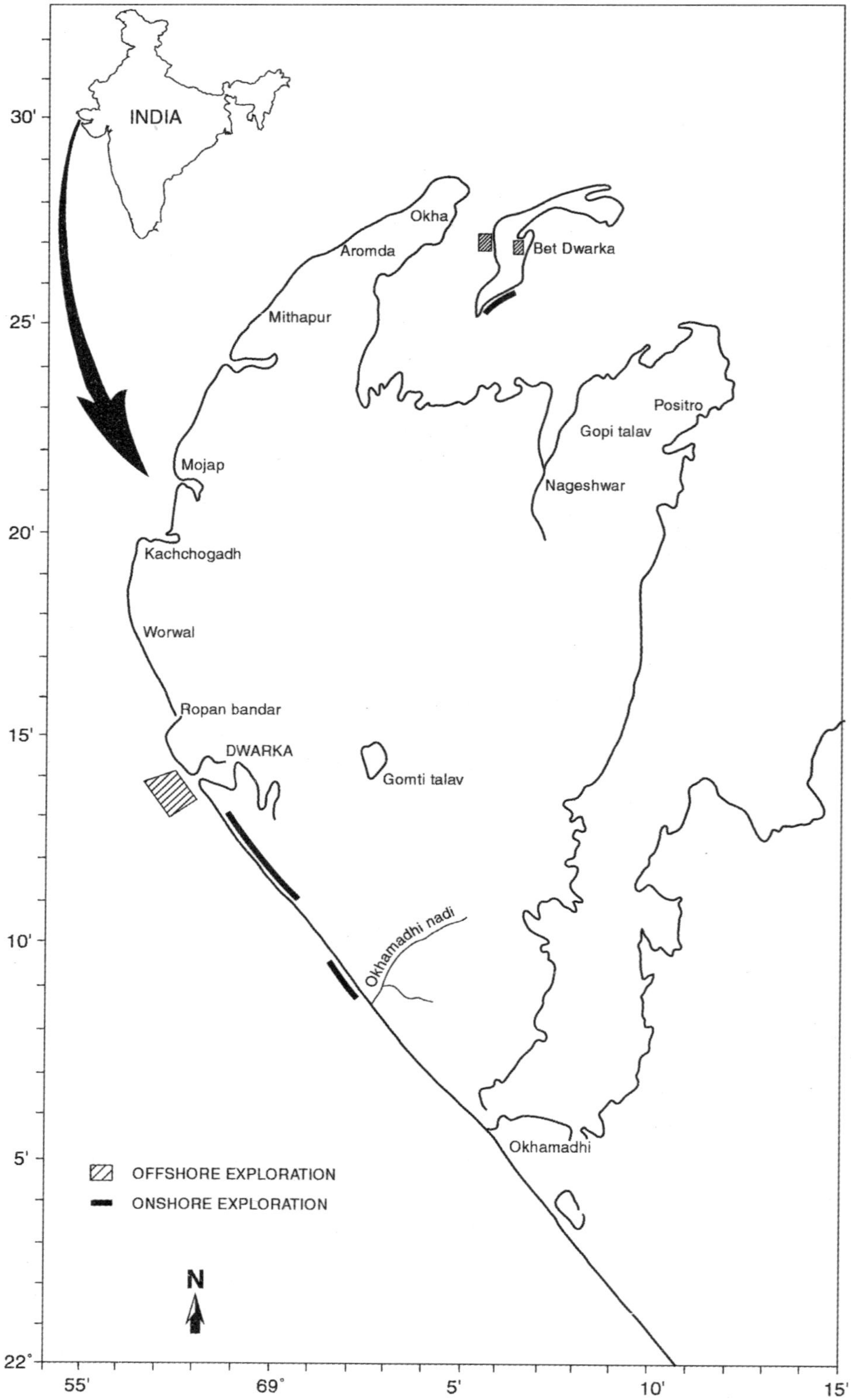

Fig. 1. Map showing archaeological sites in Okhamandal region of Gujarat.

The archaeological explorations at Bet Dwarka island during the last one-and-half decade, brought to light a large number of data on India's external overseas trade and commerce with the western and eastern countries. The Gujarat province has a distinguished record of having the oldest remains in the field of trade and commerce, legacies of which continue till date. The remains of the past maritime activities in Gujarat opened up a vast scope for the marine archaeological research in India. A massive program of marine archaeological investigations was launched in the Okhamandal area and this resulted in the recovery of a large number of antiquities related to past maritime activities. The important sites were Dwarka, Bet Dwarka, Aramda and Somnath. The archaeological remains on the Bet Dwarka island date back to the 18th century BC. During 1999-2000, NIO set up an experts committee for mid-term review and on-site visit, comprising of A.G. Untawale, R.S. Bisht, V.H. Sonawane and S.N. Rajaguru. The committee suggested to undertake onshore excavations at Bet Dwarka island to understand cultural sequence. Following their suggestions, a program for onshore excavation was launched in December 2001 and January 2002.

Bet Dwarka is the third site in Okhamandal (Fig. 1) which was systematically excavated after Nageshwar (by M.S. University, Baroda) and Dwarka (by Deccan College, Pune, and Archaeological Survey of India, Baroda Circle). Nageshwar is a proto-historic site while for Dwarka, the findings of the two excavators are contradictory. However, there is a consensus on the historical period evidence. Bet Dwarka island, which is isolated from the mainland, has a unique location. This serves as an entry point to the Gulf of Kachchh on the one hand, and it is near to the main land, on the other. This island witnessed a long cultural sequence, which commenced from the late phase of the Harappan Period. From flimsy remains, it appears that the early settlers might have visited the island scantily, as no traces of regular habitation have been found here. However, historical period witnessed sporadic settlement in different parts of the island. While comparing the historical period material of Dwarka and Bet Dwarka, no similarity in pottery, antiquity, trade and industry is observed. Sankalia (1966:14) stated that pottery from the lowest level of Dwarka appears to be local phenomena, which is confined to a small area of not more than a mile in circumference. The early historical pottery of Bet Dwarka has a lot of similarity with many other sites of the Saurashtra, and other parts of India. A number of shapes of pottery and other antiquity are comparable with findings from Amreli, Hastinapur, Prakash, Nagda, etc. Another important factor, which seems to have attracted ancient people, is the ample availability of chank shells, which were exploited in a large scale during the entire occupational periods.

1.1 PROBLEM

Religiously, Okhamandal has been an important place in a number of ways such as Dwarka, which is one of the four *Dhamas* of *Vaishanavism*, and Nageshwar is one of the twelve *Jyotirlingas* of *Shaivism*. Similarly associated with Dwarka, there are many other villages in the Okhamandal region which have religious significance (Fig. 1). Attempts were made in the early decades of the 20th century to identify the original Dwarka of the *Mahabharata* from literature, and it was in 1963 when the first attempt to dig the antiquity of Dwarka was made by the archaeologists from Deccan College, Pune. The findings of the same excavation were disputed by S.R. Rao in 1979-80, after another row of excavations within the forecourt of Dwarkadhish temple. The earliest date of Dwarka has been proposed as 1400 BC by S.R. Rao, on the basis of the discovery of the lustrous red ware from the lowest level, while the earlier excavators feel that the earliest occupation cannot be dated before the 2nd century BC. They reported a different type of pottery like painted red ware, burnished red ware, coarse red ware and black ware (IAR, 1979-80). It is amazing to note that the two excavations, which were apart not more than 25 m, yielded a different cultural sequence and raised a fundamental question on the identification of pottery. However, both the teams consisted of reputed archaeologists of India. Importantly, S.R. Rao (1990) identified two additional cultural sequences prior to the historical period, which were not recorded by the earlier excavators (Ansari and Mate, 1966).

The explorations in the Bet Dwarka island were carried out first in 1969-70 by the archaeologists of the Archaeological Survey of India (ASI), and they found the remains of proto-historic, historical and medieval periods. Subsequently, the extensive onshore and offshore explorations at Bet Dwarka were conducted by S.R. Rao from 1981, and recorded it two proto-historic, and many historical and medieval period sites (Rao, 1990). The important antiquities recovered from BDK-I (southeastern coast) include a seal (Pl. 1), two inscriptions (Pl. 2 & 3) and other Harappan pottery. Later, a team of marine archaeologists of the National Institute of Oceanography (NIO), Goa (authors are also included), conducted extensive onshore explorations and identified a historical period site in the inter-tidal zone near Khuda-Dost-Dargah, besides a large number of stone anchors and probably the remains of a Roman shipwreck in 5-8 m water-depth in the north of the present Bet Dwarka jetty (Sundaresh *et al.*, 2002). A few iron cannons were also noticed in the inter-tidal zone of the island. As mentioned earlier, the committee, consisting of scholars from various organisations, visited Bet Dwarka and recommended to undertake an excavation over the cliff, near the shore area of the southeastern coast of the island, to understand the cultural sequence as some of the pottery was noticed for the first time. Accordingly, an excavation was undertaken at Bet Dwarka during 2001-02, to obtain a cultural sequence of the island (Gaur and Sundaresh, 2003). The following cultural sequence was observed during the excavation: 1) Proto-historic Period: the remains of the Late Harappan Period were noticed in a cultivated land at Par Village of the island. This was a single-culture site. A large number of pottery, which included carinated dishes, bowls, and jars, were recovered. A few painted potsherds with black-over-red colour were also collected. The important antiquities from this trench include a copper fishhook and an antimony rod; 2) Historical Period: the remains of the Historical Period were noticed in a large area of the island. Three trenches were laid on the southeastern coast of the island. The important activity during this period was the exploitation of marine resources, like different types of shells and fishes. The excavations provided a long cultural sequence of the island. The important factor which led to a continuous habitation at Bet Dwarka was the availability of marine shells, which were exploited on a large scale and the island also served as a safe harbour in the past. The site has been dated by conventional carbon^{14}, Accelerator Mass Spectroscopy (AMS) and Thermoluminescence (TL) dating methods. Most of the results are in agreement with the cultural horizons of the island.

1.2 TRADITIONAL AND LITERARY BACKGROUND*

According to tradition, Bet Dwarka was known by various names like Shankhakar, Durjaya Dwarka, Raman Dvipa, Sokotara and Kalarakot, etc. It is traditionally believed that Bet Dwarka

* Based on the information published by S.K. Dave, 1977, Pushkarbhai Gokani, 2003 and Gazetteer of Jamnagar.

was the pleasure resort (Raman Dvipa) of Sri Krishna whose palace (Antahpura) was built here. His consorts, Satyabhama and Jambavati, are believed to have lived here. Shankhodhara is associated with *shankha* (chank shell), which is amply available around the island, and till recently chank shells were recovered by local fishermen during low tide, particularly on the western and northern coasts. Chank shell of good quality was in great demand as a non-corrosive substitute for metals in the past. In the Sanskrit text, *Padma Purana*, a story is narrated about the Shankhodhara. Vishnu, in his cosmic sleep, found about Shankhasura trying to destroy or steal the *Veda*, and the *Veda* hid itself in the sea, whereupon the people of the earth approached Brahma, the Creator, and Vishnu, the Protector, for rescuing the *Veda*. Vishnu then assumed the form of a fish (*matsya*), entered the sea and killed Shankhasura on Karttika Sukla Purnima. The *Gargya Samhita* has a different version about Shankhodhara. The great sage (Mahamuni) Trita, on his pilgrimage, reached Okha region (Ushamandal) and after taking bath in a beautiful lake, started his penance. His disciple, Kakshivahana, took this opportunity to steal a beautiful *shankha* (chank shell) kept by the side of the sage. The sage, on finding that the *shankha* was stolen by his disciple, cursed him that he should become a *shankha*. On the disciple's pleading for withdrawing the curse, the sage told him that he should continue to live in the sea but meditate on Sri Krishna who will bring him back to human form, which later Sri Krishna is said to have done.

The *Mahabharata Mausala* and *Adi Parvas* refer to Dvaraka but not to Shankhodhara, while *Skand, Vishnu, Vayu* and *Bhagavata Puranas* do refer to it. Umashankar Joshi (1946) believed that the Antaradweepa referred to in the *Mahabharata* and other ancient texts must be Bet Shankhodhara. The *Bhagavata Purana* mentions that before leaving his mortal frame, Sri Krishna put the women and children in boats and sent them to Shankhodhara, probably because the houses on its high hill were safe from storm-waves. Hirananda Shastri has called Bet Dwarka the antardweepa of the *Mahabharata* (Hirananda Shastri, 1936, 32).

Sankhodhara is mentioned for the first time in *Bhagavata Purana* and *Skand Purana – Dwarka Mahatmya*. When Col. Tod visited Bet Dwarka in 1822, he saw an image of the Buddha. In the account books of the library in Bet Dwarka, there is mention that in 1921 Smt. Sumati Murarji of Scindia Navigation Co., donated Rs. 351 to the library and transferred the image to a museum in Bombay (now Mumbai). The temple of Adinarayana at Bet is believed to have been built on a Buddhist Stupa mound but this cannot be verified now. Not far from the temple of Adinarayana is a cave in a much dilapidated condition. It might have been a Buddhist cave, according to some local residents. Jainism spread to Saurashtra under the patronage of Samprati, the grandson of Asoka. Jaina tradition says that Dvaravati was the capital of Saurashtra and the city is said to have been nine *yojanas* wide with a stone fortification wall. According to the Jaina text, the *Andhaka Vrishni*, Krishna-Vasudeva and Baladeva were the rulers of Dwarka. The Jaina Agama further mentions that the 20th Jaina Tirthankar Arishtanemi (Neminath) and Sri Krishna were cousins. The author of *Prabandha Chintamani* says in *Salivahana Prabandha* that the king of Dvaraka, namely Samudravijaya, had got installed by Neminath the image of Parsvanatha in his palace. With the submerging of Dvaraka, the palace also got submerged. Presently, there is no Jaina temple in Bet Dwarka. Viradhavala, the Saindhavas and Chavdas had occupied Bet Dwarka in the early medieval period. When Adi Shankara came to Dwarka, which lies on the mainland, he got renovated the Triloksundar temple. Dwarka, which was already a centre of *Bhagavata* cult, became a major *Vaishnava* centre after the 13th century.

Krishna's devotee, Bodana, is said to have taken away the cult image of Harimandir at Dwarka in Vikram Samvat (V.S.) 1212 (AD 1155-56). In the early medieval period, between the 10th and 13th century, the Waghers, who trace their genealogy to Sri Krishna, ruled over this area. Gajakarna became the first ruler of Bet Dwarka in AD 996. He was quite independent of the kingdoms of Saurashtra. When Vallabhacharya visited Dwarka in V.S. 1560, he found there was no image of god in Harimandir at Dwarka. He brought the Rukmini-Krishna image from Ladla village and installed it in Dwarka. It is believed that the ship heading for Haj was looted by Raja Siva Sangana's men after Sultan Mahmud Begda became the ruler of Junagadh. This gave an excuse to Mahmud Begda to order his army commander, Ajeej, to loot Okhamandal, especially Dwarka. He also destroyed a part of the temple. It is said that Raja Siva Sangana, a devotee of Krishna, was asked in a dream to save the image of the Lord. He carried the cult image with the help of Gogti Brahmins from Dwarka, and installed it in the Gosala of Sankaracharya Temple in Bet Dwarka, in V.S. 1607. Later, too, Bet was subject to attacks but the Waghers, who were the devotees of Krishna, defended it.

Late in V.S. 1616, the Raja of Jamnagar built Harimandir and got the image (lying in Gosala) installed in it. The Swamiji of Sarada Peeth got a new image from Dungarpur for the temple of Dwarkadhish at Dwarka. The Bet Harimandir was built in V.S. 1616, between the shrines of Ramachandraji and Lakshmi-Narayana. The shrines of Satyabhama and Rukmini got separated in due course of time. In V.S. 1780, the Tamachi Raja of Jamnagar renovated and enlarged the temple of Harimandir and also added shrines of Radhaji and Balamukunda to it.

Skirmishes between the British rulers and those of Bet Dwarka started in V.S. 1804, when a British ship was sunk by the Waghers. The British attacked and destroyed the fort of Bet Dwarka in V.S. 1916. In this attack six temples of Dwarkanathji and the Jambavati temple were destroyed. The image of the Lord was, however, saved by the devotees. The amount of money looted in Bet Dwarka by the British is said to be 14 crores. In V.S. 1917, Khanderao Gaekwad, the ruler of Baroda, got the temple rebuilt and the original images were installed. Early Europeans called it Sanjana – name of a notorious pirate.

The temples of *Sakti* cult also exist like a *Vaishnava* centre in Bet Dwarka because the *prameyasthana* of Vishnu is *Sakti*. There are 14 *Sakti* cult shrines namely, (1) Ambaji, (2) Icchayi, (3) Sri Abhaya, (4) Mammayi, (5) Harasiddhi, (6) Navadurga, (7) Adyesvari, (8) Chandrabhaga, (9) Lunayi, (10) Padmesvari, (11) Ashtabhuja, (12) Visota, (13) Sitala, and (14) Ajaya. But most of them are in a poor state of preservation and *Sakti* cult is not prominent anymore. Among Siva temples, Bhidabhanjan and Pancesvar temples near Sankha Talao, Banesvar and Dhingesvar temple near Banaganga are extent.

The author of *Periplus of Erythraean Sea* described this area as:

> the Gulf of Baraca, which contains seven islands, the sea-bed is in some places abrupt, and in others rocky and sharp, so that the anchors lying there are parted, some being quickly cut off, and others chafing on the bottom (Schoff, 1974).

However, Ptolemy mentions of Barake as an island in the Gulf of Kanthi which has been identified as Gulf of Kachchh. Generally, Baraca/Barake has been identified with the present town of Dwarka (McCrindle, 1879).

From the above two references, the following common points are worth notice:

1. It was an important coastal town during the Christian era.
2. It is a gulf where islands are present.
3. It is dangerous for navigation.

Archaeologically, the first point is common to the present Dwarka and Bet Dwarka but the next two points do not match with present Dwarka. However, being at the mouth of the Gulf of Kachchh and as an island, Bet Dwarka can be accurately identified with Baraca/Barake of the *Periplus of Erythraean Sea* and Ptolemy, respectively. The hypothesis also supported the present underwater explorations near present Bet Dwarka jetty, which indicate that boats from the Mediterranean countries were anchored at this point during the early centuries of the Christian Era.

1.3 GEOGRAPHICAL AND GEOLOGICAL BACKGROUND

The island is a narrow, crooked strip about 13 km long, and comprises of sand and rock. The eastern part of the island consists of sand-hills and bushes and is called Hanuman Point. Its southwest-half is rocky tableland 15 to 20 m high. The eastern end of Bet Dwarka or Shankhodhar is composed of sand-hills and bushes and is called Hanuman Point as there is a Hanuman temple nearby. The reef, north to this point is called Hanuman Dandi and extends west for 2 km to the northeast of the sand-hills that border the north side of Bet Dwarka. The island from the northeast to southwest measures about 8 km. But being a narrow and crooked piece of land, is, in its windings, about half as long again. Its southwest half is rocky tableland 15 to 20 m high. A boat can reach Hanuman Point without any difficulty from the southern side of the Chunri reef.

Between the sandy southeast side of the Bet island and the mainland of Okhamandal, the passage is very shallow, having a bank in mid-channel, which is nearly dry at low tides. The water deepens towards the southern end of the island. The inner harbour of the island is unfit for large vessels because of the rocks. There are several channels to Bet at high water. The passage round the east side of Saiani island is the best as the rocky point shows plainly. The tides also increase in velocity near Bet from 2 to 3 knots, and at Dwarka to 3 and 4 knots.

Upper Pliocene-Pleistocene-Holocene sediments comprise the geology of Bet Dwarka island. Recent sand dunes and beach sands occur at the north and northeast portion of the island, while the southern part is made of rocky cliff and platform. Full litho-stratigraphic sequence can be noticed along cliff sections, which often exceed 15 to 18 m vertically with alternation of grey to purplish coloured sandstone, shell and clays resting on a coral line limestone bed. Conventionally, the rocks of Bet Shankodhar have been considered to be ranging from Pliocene to Pleistocene. However, recent studies suggest that the lowest formation belongs to Pleistocene (Sakhawala and Shringarpure, 1990). The rest of the sequence overlining the coral line beds belong to the middle to upper Pleistocene age. The topmost Milliolite marks an uppermost Pleistocene limit before deposition of the prominent conglomeratic bed during Holocene. The beaches, marshes, mangroves and coastal sand dunes are all manifestation of recent dynamics of the sea. The island is further subjected to faults and two prominent structures – Padmteerth fault running WNW-ESE and the Sonimiyar fault running ENE-WSE – appear to have been responsible for wedging of the area between them, causing subsidence subsequent in filling and several uplifts during the recent past.

Table 1. Composite lithostratigraphic section of Bet Shankhodhar island (Sakhawala and Shringarpure, 1990).

Age	*Lithology*	*Thickness*	*Environment*
HOL OCE NE	Beach, dune sands, mud flats with tracks and trails of recent marine animals.	—	Marine
	Gritty sandstone bed	1.5 - 2	Marine
	Conglomeratic bed	2	Transitional
	Disconformity		
Mid	Miliolite limestone bed	1.5 - 2	Marine/Eolian
Dle	Calcareous sandstone bed with biogenic structure (horizontal vertical and slandering *Ophiomorpha* burrows at very high frequency) vertebrate burrows and rippe marks.	2 - 2.5	Marine to transitional marine
	Grey shale bed with shale borings and *ophimomorpha* burrows	2	Transitional marine
	Purple shale bed with *ophimomorpha* tubes	1.5 - 2	Transitional marine
	Cross-bedded calcareous sandstone bed with vertical burrows and tubes	Variable	Marginal marine
	Disconformity		
	Coralline limestone		Marine

1.4 ENVIRONMENTAL BACKGROUND

The climate of the island falls under the semi-arid zone category. The year may be divided into four seasons: (i) cold season from December to February, (ii) hot season from March to May, (iii) the southwest monsoon season from June to September, and (iv) the post-monsoon season during October and November. Rainfall records are available at the nearest station in Dwarka. The average annual rainfall of the region is 358 mm. Major rainfall is received during the southwest monsoon season, July being the month recording the highest rainfall. On an average, there are 16 rainy days in the Okhamandal region.

1.4.1 Temperature

January is usually the coldest period of the year, with the mean daily maximum temperature being 26°C and mean minimum temperature being 12°C. Temperature rises steadily from about the beginning of March till May, which is usually the hottest month, with the mean daily maximum temperature at 36°C and the daily minimum at 25°C.

1.4.2 Humidity

The air is humid throughout the year. Relative humidity is on the average about 80% during the southwest monsoon and about 60 to 75% for the rest of the year.

1.4.3 Wind

Winds are strong and blow from the southwest or west during the monsoon period. In October, they are moderate and blow mainly from directions between the southwest and northeast. Northeasterly winds also begin to appear in this month but in the next three months, easterly or northeasterly winds of moderate force prevail. In the hot season, winds strengthen and blow mainly from the southwest or west.

1.4.4 Flora

The majority of the area in Bet Dwarka has open scrub forest. These are also called "Dry Deciduous Thorny Scrubs Forests". In certain areas where human interference is less, the growth of trees are more. Otherwise, the remaining parts falling under this type are more or less treeless and barren. The trees are scattered and stunted in growth. The species of tree growing in these areas are:

(1) *Acacia Arabica* (Baval), (2) *Acacia Senegal* (Gorad), (3) *Capparis Decidua* (Karda), (4) *Diospyros Melanoxylon* (Timru), (5) *Butea Frondosa* (Khakhra), (6) *Azadirachta Indica* (Neem), and (7) *Morinda Tinctoria* (Aal).

The variety of scrubs are:

(1) *Holarrhena Antidysenterica* (Kado), (2) *Cassia Auriculata* (Aval), and (3) *Tecoma Undulata* (Ragatroydo).

Chapter–2

Chronology

Antiquities and pottery from Bet Dwarka excavations have contributed a lot in determining the time-period for the ancient settlement in the island. Bet Dwarka was habitated (which commenced in the beginning of the 2nd millennium BC and continued till today) at different places in different times. There are eight carbon[14] (Table 2), two AMS (Table 3) and three Thermoluminescence dates (Table 4) obtained from the excavated trenches, besides eight TL dates (Table 5) and three carbon[14] dates (Table 6) which were obtained from the surface samples collected during onshore explorations. The findings have been described in the forthcoming chapters and with the help of absolute dates, the following chronology has been suggested for the ancient settlement at the Bet Dwarka island.

2.1 PROTO-HISTORIC PERIOD

This is the oldest habitation located in the northeastern part of the island (near village Par) on a flat and high tableland. The pottery and antiquities clearly indicate that they belonged to the late Harappan phase and are very similar to the other late Harappan sites of the Saurashtra region. The primary reason for their establishment may be the availability of shells, which has been exploited to a great extent by the Harappans in Gujarat. Possibly, Harappans from Nageshwar migrated to Bet Dwarka island, which is situated just on the opposite, on the mainland. However, excavators at Nageshwar (Hegde *et al.*, 1990) have suggested that they are mostly Sindhi Harappans and there is no influence of the Saurashtra and Kachchh Harappans. But in Bet Dwarka, the pottery is very similar to the late Harappan sites of Saurashtra, specially Rangpur IIC. A stud handle bowl, which is a characteristic feature of Gujarat Harappan, is found here. Coarse red ware, buff ware and black ware sherds are also found at Bet Dwarka. Convex-sided bowls, carinated dishes, jars and miniature vessels, similar to the other Saurashtra Harappan sites, are also found here, apart from a few sherds of perforated jars which were observed from surface exploration. Recovery of a well-preserved copper fishhook is suggestive of the fact that fishing in deeper water was prevalent. This fishhook is very similar to other fishhooks reported from

Mohenjodaro (Marshall, 1973), Harappa (Vats, 1974), Lothal (Rao, 1979), and Padri (Shinde and Thomas, 1993) and measures 7 cm in length. However, the biggest fishhook has been reported from the Harappan level at Padri, with a total length of 14 cm. The economy of the late Harappans in Bet Dwarka was primarily based on marine resources, as also indicated by the non-fertile agricultural land of the island. The excavation has not revealed evidence of any house-planning which suggests that this island might have been their seasonal habitation and not a perennial one. Carbon[14] and TL dates from this site indicate a time-bracket for the habitation between 1600-1400 BC (Table 2).

2.2 HISTORICAL PERIOD

During the early historical period, the island was habited at many places and huge archaeological deposits were noticed at BDK-I, II, III and V. During this period, maritime activities were at the zenith and the island was probably visited by foreign traders. This period can be divided into three phases, without any significant break, on the basis of pottery and other antiquities.

2.2.1 Phase I

The evidence occurred from the lowest level of BDK-I and BDK-III where a distinct pottery, similar to the Prakash, Amreli, Hastinapur associated with NBP phase, was encountered. The habitation was concentrated on a sloppy area down towards the present shoreline and the remains of this phase have been destroyed by the sea which has been witnessed by exposure of pottery and antiquities noticed during low tide from inter tidal zone (Gaur, 1990 and Gaur *et al.*, 1994). Pottery of this phase is comprised of red ware with thick slip and burnished surface and the important findings include different types of bowls, dishes, jars, ring-footed vessels and cooking vessels. The pottery is made on a well-levigated clay. However, uniform firing is lacking because an un-oxidized core has been noticed in all the vessels. A thick coat of slip, which has been burnished, was noticed on the vessels. Important antiquities of this period comprise of a carnelian bead, terracotta toy cart, wheel, beads of fish bone, terracotta, shells and glass. A large number of shell bangles and columella were noticed from this phase. Carbon[14] and TL dates for this phase suggest a time interval between 5th to 1st centuries BC. The important finds of this phase are a few shapes of bowl, which are similar to the late Harappan pottery, specially Rangpur III. However, some more data is required in order to consolidate the aspects. The remains of houses were not encountered, which may be due to limited excavation.

The physical measurement of present high water line and the earliest level of historical period suggest that the sea level was at least lower by 2 m during this phase, as evidenced by the habitation which was concentrated towards the present inter-tidal zone, and the same has been destroyed, although little remains of the same are encountered in the layer which extends offshore.

2.2.2 Phase II

During this phase, with the rise in human population, the maritime activity also increased. Regular house-building activity was noticed as one of the trench revealed the foundation of a wall, which is L-shaped and extends towards the western and northern sides. The structures were made of irregular stone blocks and mud mortar was used as the binding material. A lot of pottery continued from Phase I. However, burnished red ware sherds were not encountered and there was a substantial decrease in dishes and ring-footed vessels. A unique shape of bowl also appeared which has a rib internally, just below the rim and the frequency of the same increases in the upper layers. Different types of bowls, which include convex-sided, and a bowl with flaring sides with a sharp rim are important pottery recorded from this phase. The introduction of a lid with round flange in the middle, which is very similar to inkpot type lid reported from many other historical period sites, is also reported from here. This particular variety of lid might have been used for covering jars and amphorae during transportation via boats. A similar type of lid has also been reported from a suspected shipwreck containing amphorae and a lead ingot in Bet Dwarka waters. However, this conclusion needs more such data to validate such a statement. The exploitation of chank shell was at peak as shell artifacts in layer 6 and 7 of BDK-I contained more than 50 per cent of the total findings. A large number of worked columella, broken bangle, beads, etc have been recorded from this site. A lot of sherds of red polished ware also occur during this phase. In general, the important shapes are bowls and jars.

Copper coins appear to be of Kushana kings, which were noticed from this phase. A lot of antiquity, including beads of terracotta, glass, shell and semi-precious stones, awls, stylus, a pendant and a duck made of bone, are the important findings. Iron artifacts were found extensively from this phase, which include arrowheads, sickles, and different types of nails. On the basis of archaeological findings and absolute dates, this phase may be dated between 1st century BC and 2nd century AD.

2.2.3 Phase III

This phase is represented by the upper layers in BDK-I, II and III. The extensive structural activities noticed during this period are documented by houses consisting of large rooms, measuring 4 × 4 m, recorded in BDK-I. The structures were made of small limestone blocks and mud mortar was used as the binding material. Working floor with hearth was also noticed from this phase. Pottery of the earlier phase continued but the clay used during this phase was not well-levigated. A lot of sherds of red polished ware also occurred and the frequency of inkpot-type lid increased substantially. Important antiquities of this phase include beads of glass, terracotta, shells and dentalium shell. Copper pendant, earring and finger rings are the other important findings. A potsherd is found engraved with a *brahmi* letter 'A', which may be datable to the 3rd century AD. On the basis of archaeological findings and carbon dates, this phase may be dated between 2nd and 4th century AD.

Another important point worth mentioning here is that the people of Bet Dwarka had greater contact with Saurashtra people than people of the Okhamandal region. The excavations at Dwarka by Deccan College, Pune (Ansari and Mate, 1966) and Archaeological Survey of India (IAR-1979-80), suggest that historical period pottery is different from the pottery of Bet Dwarka. Bet Dwarka pottery has much more similarities with Saurashtra pottery of the early historical period.

The present excavation has thrown light on the cultural sequence of the Bet Dwarka island. Around 17th century BC, late Harappan people had established their settlement and they perhaps migrated from Nageshwar, which is close by. They exploited marine resources such as fishes and chank shells. It appears that the late Harappans of Bet Dwarka island had plenty of interaction with Saurashtra Harappan people and they might have visited ports on the coast of the northern Saurashtra region. The scanty habitational deposit suggests that the site was abandoned after a couple of centuries of the settlement. The island was again habited during the 8th century BC on the southeastern coast of the island. However, at later stages the habitation extended to a vast area. Hectic maritime activities were witnessed during this period in which Mediterranean boats also visited the island. The reference of Baraca may be identified with Bet Dwarka island. Perhaps a Roman ship also wrecked here and that may be one of the reasons that the author of *Periplus of Erythraean Sea* has mentioned about the difficult navigation in the Gulf of Baraca. The island continued to be an important centre of maritime activity till the emergence of Okha port in the Okhamandal area. The discovery of a large number of anchors of different types near the present jetty suggests that this point served as an anchoring point of the ships for a long time.

Table 2. C^{14} dates from Bet Dwarka island sample collected during excavations in 2001 December (Gaur and Sundaresh, 2003).

Sl. No.	*Site*	*NIO Sample nos.*	*Depth in cm*	*Layer BSIP*	*Lab Number Year in BP*	*C^{14} Date*	*Calibrated Date*
1.	BDK-I	BDK-I/charcoal/2001/20	70	4	2010	3600±90	4070-3730
2.	BDK-II	BDK-II/shell/2001/21	240	8	1998	1940±80	1990-1820
3.	BDK-II	BDK-II/shell/2001/22	275	10	1996	2000±80	2040-1870
4.	BDK-III	BDK-III/charcoal/2001/23	70	4	2005	2200±100	2340-2060
5.	BDK-III	BDK-III/charcoal/2001/24	225	9	2009	2590±100	2780-2500
6.	BDK-III	BDK-III/shell/2001/25	220	9	1997	2000±80	2040-1870
7.	BDK-VI	BDK-VI/shell/2001/26	50	2	2000	3140±100	3470-3260
8.	BDK-VI	BDK-VI/shell/2001/27	20	1	1993	3470±80	3830-3640

Table 3. AMS age data for organic samples from a trench at Bet Dwarka (Rajendran *et al.*, 2003).

Sample ID	*Trench No.*	*Material Dated*	*$^{13}C/^{12}C$ Ratio*	*^{14}C Age Years BP*	*Calendar Age (2 Sigma Range)*	*Calendar Years (2 Sigma Range)*
BDK-2-L	BDK-II	Charcoal	–24.6‰	1859±60	1925-1620	AD 25-AD 328
BDK-2-T	BDK-II	Charcoal	–25.8‰	1980±40	2000-1860	50 BC-AD 100

Calendar ages estimated following Stuiver *et al.*, 1998.

Table 4. TL dates from Bet Dwarka island supplied by Wollogong University of Australia (Vora *et al.*, 2002).

Sl. No.	*Site*	*Lab Ref.*	*Uncorrected TL Dates*	*Corrected for Fading*
1.	BDK-VI	W-2876	3260±470	3380±490
2.	BDK-I	W-2877	2460±330	2790±370
3.	BDK-VI	W-2878	2300±200	2430±210
4.	BDK-I	W-2879	1380±150	1440±160
5.	BDK-I	W-2880	1960±160	2140±170
6.	BDK-I	W-2881*	740±50	890±60
7.	Khuda Dost site	W-2882	1000±170	1060±180
8.	BDK-II	W-2883	1270±380	1370±410
9.	BDK-I	W-2884	970±120	1060±130

Note * This sample (W2881) exhibited a TL fading factor of more than 20% over the period of the test. This casts a degree of doubt upon the reliability of the final TL age computed.

Table 5. Dates of surface sample from Bet Dwarka island.

Sl. No.	*Site*	*Material*	*Lab ref.*	*C^{14}/TL Dates*
1.	BDK-I	Shell	BS-1898	2040±80
2.	BDK-I	Shell	BS-1899	1910±80
3.	BDK-I	Potsherd	W-2571	860±130

Table 6. TL dates from Bet Dwarka sample collected during excavation in Season 2001 December. The dates have been supplied by Dr. A.K. Singhvi of PRL.

Sl. no.	*Sample No.*	*Q (min)*	*I (min)*	*ED (Gy) Q + I*	*Total Dose (D(uGy/a)*	*Age (yrs)*
1.	BDK-II (L-2)	0.90±0.13	2.59±0.04	8.54±0.41	2761±300	3093±367
2.	BDK-II (L-6)	1.27±0.14	1.26±0.1	6.17±0.58	3517±407	1754±261
3.	BDK-II (L-11)	1.23±0.1	1.87±0.16	7.56±0.63	3183±649	2375±523
4.	BDK-II (L-9)*	1.92±0.5	0.49±0.11	5.88±1.4	3427±670	1716±530

* This sample was sent to Dr. C.P. Rajendran from CESS for cross-checking with C^{14} dates of this period.

Chapter–3
Cuttings and Structures

The southeastern coast of the Bet Dwarka island has maximum deposits of archaeological remains. A long section, more than a kilometer in length exposed to the sea, witnessed a large amount of damage to the archaeological remains. At this location, three trenches, namely BDK-I, II and III, were exposed to the natural soil. Trench BDK-IV was laid on an agriculture land. However, except on the surface, no cultural deposit was noticed during the excavations. BDK-V is located on the southwestern coast of the island, which is situated in the inter-tidal zone. The last trench, BDK-VI, was laid in the northeastern coast of the island (Fig. 2). This is a late Harappan site in the island. The excavation was carried out till the archaeological findings continued and till few centimetres into virgin soil in each trench. The layers were distinguished on the basis of colour, composition and texture. A brief description of the findings from each sites is given below.

3.1 BDK-I

The trench was exposed on the southeastern side of the island (Pl. 4). The excavation was carried up to a depth of 2.65 m and total nine layers were marked (Fig. 3 and 3a). The foundation of one structure was noticed in this trench (Pl. 5). The structure is made of irregular stone blocks and the binding material used is mud. The structure has an extension towards the southern side (Fig. 4). It appears to be a part of a room of house complex. The size of this room is 3 × 3 m, with a door that appears to have been on the northern side. However, the same had been enclosed after sometime. Two other structures adjoining this one were noticed on either sides. A hearth and flooring was noticed on the northern side of the structure, which might have been a part of the kitchen. The important antiquity contemporary to this structure were a few areca nut-shaped terracotta beads, a copper earring, a broken decorative sandstone block besides shell artifacts like bangles and beads.

Two copper coins of the Kushana Period, one each of awl and stylus of bone, were recorded from layer 6. A large number of iron objects, including nails, sickles, and arrowheads were

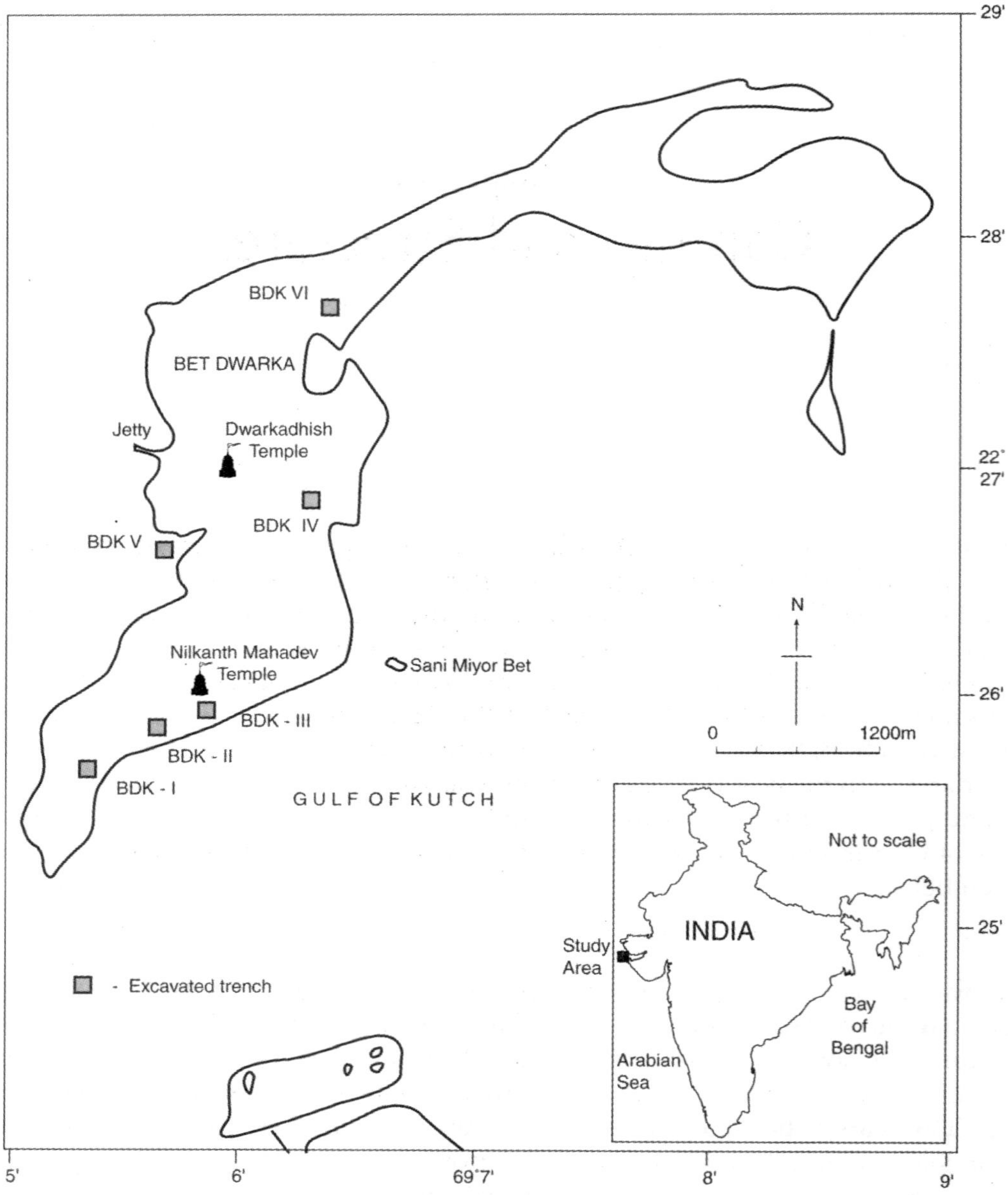

Fig. 2. Location of the trenches in Bet Dwarka island.

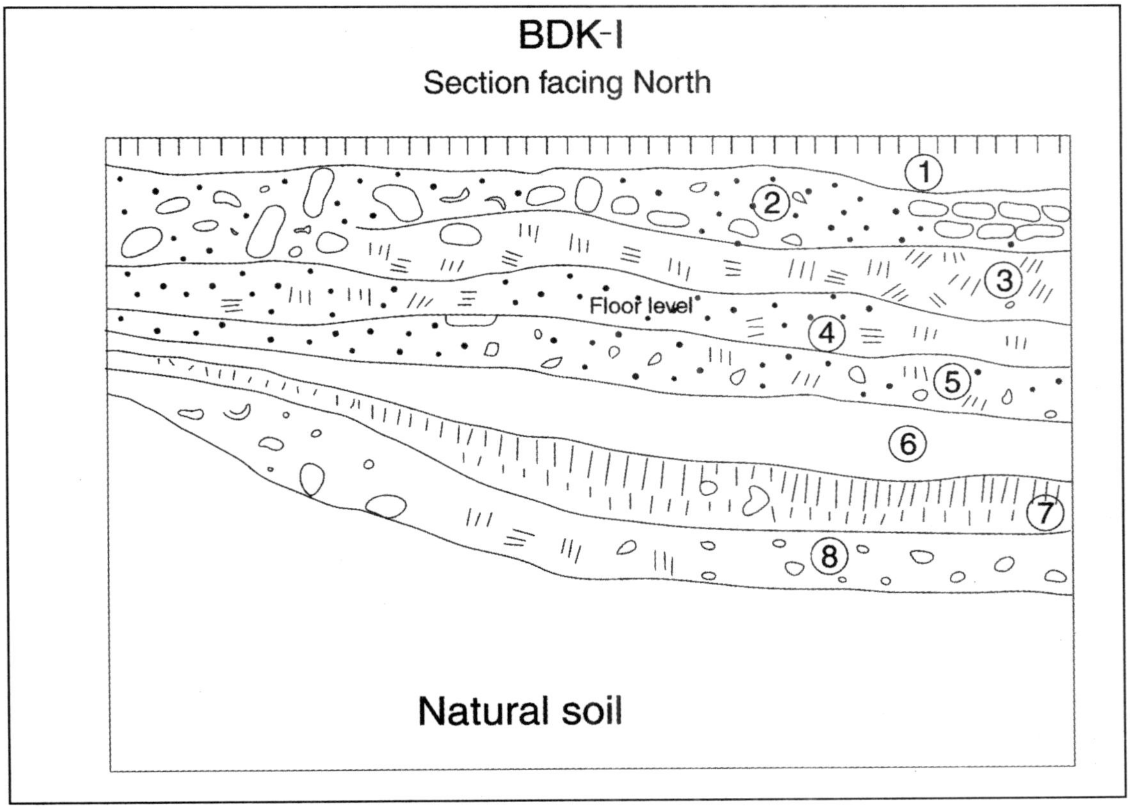

Fig. 3. Section of the trench BDK-I.

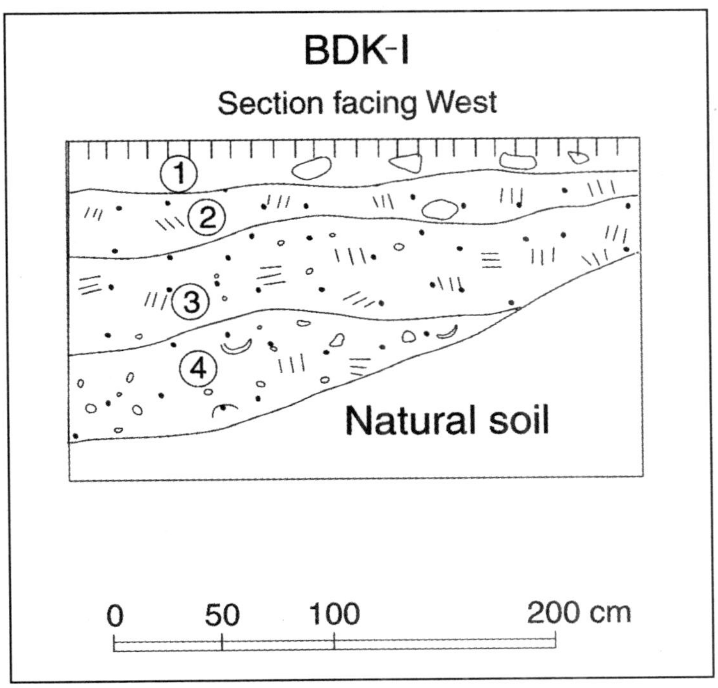

Fig. 3a. Section of the trench BDK-I.

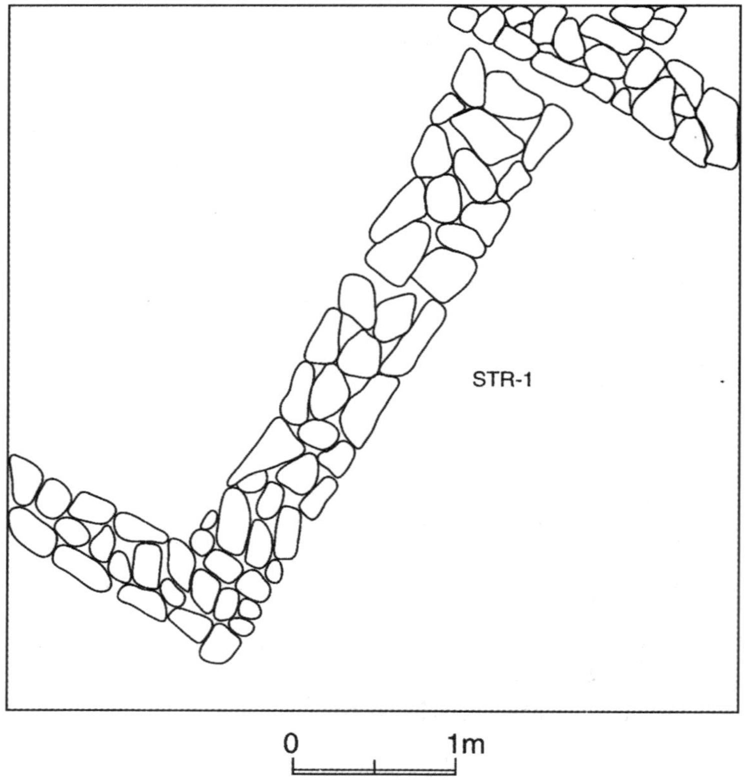

Fig. 4. Plan of stone structure from the trench BDK-I.

collected. The layers 6 and 7 yielded more than 50% of shell artifacts including a large number of columella and apex portions of *turbinella pyrum*; the rest are potsherds. The important potsherds include red polished ware, plain red ware and a few sherds of black ware. The important shapes are jars of different sizes, bowls of various types such as bowls with turned sharpened rim, bowls with featureless rim, bowls with an internally ribbed rim, dishes, lids, basins and cooking vessels. Basins of different sizes with often a flange on the exterior were also found.

The earliest habitation in BDK-I and II started on the slope of the hill and extended towards the shore area; presently the remains of the lowest habitation is limited to not more than a meter in width, parallel to the shore and foot of the hill, while the area towards the offshore has already been destroyed by the sea. The lowest cultural level in the trench is lower than the present high water line by about 80 cm.

Details of Layers

A total of nine layers were identified and a brief description of each layer is given below:

Layer 1 consists of loose soil, light brown in colour. Small stone pebbles were also noticed. Maximum thickness of the layer is 12 cm.

Layer 2 is represented by light brown colour with a large number of stone rubbles and loose soil with lots of *kankar*. The maximum thickness of this layer is 40 cm.

Layer 3 consists of compact and light brown soil. This layer also has small shells and gravel. The maximum thickness of this layer is 15 cm.

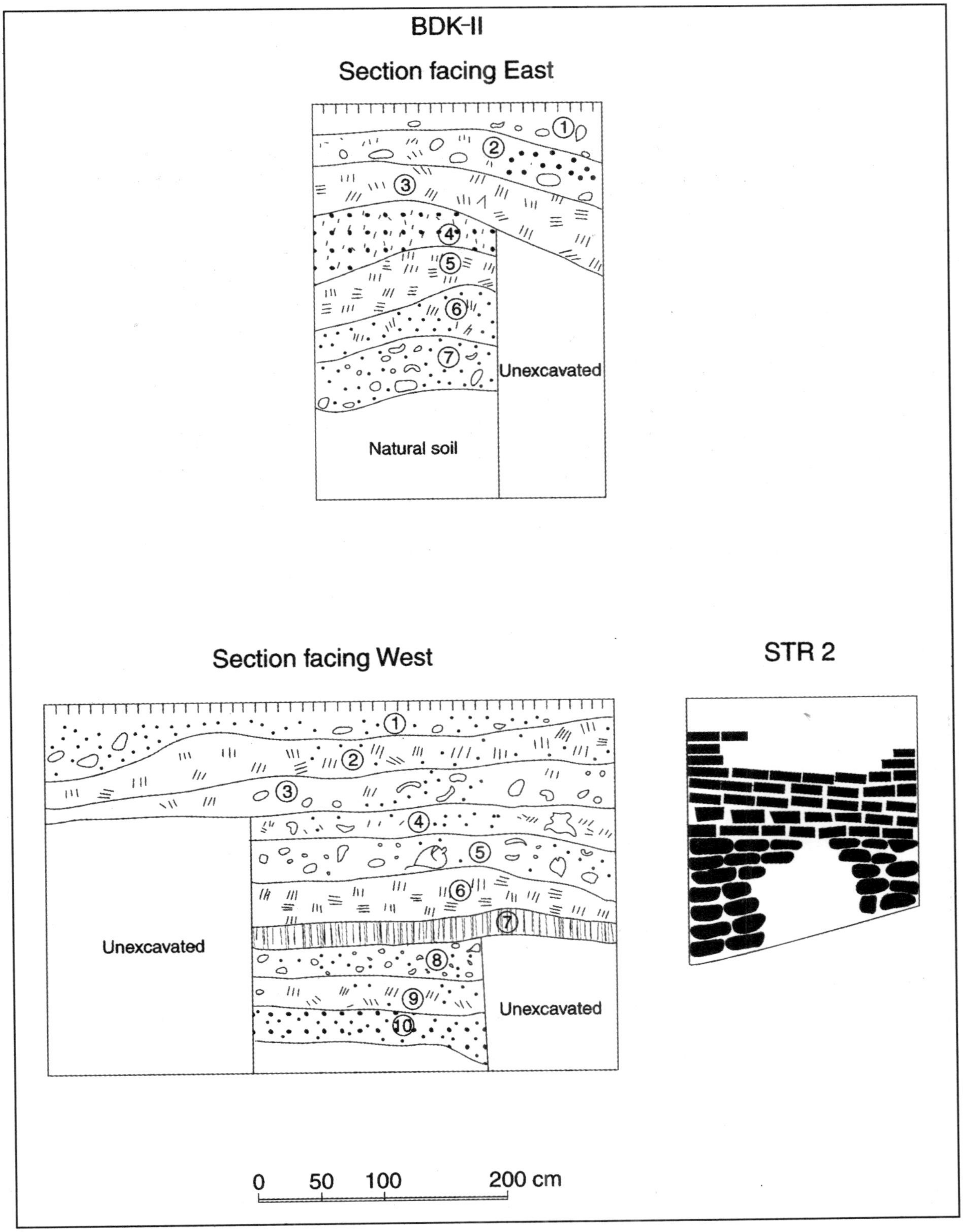

Fig. 5. Section of the trench BDK-II.

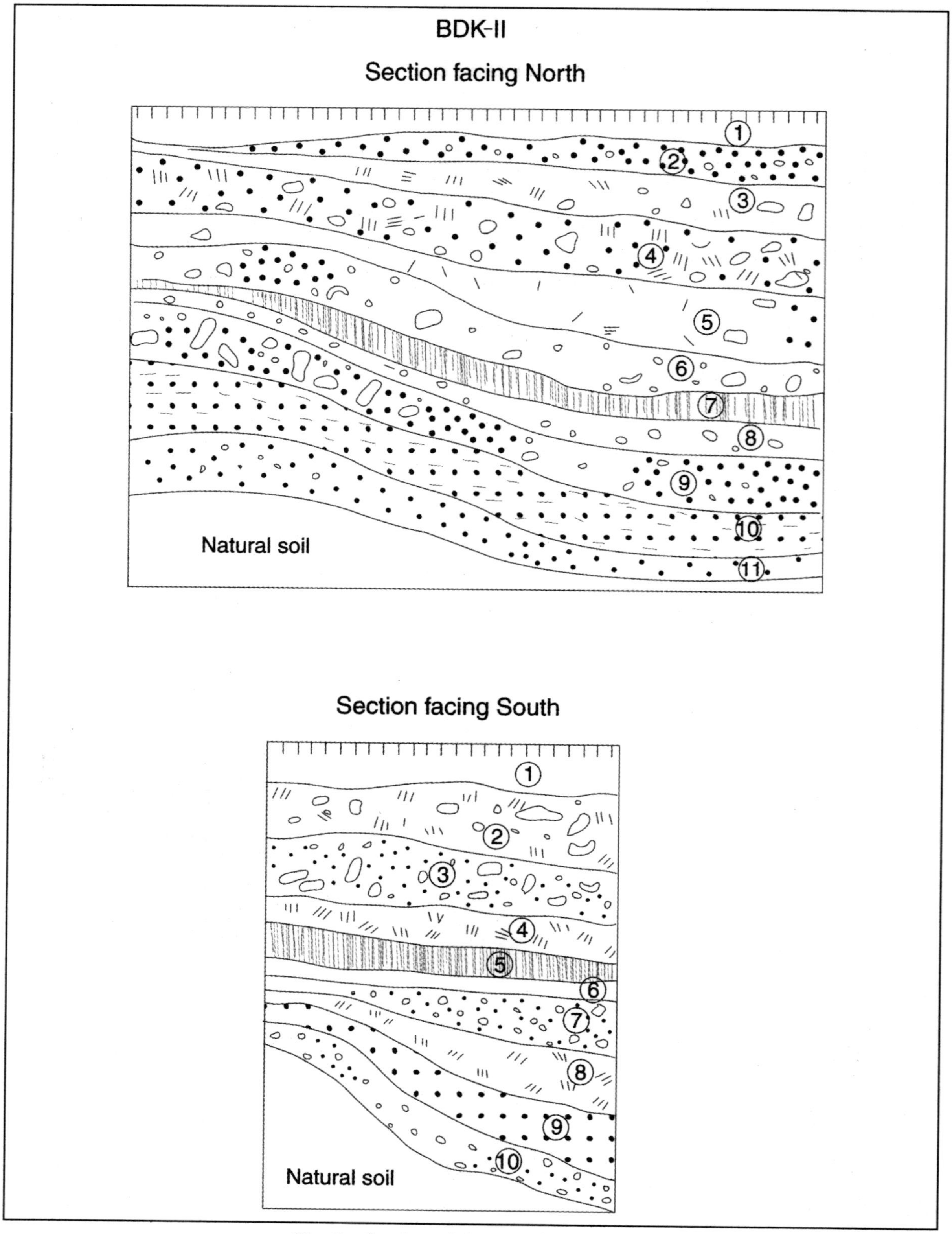

Fig. 5a. Section of the trench BDK-II.

Layer 4 comprises of very compact clay and is dark brown in colour. Several ashy patches are also noticed. A rammed working floor is also noticed in this layer. The maximum thickness is 20 cm.

Layer 5 is represented by a rammed thick floor. It is yellowish in colour with lots of lime *kankar* and its maximum thickness is 20 cm.

Layer 6 is represented by a loose and brown colour soil. A few ashy patches are also noticed in this layer. The maximum thickness of this layer is 25 cm.

Layer 7 consists of ashy loose soil. A large number of chank shells are reported from this layer. The maximum thickness is 28 cm.

Layer 8 consists of loose soil, grey in colour. The layer also has stone rubbles. The maximum thickness is 35 cm.

Layer 9 comprises of compact greenish clay. It lies on the sloppy virgin layer. A maximum thickness of 20 m towards the offshore was noticed.

3.2 BDK-II

The trench was laid at the highest point in the southern coast of the island (Pl. 6). It measures 5 × 2.5 m. A total deposit of 3.45 m was noticed in this trench, and 11 layers were identified (Fig. 5 and 5a). The initial habitation lied on a sloppy area, which was extended in a similar manner as of BDK–I; however, at a later stage the habitation also extended shoreward. The foundation of one structure was noticed in the southeast corner of the trench (Pl. 7). The structure was sealed with layer 3 and the foundation of the structure runs up to layer 4 (Fig. 6). A number of disturbed blocks were noticed in layer 3 and 4, which are the remains of some of the collapsed structures. Shell artifacts, including beads and broken bangles, were recovered from this trench. A large number of pottery was collected from all the layers. The pottery comprises of red polished ware, red ware and a few sherds of black ware. The important shapes are bowls, basins, jars, dishes, different types of lids and cooking vessels. One of the sherds of the red polished ware bowl bears the inscription of a *Brahmi* letter "A". A few other graffiti marks were noticed. A large number of iron artifacts were also collected from this trench, which include sickles, nails, arrowheads, rings, etc. The lowest cultural level in the trench is lower than the present high water line by about 70 cm. Layer 9 has been identified as liquefied material, which could be the result of an earthquake (Rajendra *et al.*, 2003). A full fledge study on the remains of earthquake from Bet Dwarka has been published in *Current Science* and the same has been included here with slight modification as *Annexure V*.

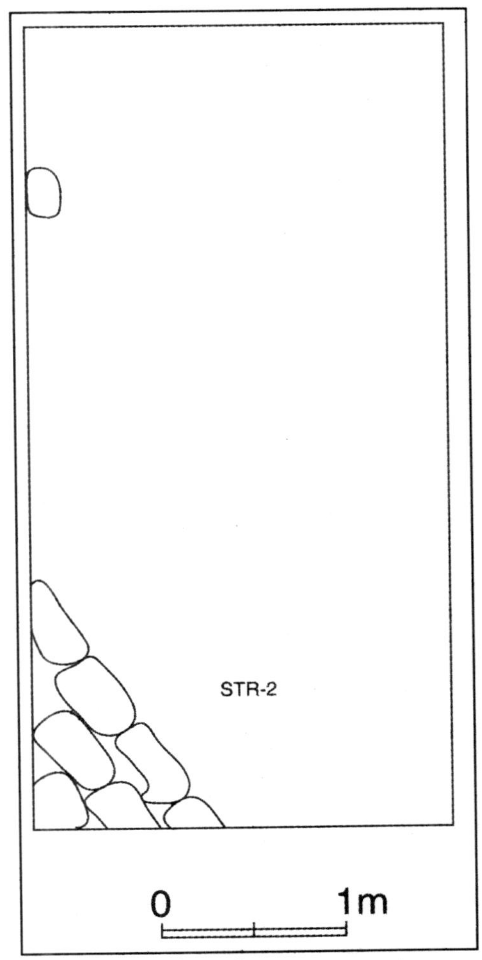

Fig. 6. Plan of a stone structure from BDK-II.

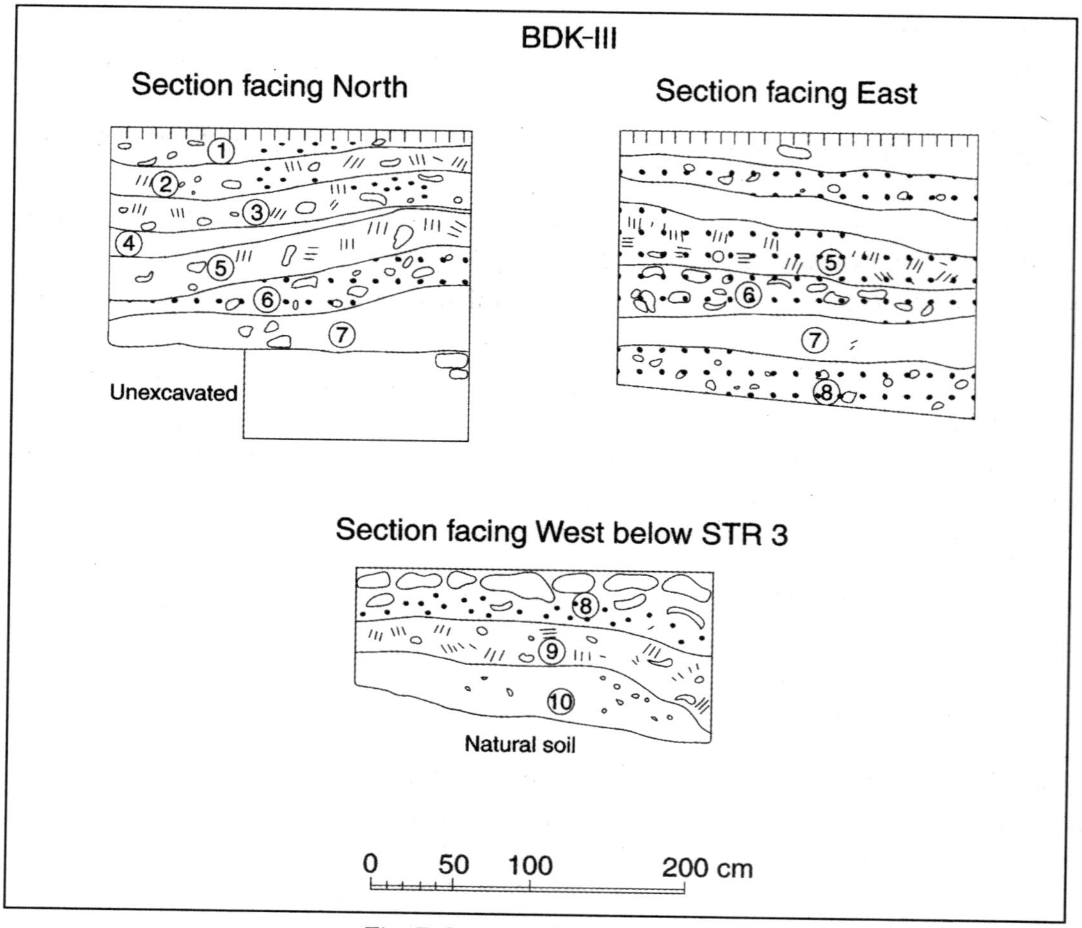

Fig. 7. Section of the BDK-III.

DETAILS OF LAYERS

A total of 11 layers were identified and a brief description of each layer is given below:

Layer 1 consists of loose soil with light brown clay. The layer disappear towards the northern side. The maximum depth is 60 cm.

Layer 2 has whitish colour clay with a loose texture. A few stone rubbles were also noticed. The maximum depth is 20 cm towards the southern side.

Layer 3 is greyish in colour with a loose texture. A few stone rubbles were noticed in the layer. The maximum thickness is 25 cm at highest point in the western side.

Layer 4 consists of thick deposits of small stones with a whitish colour clay. The texture of clay is loose. The maximum thickness is 20 cm at highest point.

Layer 5 is represented by a huge deposit of stones which are reddish in colour and have a compact texture. The maximum thickness is 30 cm on the southern side.

Layer 6 comprises of compact soil, yellowish and reddish in colour. The maximum thickness at highest point is 20 cm. A working floor on the eastern section in this layer was also noticed.

Layer 7 consists of compact and rammed material, reddish in colour. The maximum thickness is 25 cm.

Layer 8 is represented by compact hard clay, greenish in colour. The maximum thickness is 20 cm on the southern side.

Layer 9 consists of light brown colour clay which is compact is nature. Small patches of ashy layers were also noticed. The maximum depth is 30 cm on the southern side.

Layer 10 comprises of black sand, which is loose in nature. The maximum thickness on the northern side is 23 cm. It is said that this layer represents the liquified material of earthquake.

Layer 11 consists of compact clay with small gravels. The maximum thickness is 28 cm. It is greenish in colour. The layer lies on a natural sloppy formation.

A working floor on the eastern section was also noticed in this layer. The maximum thickness of the layer is 25 cm.

3.3 BDK-III

The trench was laid towards the eastern side of trench BDK-II, and very near to the present water pump house. It measures 5 × 2.5 m. A total deposit of 2.35 m was noticed and ten layers were identified (Fig. 7). The foundation of a structure was also noticed, which is sealed by layer 6 and it ran through into layer 7 and 8 (Pl. 8). The structure is made of bigger limestone blocks as compared to other structures of BDK-I and II. The exposed portion of the structure is L-shaped (Fig. 8), which possibly extends towards the south and west direction and probably it is a part of a house complex. Shell artifacts, including beads and bangles apart from lots of waste of shells, were noticed. One unidentified small copper coin was also recorded from this trench. A number of terracotta beads, balls, a toy-cart and a wheel with painted spokes were noticed from the lower level. A carnelian bead, glass beads and a pestle were important findings, besides a few iron artifacts. As usual, lots of pottery including plain red ware, red polished ware, red burnished ware, black ware and a few grey ware sherds were found. The important shapes are jars, basins, dishes, bowls, cooking vessels and lids.

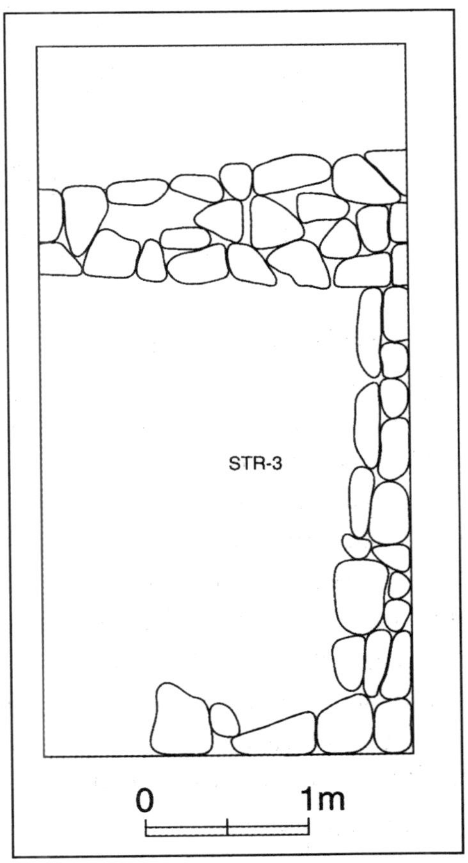

Fig. 8. Plan of stone structure from BDK-III.

Details of Layers

Total ten layers were identified. A brief description of each layer is given below:

Layer 1 consists of loose soil, dark grey in colour. The maximum thickness is 15 cm on the southern side.

Layer 2 has whitish loose soil with a few rubble stones. The maximum thickness is 40 cm.

Layer 3 has whitish loose soil with small stone rubbles. It has a maximum thickness of 12 cm on the southern side.

Layer 4 consists of compact clay, dark green in colour. It has a maximum deposit of 30 cm in the southeast corner.

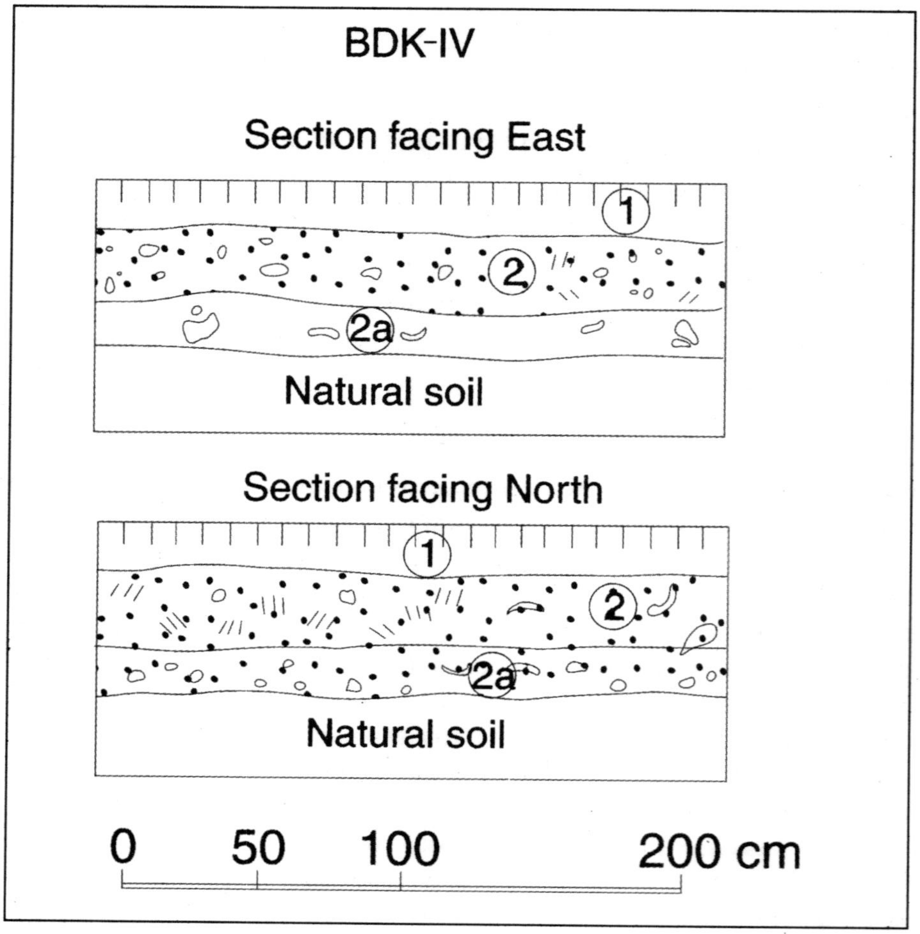

Fig. 9. Section of the BDK-VI.

Layer 5 consists of fine-grained compact clay, green in colour. It evenly slopes down towards the northeastern side of the section. The thickness of this layer is 25 cm.

Layer 6 consists of stone rubbles with loose clay. The maximum thickness is 60 cm in the southwest corner.

Layer 7 consists of comparatively compact clay, light brown in colour. A few stone rubbles were also noticed in it. The maximum thickness is 20 cm.

Layer 8 consists of green colour clay with a dark reddish colour working floor. The maximum thickness is 50 cm in the southwest corner of the trench.

Layer 9 is compact, green in colour with a few stones and has a maximum thickness of 20 cm in the northern side of the trench.

Layer 10 lies over natural bed. It is blackish in colour and its maximum thickness is 30 cm in the north side of the section.

3.4 BDK-IV

The trench was laid in an agricultural land on the eastern side of the island, which is known as Sundaravan, located towards the south of the village Balapur (Pl. 9). From the surface, a large number of pottery was collected earlier. However, after excavation no archaeological artifacts were recovered and the excavation was stopped after digging up to 75 cm.

3.5 BDK-V

The site lies near Khuda-Dost-Dargah, on the western coast of the island (Pl. 10). This site submerged during high tide. During low tide, the section facing towards the sea was scraped off and potsherds and broken shell bangles were recovered from this place.

3.6 BDK-VI

The trench was laid in an agricultural land, east of the village Par and near a mosque (Pl. 11). The antiquities collected earlier from here belong to the Late Harappan Phase, and the aim of the present excavation is to record the total deposit of the site. Hence, a trench measuring 2.5 X 2.5 was laid here. A total deposit of 95 cm and two layers were identified (Fig. 9). A big stone block on the western section of the trench was encountered, which could be the remains of some structure (Pl. 12). However, continuity of the same could not be traced out. The important findings from here include a big copper fishhook and a copper antimony rod, besides a large number of dentalium beads, broken shell bangles and sand waste of shells. Important pottery recovered includes plain red ware, painted red ware, buff ware and black ware. The important shapes include carinated dishes, convex-sided and stud-handled bowls, jars and miniature vessels.

Description of Layers

Layer 1 is represented by loose, white sandy clay. Loose *kankars* were also noticed. It has a maximum thickness of 50 cm.

Layer 2 is the same as above except a little compact white sandy clay has been noticed. This layer lies over a hard *kankar* natural bed. The maximum thickness is about 48 cm.

Chapter–4
Antiquities

A large number of antiquities have been recovered from Bet Dwarka island since 1983, which include seals, inscriptions and chert blades, besides a large number of potsherds. During the present excavation, antiquities such as terracotta, marine shells, bone, iron and copper have been recovered from stratified deposits. The descriptions of finished artifacts are given below. However, detail findings of shell artifacts are also dealt with in *Annexure IV*.

4.1 TERRACOTTA BEADS

Terracotta beads are generally found from every archaeological site (proto-historic onwards) in the Indian sub-continent. It is believed that stone and glass beads were meant for the rich and terracotta beads were greatly in demand by the common man in ancient India (Sharma, 1969). The plasticity of the material for any form to suit the masses was another factor in its popularity. The diversity in the forms is, therefore, noticed in the beads of this material. The most predominant type amongst this class is the pear-shaped one with a truncated apex, generally called areca nut-type, on account of the size and shape it resembles. Prepared on the fast wheel and produced perhaps on mass scale, this type is one of the commonest found in India. From Bet Dwarka, 11 terracotta beads have been recovered during excavations (Fig. 10, Pl. 13). The perforations are generally very large and regular. A brief description of the beads is as follow:

1. Beads with lenticular, circular and pear-shaped, blunt edges. Treated with black slip. A circular depression on the top is present. A thick axial hole is noticed. This is the biggest TC bead found so far from here. The diameter is 4 cm and thickness 2 cm. BDK-I.
2. Truncated bi-cone circular bead. A groove on the lower side is noticed around the hole. Uneven surface; not well-fired. The surface is yellowish in colour. The diameter is 2.1 cm and thickness 1.7 cm. BDK-II.
3. Broken pear-shaped bead. Treated with black slip. The diameter is 2.3 cm, remaining thickness is 0.7 cm. BDK-III.

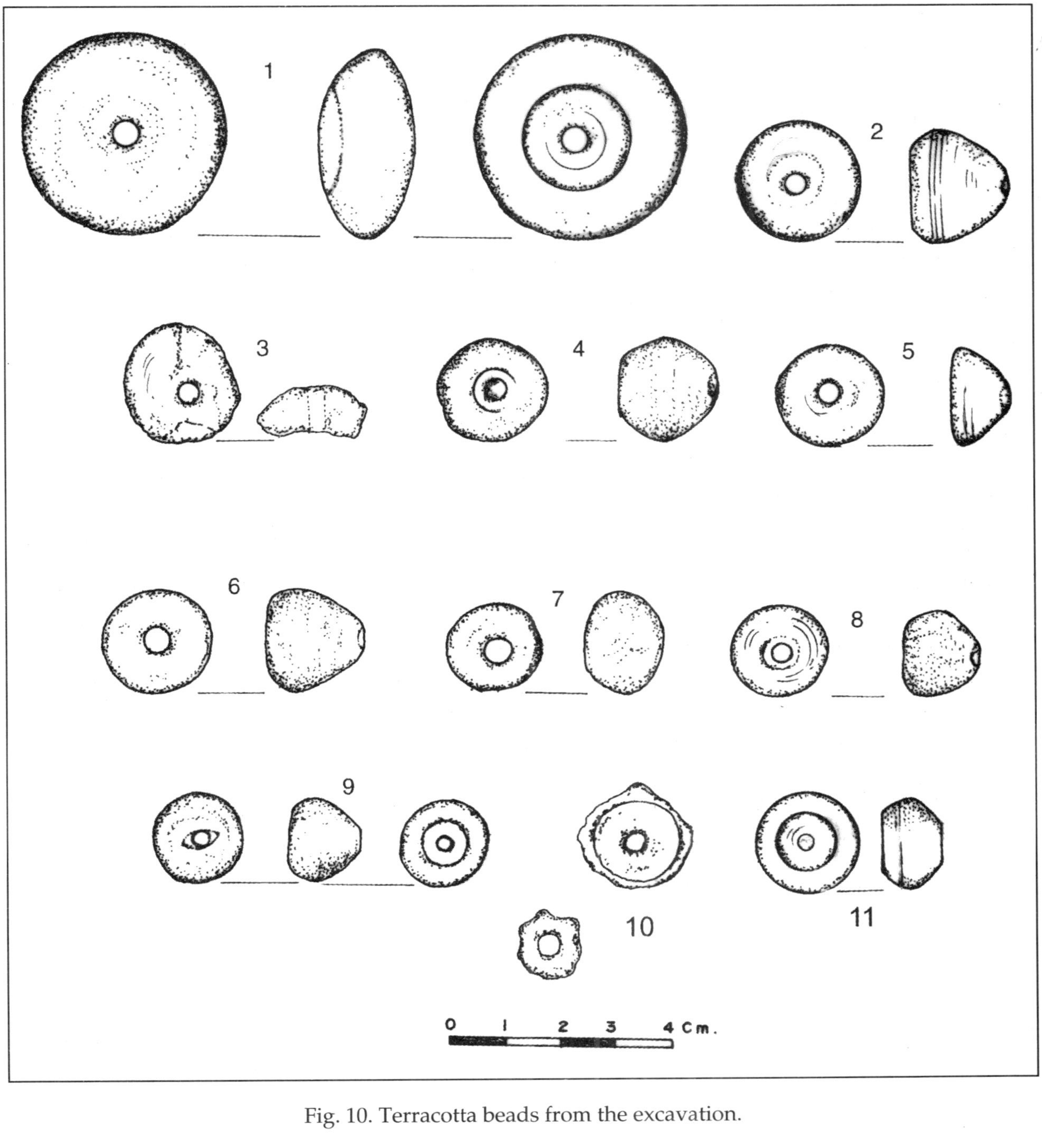

Fig. 10. Terracotta beads from the excavation.

4. Bead made of sun-dried clay. Spherical-shaped; uneven surface; light brown in colour. The diameter is 2.0 cm and thickness 1.8 cm. BDK-III, surface find.
5. Small areca nut-shaped. Two grooves on the upper edges. The top is even and smooth. This is not well-fired and the surface colour is yellowish black. Its diameter is 2 cm and thickness 1.1 cm. BDK-I.
6. Pear-shaped bead with a groove on the upper side; smooth surface; treated with black-slip. The diameter is 2.0 cm and thickness 1.7 cm. BDK-I.
7. Spherical-shaped bead with an uneven surface and wide hole in the middle; red slipped. The diameter is 1.7 and thickness 1.4 cm. BDK-III.
8. Small areca nut type bead, truncated at top with a blunt carinated profile; smooth surface; treated with black slip. The diameter is 1.8 cm and thickness 1.3 cm. BDK-I.
9. Standard pear-shaped bead, truncated at top with a medial groove; rough surface and treated with black slip. The diameter is 1.6 cm and thickness 1.3 cm. BDK-I.
10. Broken bead, ill-fired and black slipped with a rough surface. The diameter is 1.9 cm and thickness 0.6 cm. BDK-II.
11. Spherical-shaped bead with a groove on the upper side. It has a smooth surface and is treated with black slip. Its diameter is 1.9 cm and thickness 1.6 cm. BDK-II.

4.2 SHELL BEADS

There are six shell beads and four of them are circular-shaped, like a ball with an across perforation in the middle (Fig. 11 and Pl. 14). The last one is a long bead with a square section and perforation in the middle. With all probability, these beads have been made from the columella part of *Turbinella pyrum*, as they are similar to those found from Harappan and historical period sites across the sub-continent.

1. Upper side is spheroid in shape and lower side is flattish with a smooth surface. A thin perforation in the middle is present. Its diameter is 1.4 cm and height 1.3 cm. BDK-III.
2. Spheroid in shape, the shell bead has a fine finish. A very thin hole in the middle is present. Its diameter is 1.4 cm and height 1.3 cm. BDK-II.
3. Short barrel circular-type bead. It does not have a perfect finish. A very thin hole in the middle is present. Its diameter is 0.85 cm and thickness 0.75 cm. BDK-III.
4. The bead is thin with a square section. There is a hole in the middle. Its length is 0.2 cm and width 0.4 cm. BDK-III.
5. Long cylindrical squarish bead. The hole is not perfectly drilled. Its length is 2 cm and width 0.6 cm. BDK-II.

4.3 GLASS BEADS

There were 13 glass beads recovered from the excavations (Fig. 11, Pl. 15). The colours represented include blue, blue-green, green, black and yellow. The blue glass beads are present in a majority. The beads of glass have been reported from every historical period site in the Indian sub-continent, and they are dated between 5th century BC and 3rd century AD in the Bet Dwarka island. The description of nine beads is as follows:

1. Light bluish-green glass bead, which is long, convex and hexagonal type. On one side the edge of hole is blunt and on the other side sharp. Length is 1.9 cm and diameter 1.5 cm. BDK-I.

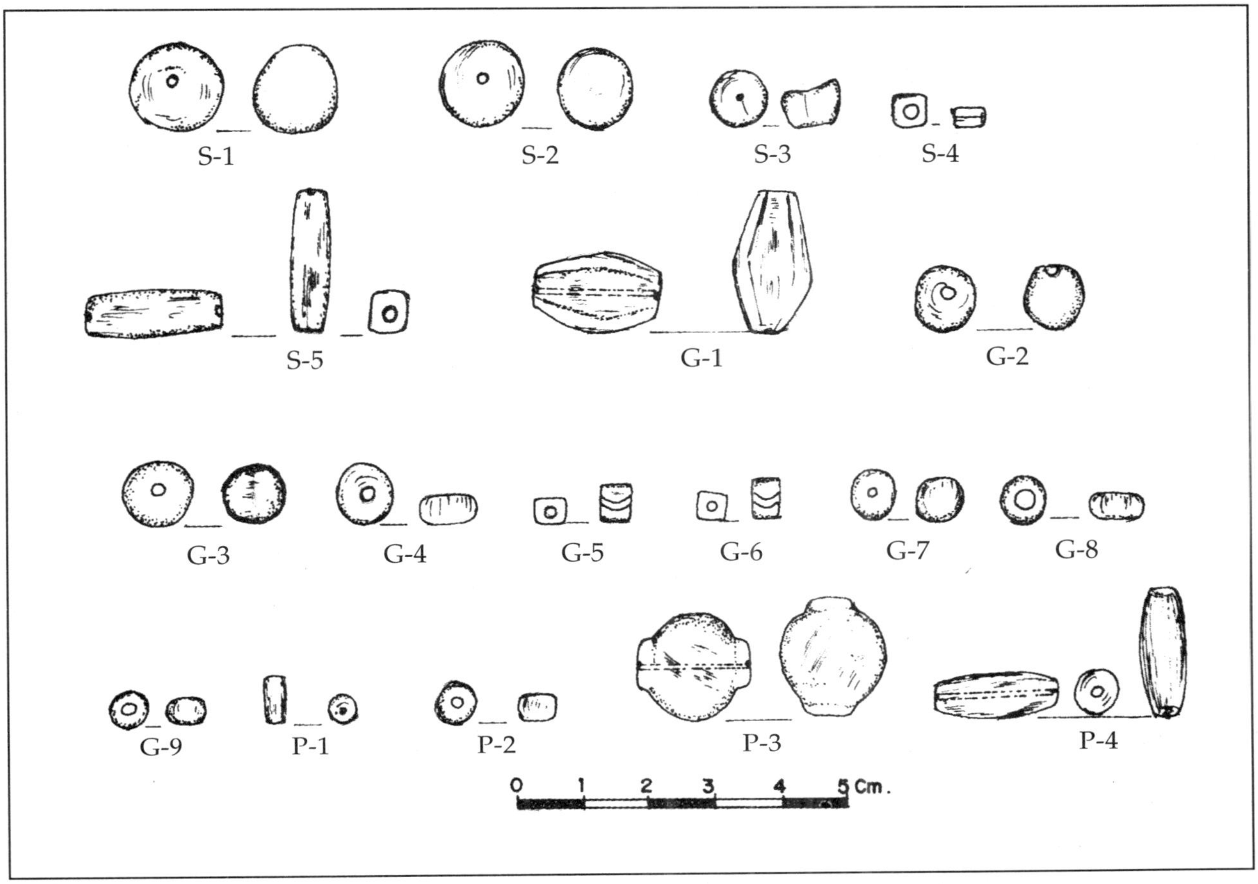

Fig. 11. Shell, glass and stone beads (S-Shell, G-Glass and P-Stone).

2. Green glass bead; spheroid type; it is broken. Its diameter is 0.8 cm and height 0.8 cm.
3. Black opaque glass bead, spherical in shape. The edge of one side of the hole has threading marks; surface is porous. Its height is 1.0 cm and diameter 1.1 cm. BDK-I.
4. Dark blue glass bead with a spherical shape, wide hole and etched. On the exterior, a few white colour lines are also noticed. Its diameter is 0.8 cm and thickness 0.5 cm. BDK-III.
5. Blue glass bead, which is a diamond-faceted square and is etched. Its length is 0.6 cm and thickness 0.4 cm. BDK-III.
6. Dark blue glass bead, long and cylindrical in shape. It is etched. Its length is 0.4 cm and height 0.7 cm. BDK-III.
7. Dark blue glass bead. It is standard spherical type. Its diameter is 0.8 cm and height 0.7 cm. BDK-III.
8. Yellow transparent glass bead which is small, barrel, circular type with a wide middle hole, and fine finish. Its diameter 0.7 cm and length is 0.4 cm.
9. Micro-bead with a spherical shape of green glass bead. Its diameter is 0.4 cm and length 0.3 cm. BDK-III.

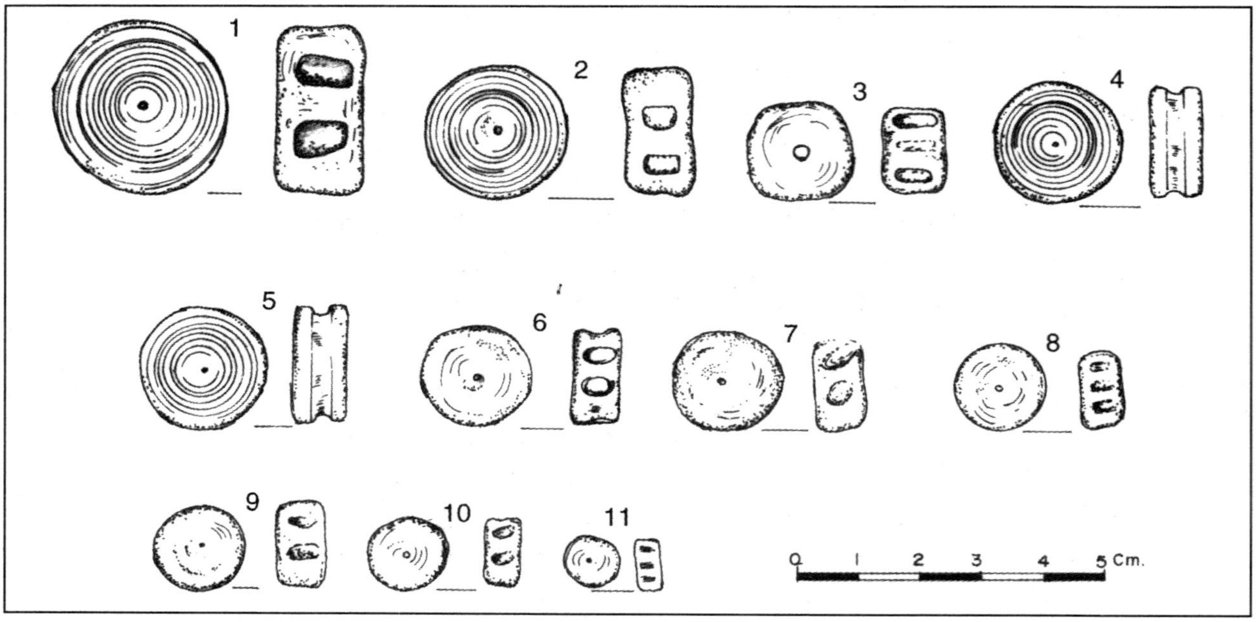

Fig. 12. Fish bone beads.

4.4 STONE BEADS

Four stone beads have been found during the excavations (Fig. 11 and Pl. 15). One each of them is from carnelian, amethyst, red jasper and black stone. These types of beads are found extensively across the country. A brief description of each bead is given below:

1. Long barrel, circular-type red jasper bead with blunt edges. Its length is 0.7 cm and diameter is 0.3 cm. BDK-III.
2. Black stone bead which is short barrel, circular type. A hole in the middle is present. Its diameter is 0.6 cm and length 0.4 cm.
3. Bi-cone circular and tabular type amethyst bead; purple in colour. Its length is 1.7 cm, width 1.6 cm and thickness 0.8 cm. BDK-II.
4. Long barrel-type carnelian bead; edges are blunt; has a wide hole which is not in the middle. Its length is 1.9 cm and diameter 0.6 cm. BDK-III.

4.5 FISH BONE BEADS

Fish bone beads have been found in large quantity from all the three trenches of the historical period (Fig. 12 and Pl. 16). They are of various sizes, depending upon the availability of fish bones. These are primarily of spinal bone, which can be used as bead without any modification. However, a few beads have designs on the outer surface as well. Their shapes indicate that these could have been used as earring; such types are also used by the *Rabari* community of Gujarat. A few beads suggest some deliberate groove on the surface. The details of a few fish bone beads are given below:

1. Short barrel-shaped; no modification was carried out in this bead; four deep holes seen on the exterior, which are on the ribs. Its diameter is 3.0 cm and thickness 1.5 cm. BDK-II.
2. Short barrel-shaped, truncated on both sides with a fine finish. Its diameter is 2.3 cm and thickness 1.2 cm. BDK-II.

3. Squarish barrel-shaped; truncated on both sides. Its diameter is 2.0 cm and thickness 1.0 cm. BDK-I.
4. Short barrel-shaped, circular bead. A fine and wide groove on the exterior is present. Its diameter is 2.1 cm and thickness 0.9 cm. BDK-III.
5. Short barrel-shaped, circular bead with a wide and fine groove on the exterior. Its diameter is 2.0 cm and thickness 0.9 cm. BDK-III.
6. Short barrel-shaped; middle of the exterior has continuous and regular depression. This type of bead was used for widening the ear hole for wearing of earring. Its diameter is 1.9 cm and thickness 0.9 cm. BDK-I.
7. Short barrel, circular-shaped; four deep holes on the exterior. Its diameter is 1.6 cm and thickness 0.8 cm. BDK-I.
8. Short barrel-shaped; truncated on both sides. Its diameter is 1.4 cm and thickness 0.7 cm. BDK-II.
9. Short barrel-circular shaped; four deep holes were noticed on the exterior. Its diameter is 1.4 cm and thickness 0.8 cm. BDK-III.
10. Short barrel, circular-shaped broken bead; holes found on the exterior. Its diameter is 1.3 cm and thickness 0.7 cm. BDK-II.
11. Small bead with short barrel, circular-shaped; holes on the exterior have been noticed. Its diameter is 0.9 cm and height 0.5 cm.

4.6 BONE ARTIFACTS

There are four bone artifacts found – one bird (duck), a pendant, an awl and a stylus (Fig. 13 and Pl. 17). The bird is of great interest; it is formed with small alteration. Each bone object has been polished. A brief description of the bone objects is as follows:

1. A broken duck figure on bone; the head of the figure is broken; it has been polished; on both sides, three grooves represent feathers; a small tail is also seen. Its length is 3.6 cm, height is 2.6 cm and thickness 1.8 cm. BDK-II.
2. Bone pendant; on the obverse three circles with one dot in each circle is present; two thick grooves on one end and the other end pointed; reverse is plain. Its length is 3.7 cm, width 1.5 cm and thickness 0.5 cm. BDK-II.
3. Awl with a fine working point and a polished surface (similar to Hastinapur Pl. LX, no. 2, Prakash 1955 Pl. XXIX, no.5). Its length is 5.3 cm and thickness 0.7 cm. BDK-I.
4. Broken stylus; traces of chipping are prominently seen. Its length is 2.9 cm, diameter 0.6 cm and depth 60 cm. BDK-I, layer 3.

4.7 TERRACOTTA OBJECTS

Terracotta artifacts are comparatively less from Bet Dwarka excavations. Besides the ten beads, a broken toy cart wheel and an animal figure are some important objects that have been recovered during the excavation (Fig. 14, 14a and 14b, Pl. 18-19). A brief description of each object is given below:

1. Wheel of a toy cart in red ware; it is treated with a thick coat of red slip. The hubs on either sides are projected. It is well-fired and of medium fabric. It is similar to TC wheel from Prakash (Pl. XXVI, no.2). Its total diameter is 5.1 cm, diameter of the hub is 2.0 cm, diameter of the hole is 0.5 cm. BDK-III.

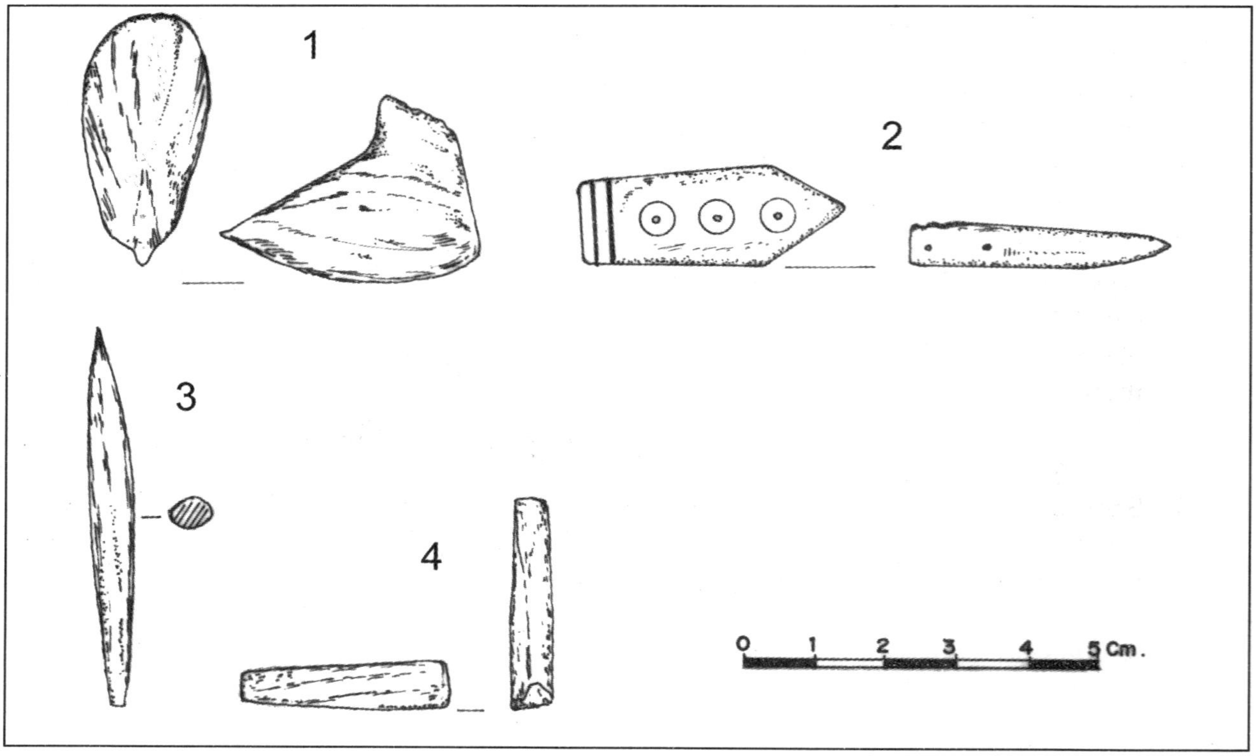

Fig. 13. Bone artifacts.

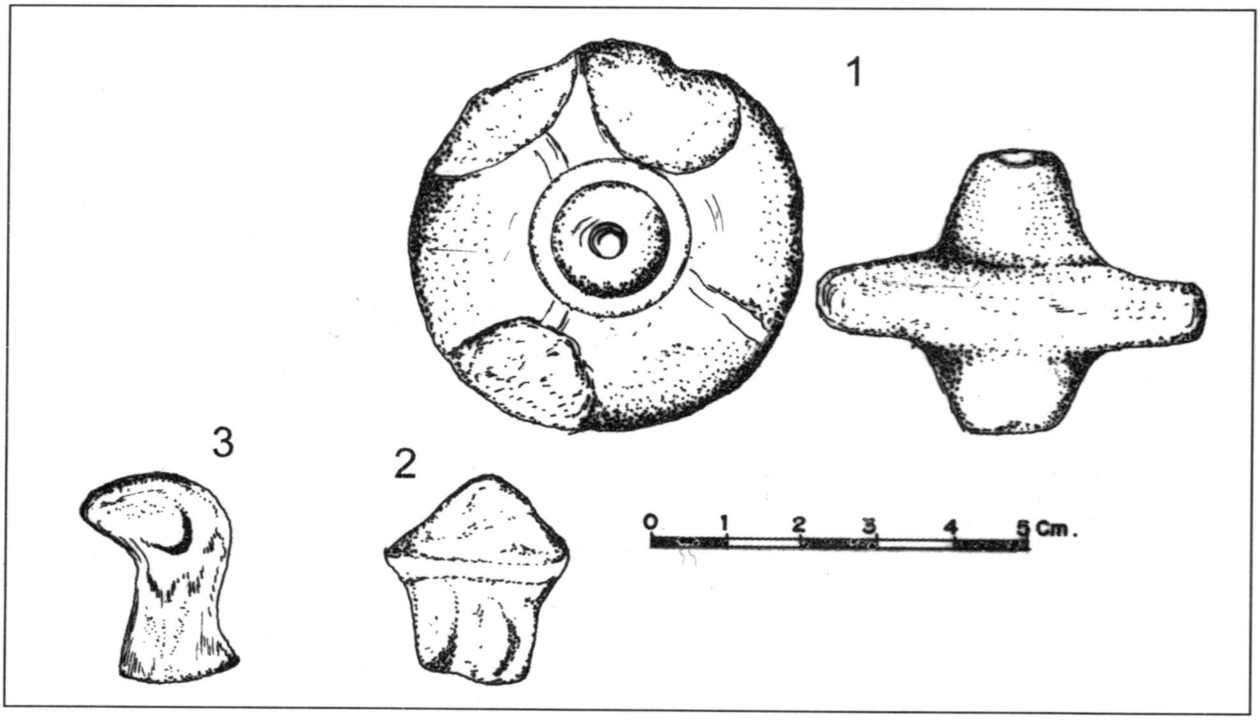

Fig. 14. Terracotta artifacts.

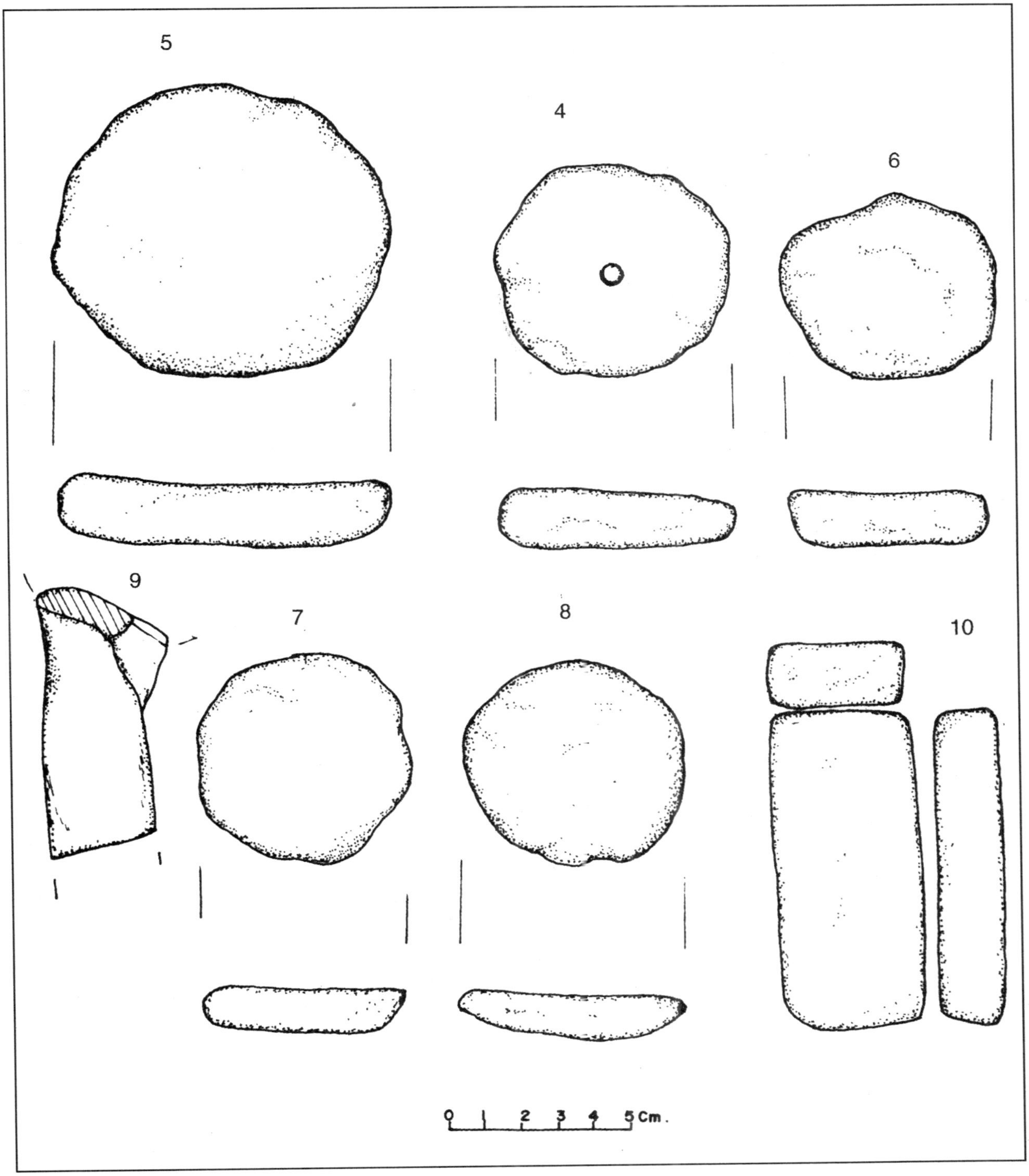

Fig. 14a. Terracotta artifacts.

2. Upper part of a stop or a knob of red ware. It is well-fired and is of medium fabric. It is treated with red slip. Its height is 3 cm, diameter of projection is 2.5 cm and diameter of stem is 1.5 cm. BDK-II.
3. Unidentified figure of an animal; the ears have been made by pressing the original clay surface, with the help of the tips of the fingers. It is made on red ware and treated with red slip; it is of medium fabric and is ill-fired. Its height is 3 cm and thickness 1.2 cm. BDK-II.
4. Spindle whorl made of red ware pottery; on one side, it is slightly concave with a central hole. Its diameter is 3 cm and thickness 0.7 cm. BDK-VI, surface area.
5. Hop-scotch made on red ware pottery. The diameter is 5 cm and thickness 0.6 cm. BDK-I.
6. Small hop-scotch made on red ware pottery. The diameter is 3 cm and thickness 0.7 cm.
7. Hop-scotch made on red ware pottery. The diameter is 3.5 cm and thickness 0.6 cm.
8. Hop-scotch made on red ware pottery. The diameter is 3.3 cm and thickness 0.6 cm.
9. Leg portion of a human figure; dull red in colour. Length is 7.7 cm, depth is 174 cm and diameter 3 cm. BDK-II, layer 6.
10. Terracotta rubber stone; dull red ware; black core noticed; it is ill-fired. Length is 9.3 cm, thickness 1.8 cm, width 4.1 cm and depth 163 cm. BDK-II, layer 5.
11. Toy cart (?) broken on the front side and made on red ware. The cart is a model of a cargo cart as it has good space for keeping cargo. It has been made from 3-4 parts joined together. The vacant space measures 7 × 6 × 3.5 cm while the upper hole measures 4.5 × 4 cm. The maximum height is 6 cm, width is 8.4 cm and remained length is 8 cm. The upper edge of the back portion has been designed with three small projections. BDK-III.

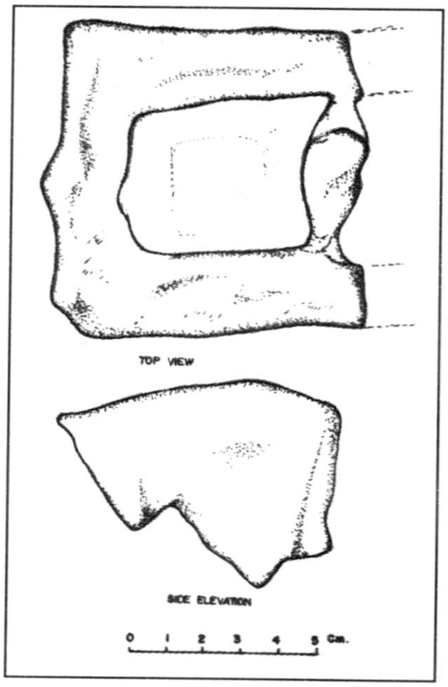

Fig. 14b. Terracotta artifacts.

4.8 TERRACOTTA & STONE BALLS

A large number of terracotta and stone balls were recovered during the excavations (Fig. 15 and Pl. 20). They are restricted to only historical period sites on the southeastern coast of the island. A brief description of each one is given below:

1. Stone ball with smooth surface; yellowish in colour. Diameter 2.8 cm. BDK-VI 65-70 cm, layer 2.
2. Stone ball with irregular shape; whitish in colour. Diameter is 2.5 cm and depth 130 cm. BDK-III, layer 6.
3. Stone ball with smooth surface; whitish in colour. Diameter is 2.1 cm and depth 150 cm. BDK-III, layer 7.
4. Stone ball with irregular shape; yellowish in colour; smooth surface. Diameter is 2.1 cm and depth 100 cm. BDK-II, layer 3.

Pl. 1. Late Harappan seal made on conch shell, discovered during marine archaeological explorations in 1986 (after S.R. Rao, 1987).

Pl. 2. Inscribed potsherd recovered during onshore explorations from Bet Dwarka (S.R. Rao, 1990).

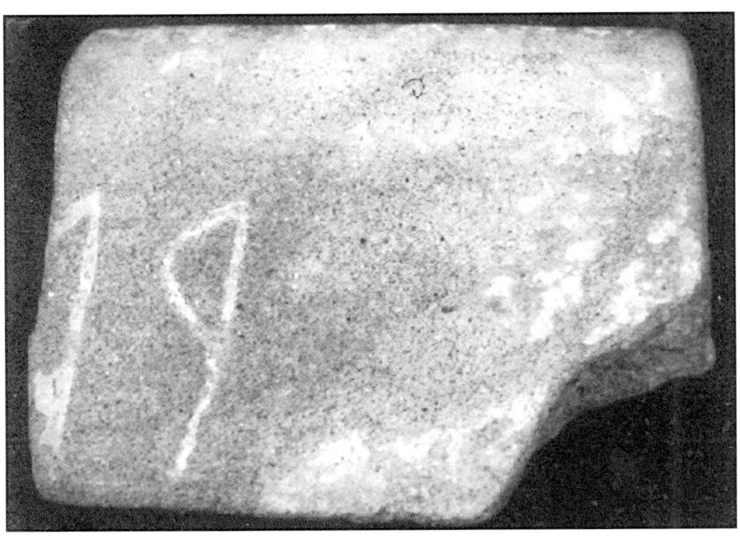

Pl. 3. Graffiti marks on a potsherd from Bet Dwarka discovered during onshore explorations (Sundaresh and Gaur, 1998).

Pl. 4. The trench BDK-I.

Pl. 5. Structures exposed in BDK-I.

Pl. 6. The trench BDK-II.

Pl. 7. Structure exposed in BDK-II.

Pl. 8. Structure exposed in BDK-III.

Pl. 9. Trench BDK-IV.

Pl. 11. Trench BDK-VI.

Pl. 10. Trench BDK-V.

Pl. 12. A large stone in trench BDK-VI.

Pl. 13. Terracotta beads.

Pl. 14. Shell beads.

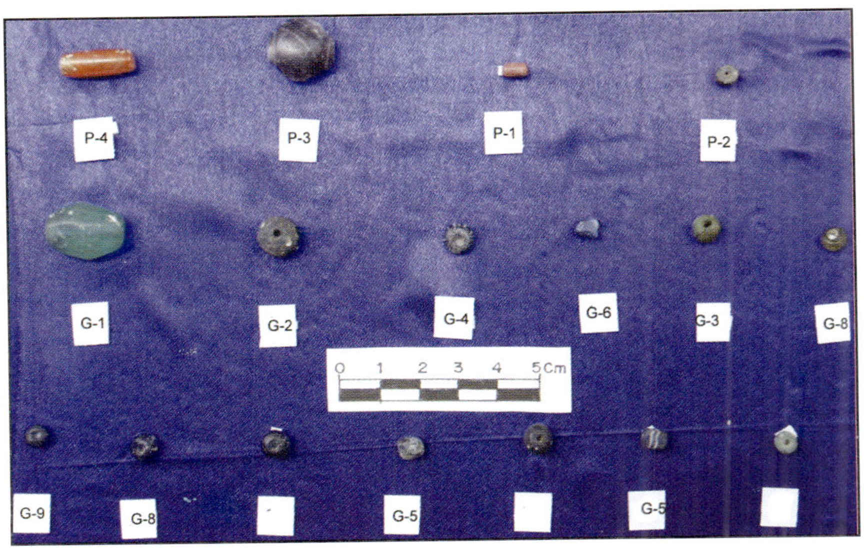

Pl. 15. Glass and Stone beads (G-Glass and S-Stone).

Pl. 16. Fish bone beads.

Pl. 17. Bone artifacts.

Pl. 18. Terracotta artifacts.

Pl. 19. Terracotta artifacts.

Pl. 21. Stone artifacts.

Pl. 21. (A) Stone artifacts.

Pl. 21. (B) Stone artifacts.

Pl. 20. Terracotta and stone balls.

Pl. 22. Copper artifacts.

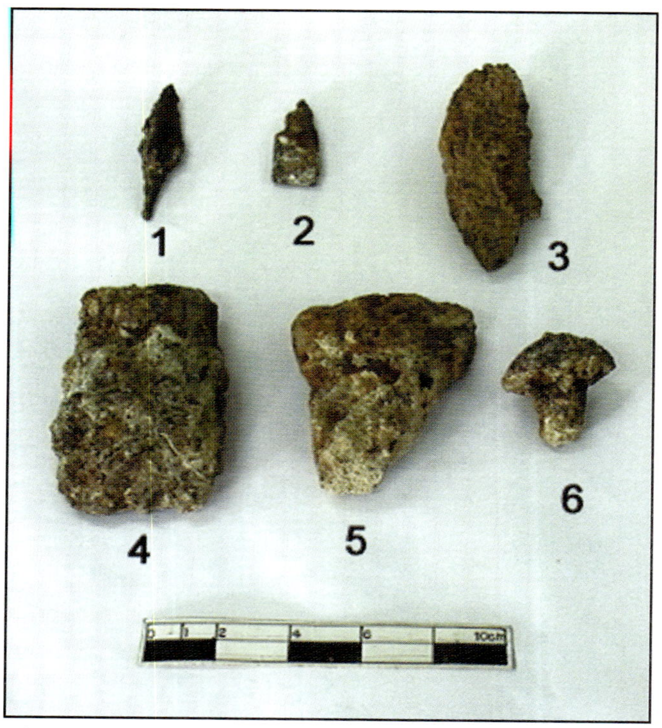

Pl. 23. Iron objects.

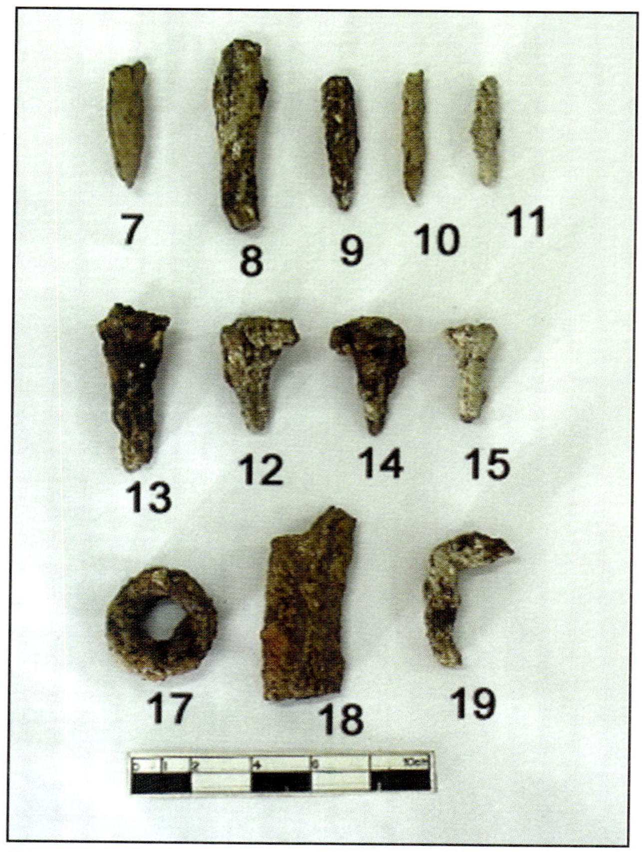

Pl. 24. Iron objects.

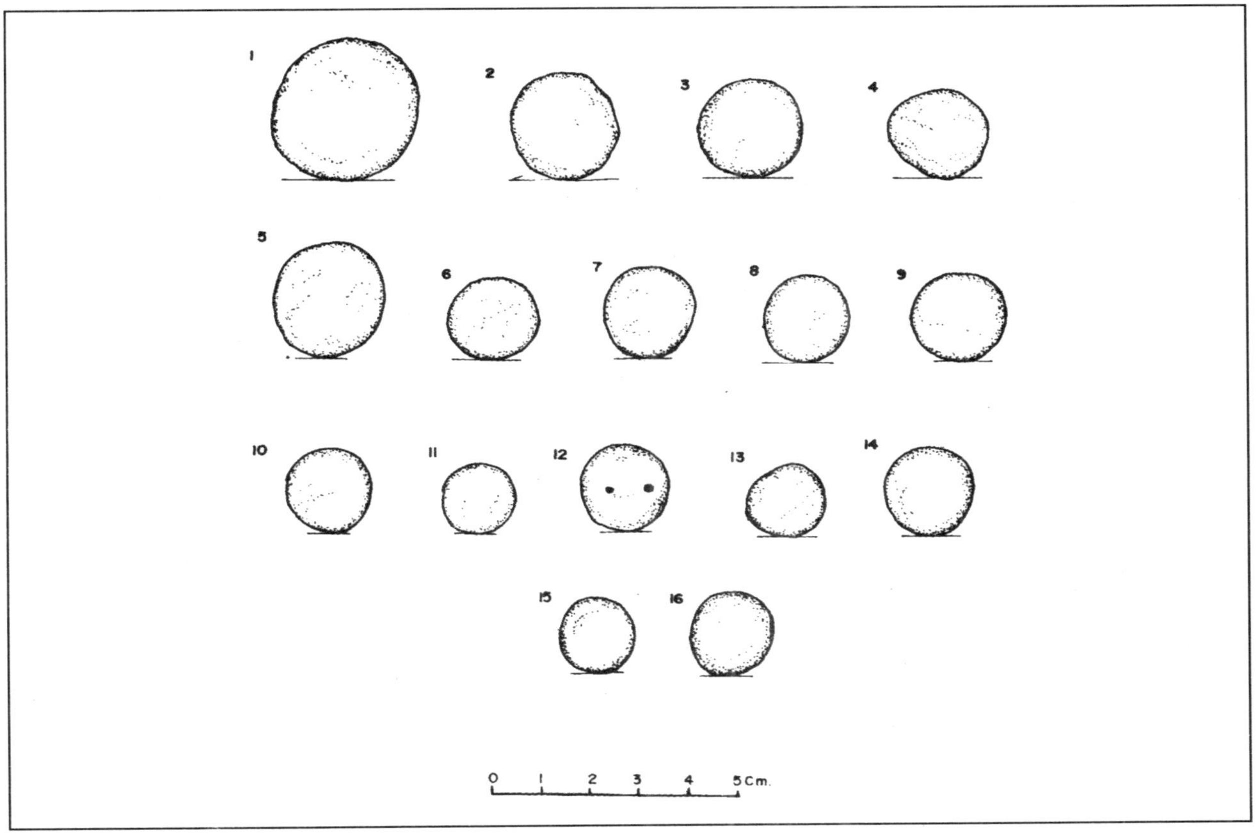

Fig. 15. Terracotta and stone balls.

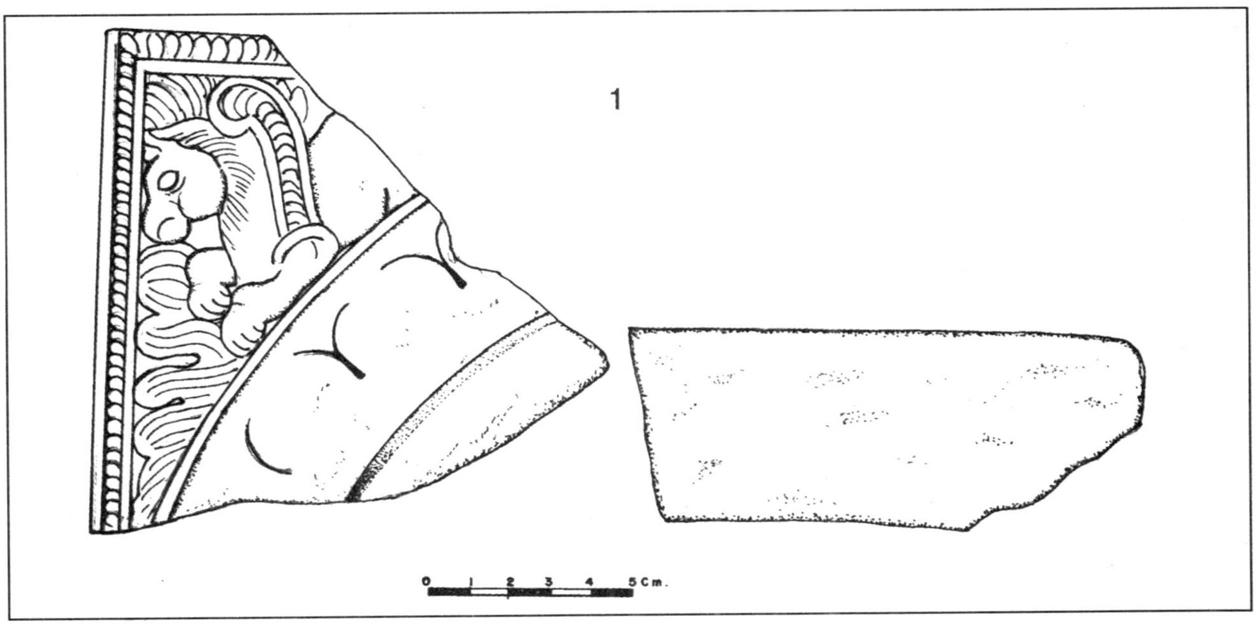

Fig. 16. Stone artifacts.

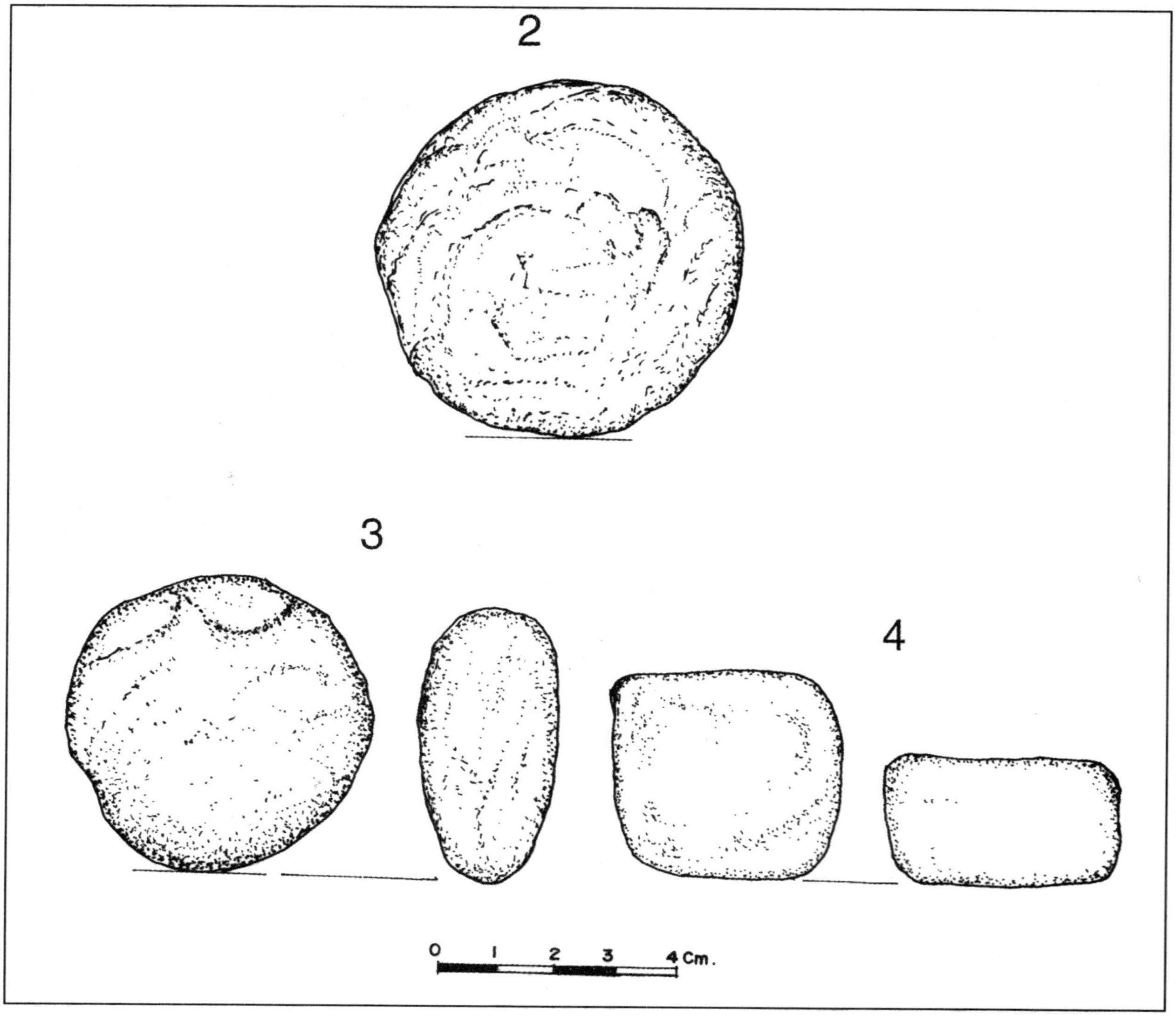

Fig. 17. Stone artifacts.

5. Terracotta ball with a smooth surface; reddish in colour. Diameter is 2.2 cm and depth 80 cm. BDK-I, layer 4.
6. Terracotta ball; well-fired and of medium fabric. Diameter is 2.0 cm and depth 130 cm. BDK-III, layer 6.
7. Stone ball with a smooth surface. Diameter is 2.0 cm and depth 130 cm. BDK-III, layer 6.
8. Stone ball with irregular shape with smooth surface; yellowish in colour. Diameter is 2.0 cm and depth 25 cm. BDK-II, layer 2.
9. Stone ball with smooth surface; yellowish in colour. Diameter is 1.9 cm and depth 261 cm. BDK-II, layer 10.
10. Broken stone ball with a smooth surface; greyish in colour. Diameter is 1.9 cm and depth 75 cm. BDK-III, layer 4.

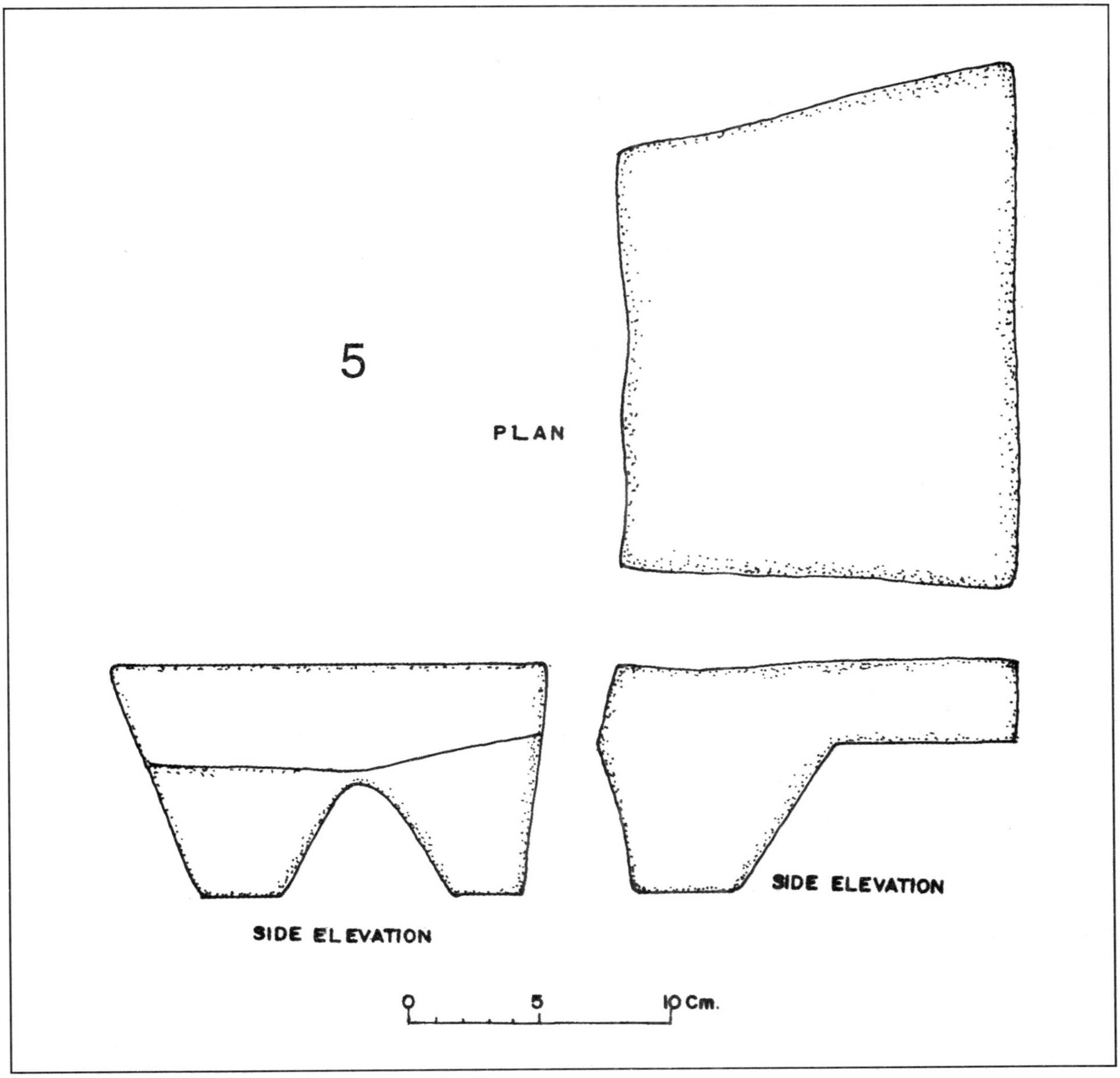

Fig. 18. Stone artifacts.

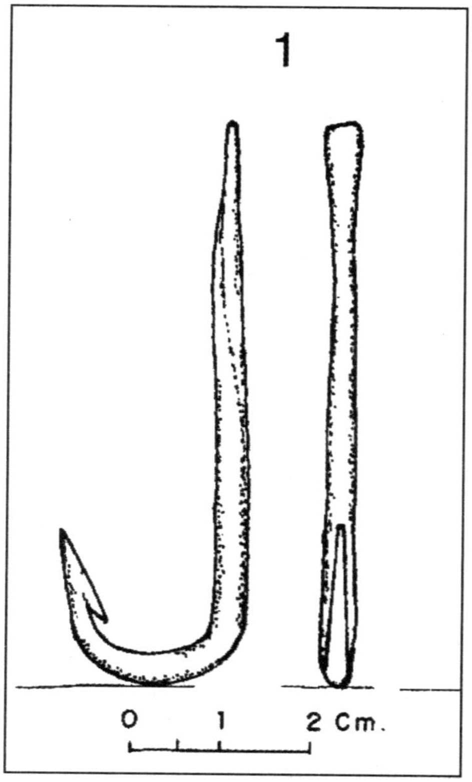

Fig. 19. Copper fishhook.

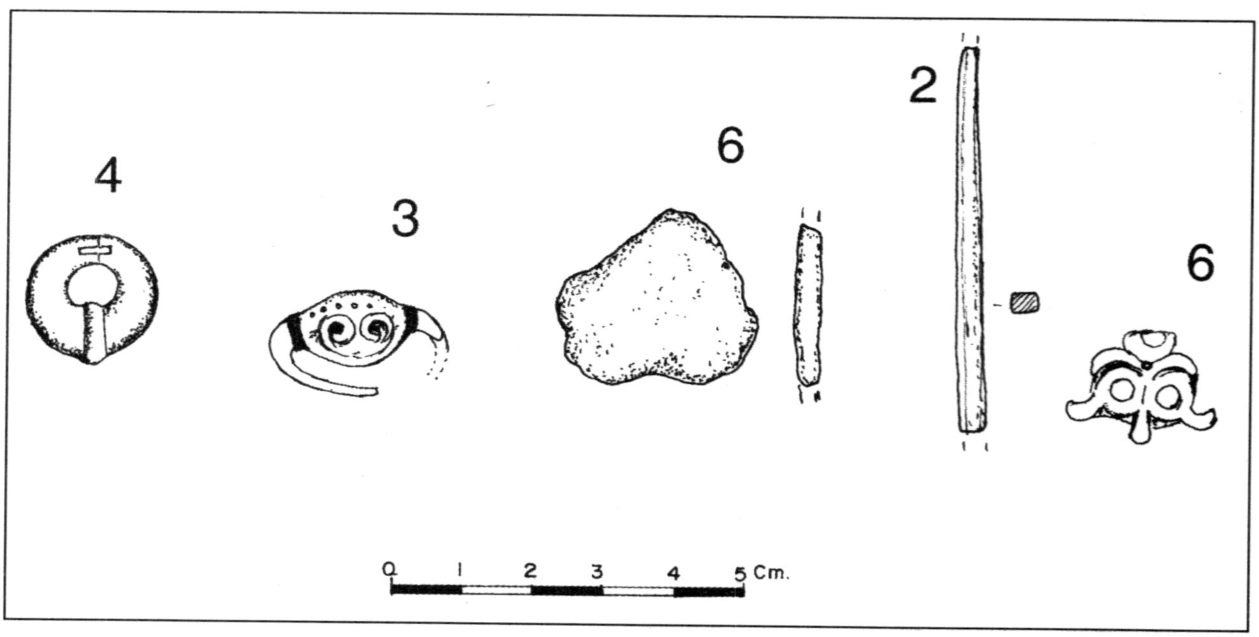

Fig. 20. Copper artifacts.

11. Broken terracotta ball of small size, well-fired and of medium fabric. Diameter is 1.4 cm and depth 130 cm. BDK-III, layer 6.
12. Stone ball with irregular shape and smooth surface. Diameter is 1.9 cm and depth 80 cm. BDK-I, layer 4.
13. Ball of sun-dried clay; depression on one side noticed. Diameter is 1.7 cm and depth 44 cm. BDK-III, layer 3.
14. Stone ball of irregular shape with smooth surface. Diameter is 2.1 cm. BDK-III.
15. Small, irregular terracotta ball with smooth surface. Diameter is 1.6 cm and depth 130 cm. BDK-III, layer 6.
16. Broken terracotta ball; reddish surface. Diameter is 1.7 cm and depth 60 cm. BDK-III, layer 3.

4.9 STONE OBJECTS

Very few stone artifacts have been recovered, and among them a decorative piece of sandstone (Pl. 21) and a four-legged quern are included (Fig. 16-18). A brief description of each object is as follows:

1. A broken decorated sandstone slab. It appears that the centre is marked with a circle having a *Purna Ghata* symbol. One remained corner design contain a seated lion with prominent mans. The left space is filled with floral designs. The outer boundary has regular cross lines. The length of the remained portion is 12.5 cm, width is 12.2 cm and height is 5 cm. BDK-I, layer 3.
2. A single example of sling ball from BDK-I. It is of sandstone and is circular in shape. Diameter is 6 cm and depth 60 cm. BDK-I, layer 3.
3. Discular-spheroid, sandstone. The flat sides retain the original surface. Diameter is 5.3 cm, thickness 2.7 cm and depth 2.55 cm. BDK-II, layer 11.
4. Cubical weight of locally-available sandstone. Length is 3.9 cm, width 3.7, the height varies from 3 to 2.2 cm and depth 70 cm. BDK-I, layer 5.
5. Four-legged quern made of basalt, which is broken on one side. One end of the upper surface protrudes beyond the axis of the legs. Available length is 16 cm, width 19.5 cm, thickness 3.5 cm and depth 160 cm. BDK-III, layer 7. It is similar to the one found at Prakash 1955 (Pl. 20, no. 3).

4.10 COPPER OBJECTS

Besides copper coins, six copper objects were discovered from the Bet Dwarka excavations. The most important finding is a copper fishhook from late Harappan Phase and it is well-preserved and one of the biggest fishhook from this phase. The details and comparative study of fishhook has been published (Gaur and Sundaresh, 2004), and the revised version of the same is included in this report as Annexure II. An antimony rod, pendant, earring and a figure are other important findings from the excavations (Fig. 19-20 and Pl. 22). A brief description of each finding is given below:

1. Fishhook with barbed point, straight sunk without forming any curve. However, the top is beaten up and made wide and thin, perhaps for holding thread. Some of the Mesopotamian sites like Ur, yielded similar type of fishhooks. Several Harappan sites reported fishhooks, which are barbed, and range from 1.25 to 7 cm in length (Sarkar, 1953). Fishhook from Bet Dwarka is one of the biggest recorded from Harappan sites.

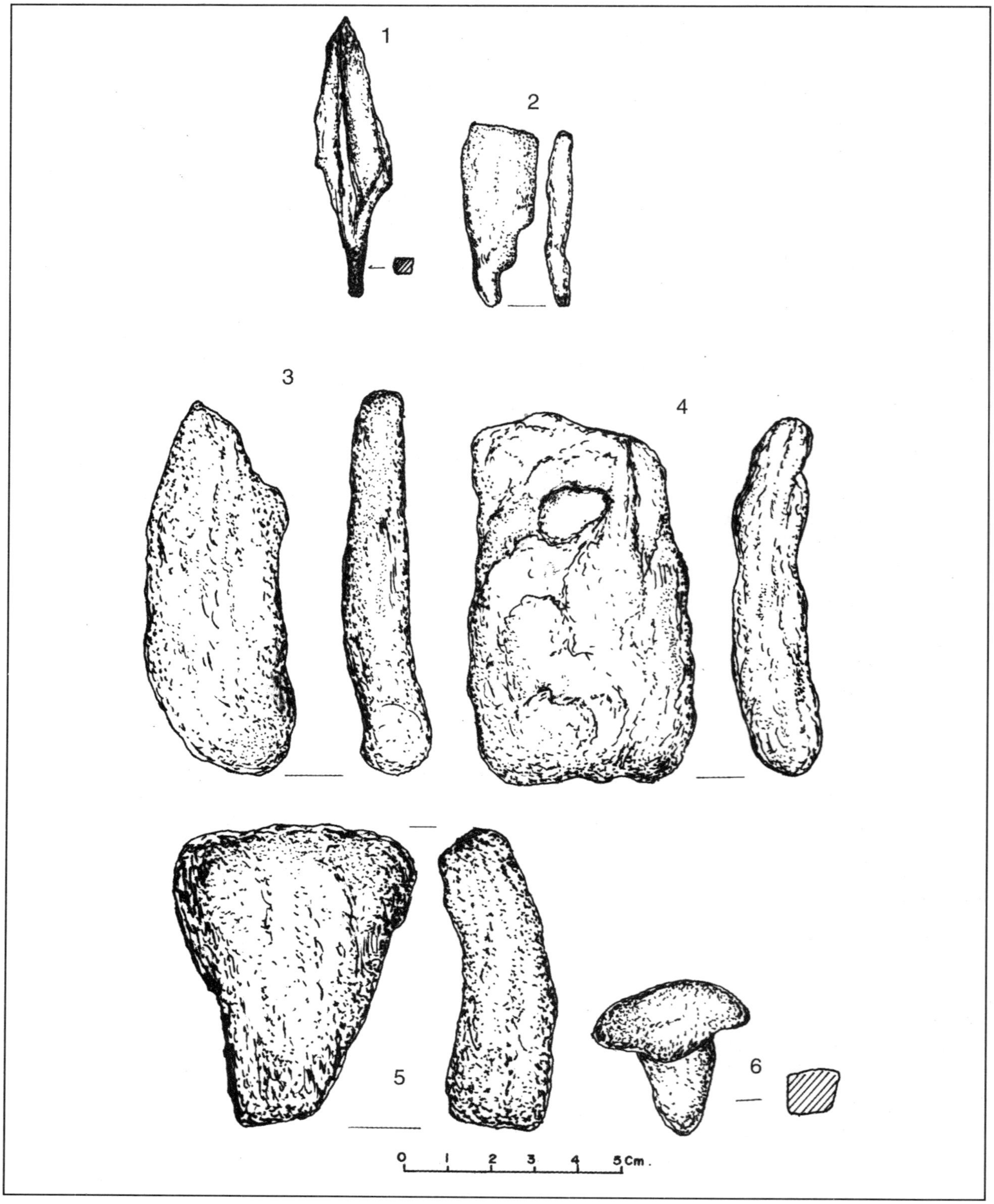

Fig. 21. Iron objects.

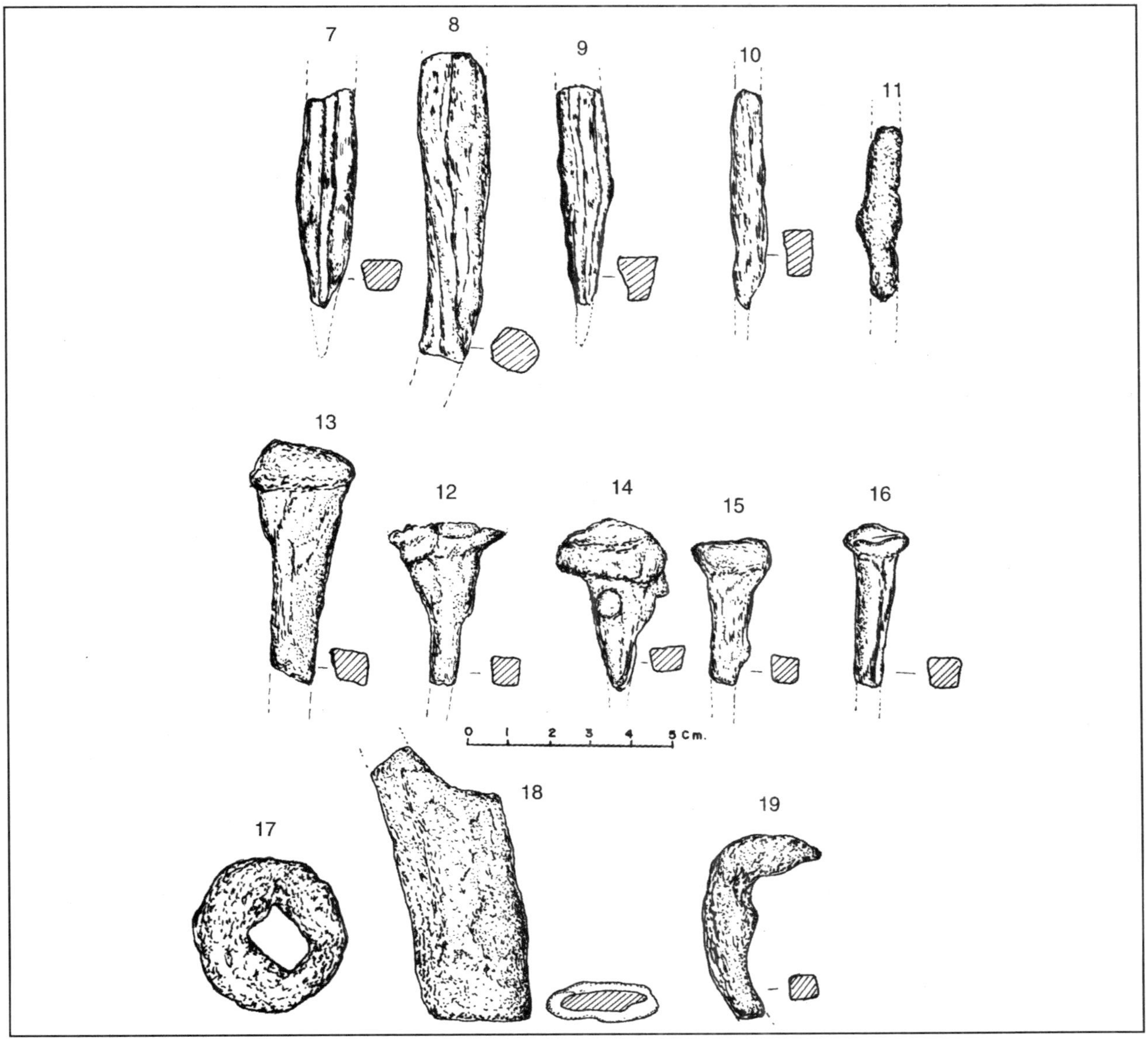

Fig. 22. Iron objects.

Length is 6.5 cm, barbed point of 1.1 cm, section of sank is round. BDK-VI. (A full fledged study on this fishhook has been published in *Current Science* and the same has been included as Annexure I.)

2. Antimony rod of rectangular section. One half is thinner than the other one. Similar types of antimony rods have been reported from several Harappan sites and from other places. Length is 5.5 cm and thickness 0.4 cm. BDK-VI.
3. Broken finger ring with a bank of round section. It is in broad oval shape with floral designs on the upper side. Diameter is 1.5 cm. BDK-III.
4. A thick earring. It can be placed in the ear by turning the two sides away from each other, as they are joined with a groove and socket. The ring has the evidence of gold coating. Outer diameter is 1.9 cm and inner is 0.7 cm. BDK-I.

5. Broken part of some unidentified copper object. Maximum length is 2.6 cm and thickness 0.3 cm. BDK-III.
6. Copper pendant with a mythical animal design. A hole on the upper side is present. Height is 1.6 cm and thickness 0.2 cm. BDK-III.

4.11 IRON OBJECTS

A large number of iron artifacts were recovered from all the phases of the historical period settlements of Bet Dwarka. The most prominent among them are nails, sickles and arrowheads (Fig. 21-22, Pl. 23-24). The iron objects have been heavily encrusted and only a few have preserved core. A brief description of the iron objects is given below:

1. Arrowhead with a thin long tang. It has a sharp, pointed top; heavily rusted. Length is 6.4, width 1.6 cm and depth 60 cm. BDK-I, layer 4.
2. Arrowhead with broken tang. It is bend towards the top point and heavily rusted. Length is 4.1 cm, width 1.6 cm, thickness 0.5 cm and depth 90 cm . BDK-I, layer 7.
3. Sickle fragment. It is heavily rusted. Remained length is 9.0 cm, width 3.1 cm and thickness 1 cm.
4. Celt-like axe head and broadening lower side and heavily encrusted. Length is 8.7 cm, width 5 cm, depth 120 and thickness 1.2 cm. BDK-I, layer 6.
5. Celt-like axe head. It forms a triangular shape. There is a slight bend towards the lower side. Length is 6.8 cm, width 5.5 cm/1.6 cm and thickness 2.2 cm.
6. Broken nail. Core is well-preserved. Length is 3.2 cm, diameter of nail is 0.9 cm, diameter of head is 2.00 cm and depth is 30 cm. BDK-II, layer 2.
7. Small broken point side nail is well-preserved; prominent head, roundish on top. Length is 4.1 cm, diameter of pointed side is 0.8 cm, diameter of head is 1.6 cm and depth is 89 cm. BDK-III, layer 3.
8. Nail without head; squarish in section; thickly encrusted. Maximum length is 5.2 cm, width and thickness are 1.2 cm on the upper side.
9. Nail with broken head; heavily encrusted; appears to be squarish in section. Length is 7.3 cm. Upper side thickness is 1.5 cm; lower side is 1.2 cm and depth is 100 cm. BDK-I, layer 6.
10. Pointed nail without head; core is well-preserved. Length is 5.2 cm, diameter is 1.5 cm and depth 7 cm. BDK-I, layer 1.
11. Fragmented nail without head; heavily encrusted. Length is 4.1 cm, diameter in middle is 1.1 cm and depth 2.05 cm. BDK-II, layer 8.
12. Broken nail with broad head. Head is roundish on top. Head diameter is 3.2 cm, shaft diameter is 1.4 cm and depth 242 cm. Remained length is 3.5 cm. BDK-II, layer 10.
13. Nail with head which is flat on top; lower side nail is broken; heavily encrusted. Length is 5.7 cm, diameter of head is 2.6 cm, diameter of the lower side of nail is 1.2 cm and depth is 225 cm. BDK-II, layer 8.
14. Small nail with broad head; top head is of convex type. Length is 4.3 cm, diameter of head is 2.4 cm, diameter at lower side is 0.7 cm and depth is 271 cm. BDK-II, layer 10.

Pl. 25. Copper coins.

Pl. 26. Late Harappan pottery from BDK-VI.

Pl. 27. A sherd of bowl with a brahmi letter "A".

Pl. 28. Miniature vessel in red polished ware.

Pl. 29. Historical period lids.

15. Fragmented nail with wide head; heavily encrusted. Length is 4 cm and diameter is 3.1 cm and depth 130 cm. BDK-III, layer 6.
16. Broken nail with heavy encrustation. The section of the nail appears to be squarish. Length is 4 cm, diameter of head is 2.5 cm, thickness of lower part is 0.8 cm and depth 110 cm. BDK-III, layer 5.
17. Head of the nail; heavily encrusted. A hole was created for inserting nail in the head. Length is 3.8 cm, thickness 1.5 cm and depth 185 cm. BDK-III, layer 8.
18. Sickle fragment; core is well-preserved. Length is 6.4 cm, width 2.7 cm, central thickness is 1 cm and depth 75 cm. BDK-I, layer 4.
19. Broken clamp with heavy encrustation. Length is 4.9 cm, diameter is 1.4 cm and depth 245 cm. BDK-II, layer 10.

4.12 COPPER COINS

There were five copper coins discovered during the excavations. A few copper coins of the Kushana Period were discovered earlier from surface exploration (Sundaresh and Gaur, 1998). Two each copper coins have been found from BDK-I and III and one coin was discovered from the surface near BDK-III (Pl. 25). The description and details of each coin is given below:

1. *Obverse:* Three arched hills with a wavy line below and floral dotted design in dotted circle.

   Reverse: Standing figure of an animal. A small Swastika symbol has been noticed between the two legs of an animal. Above the animal, a six-arched Ujjaini symbol is also noticed. BDK III, depth 110 cm, layer 5.
2. Kushana coin

   Obverse: King is standing to the left, wearing a diadem and helmet, sacrificing at an altar. He also holds a spear in his raised left hand. He is wearing a tunic. The Greek legend *Shao ka* is readable and remaining legends have been worn out.

   Reverse: It has been heavily encrusted. However, a standing human figure can be identified. Script is noticed but is not readable. BDK-I, depth 80 cm, layer 6.
3. Kushana coin

   Obverse: King is standing to the left, wearing a diadem and helmet, sacrificing at an altar. He also holds a spear in his raised left hand. The script is not readable.

   Reverse: A male deity figure is standing. Some Greek legend is present but it is not readable. BDK-I, depth 80 cm, layer 6.
4. Copper coin, heavily corroded on both sides and found associated with previous one so it may also belong to the Kushana Period. However, nothing is decipherable. BDK-III, depth 10 cm, layer 1.
5. Copper coin, unidentified, as a symbol or figure could not be traced.

Chapter–5

Pottery

Bet Dwarka was a very important centre of the ceramic industry and it supplied clay vessels to the Kachchh and Saurashtra regions by boats till recently. However, the introduction of steel vessels forced the local inhabitant to adopt other professions for survival. A pond in the middle of the island, having very fine clay, was used for pottery manufacturing right from the arrival of man on the island. As defractometric study has suggested, the mineral composition of the pottery had a close affinity to the local clay. This compositional similarity provides the evidence to suggest that the recovered pottery from Bet Dwarka is exotic. Thus, it appears that the proto-historic and historic people of Bet Dwarka were well aware of the properties of local clay and its utility as pottery raw material (Hashimi *et al.*, 1994). Earlier onshore and inter-tidal zone explorations in the Bet Dwarka island revealed a large number of pottery of proto-historic period and historical period from various places. The pottery of proto-historic period was noticed at two sites, namely BDK-I and VI, which was similar to those found at Rangpur IIB-IIC. A potsherd from BDK-I was dated by thermoluminesence to 3520 years BP (Rao, 1988). However, recent excavations did not reveal any potsherd of proto-historic period from BDK-I, while BDK-VI have complete deposit of the proto-historic period. The entire pottery from BDK-I, II, III and VI has been divided into two periods. Period I is represented by the late Harappan assemblage at BDK-VI, and Period II by the historical period (5th century BC to 3rd century AD) at BDK-I, II and III.

5.1 PERIOD I

A small trench in an agriculture field in Balapur village of Bet Dwarka island represents Period I, assignable to the Late Harappan Period (Gaur, 1990 and Gaur *et al.*, 1994) and may be associated with Rangpur IIB (Rao, 1962). The habitation appears to be short-lived as the total deposit at the highest point was 90 cm. Earlier surface explorations revealed the remains of perforated jars, dish, dish-on-stand and goblet in red ware. A few convex-sided, painted potsherds of bowls

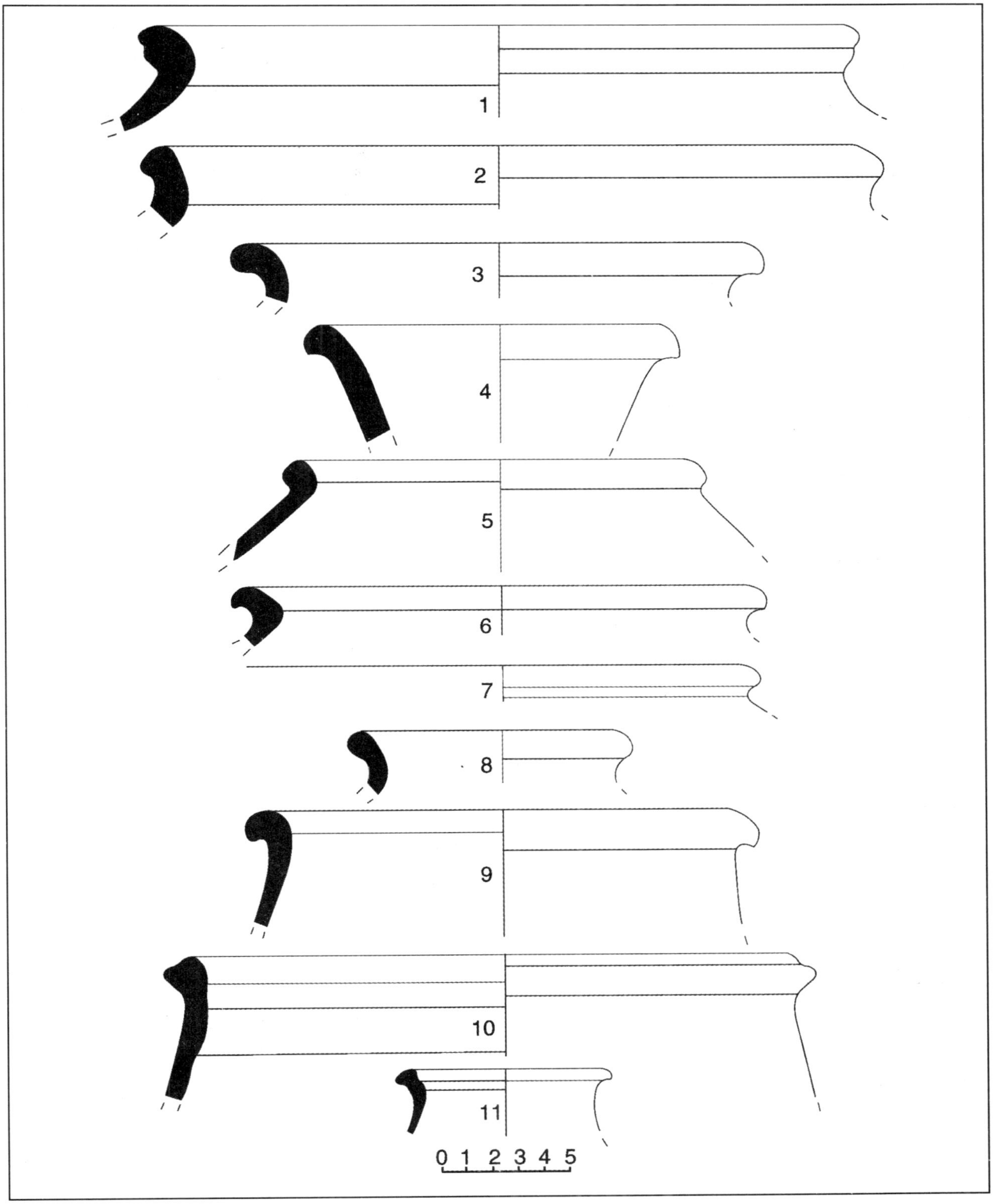

Fig. 23. Late Harappan pottery from BDK-VI.

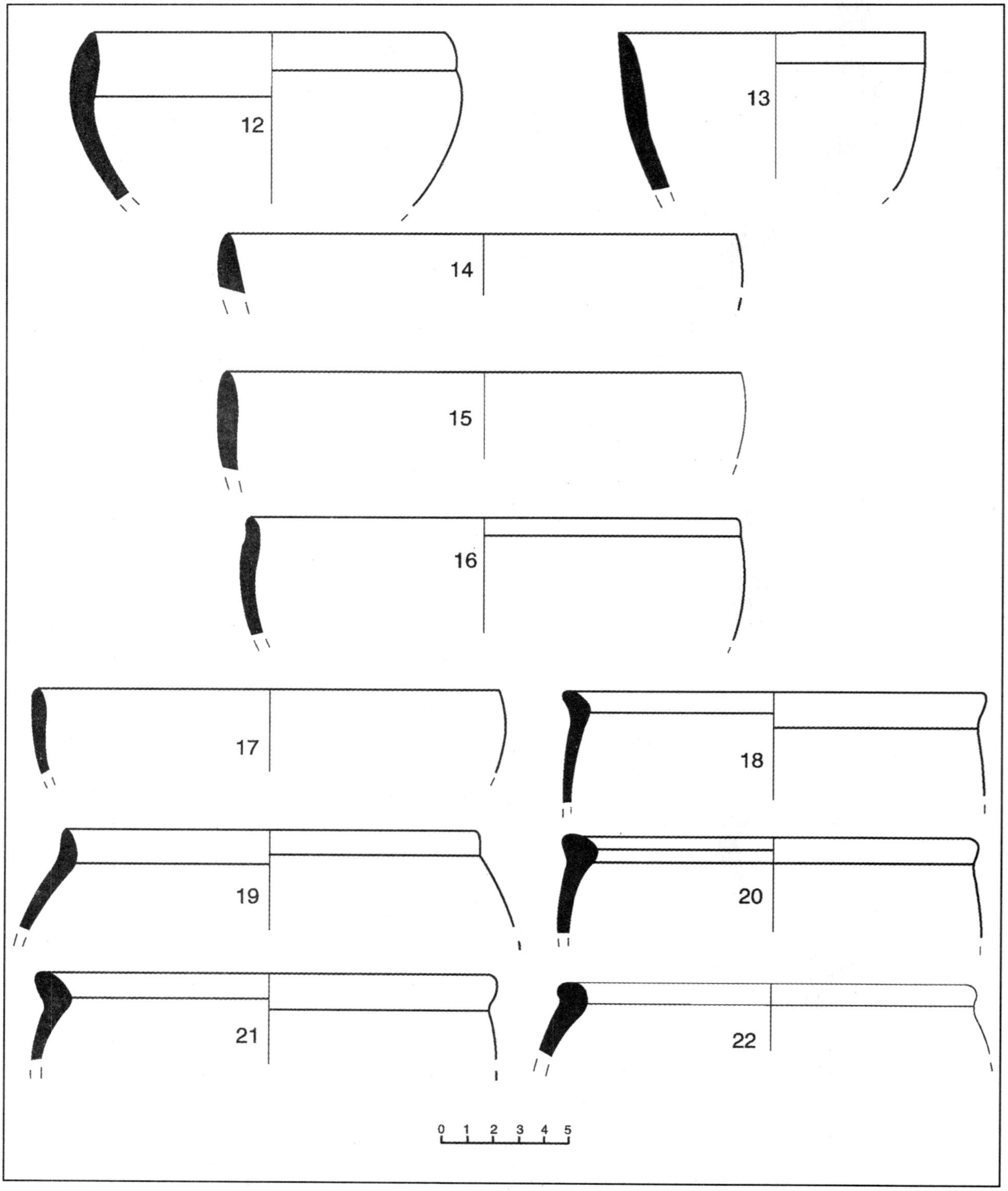

Fig. 24. Late Harappan pottery from BDK-VI.

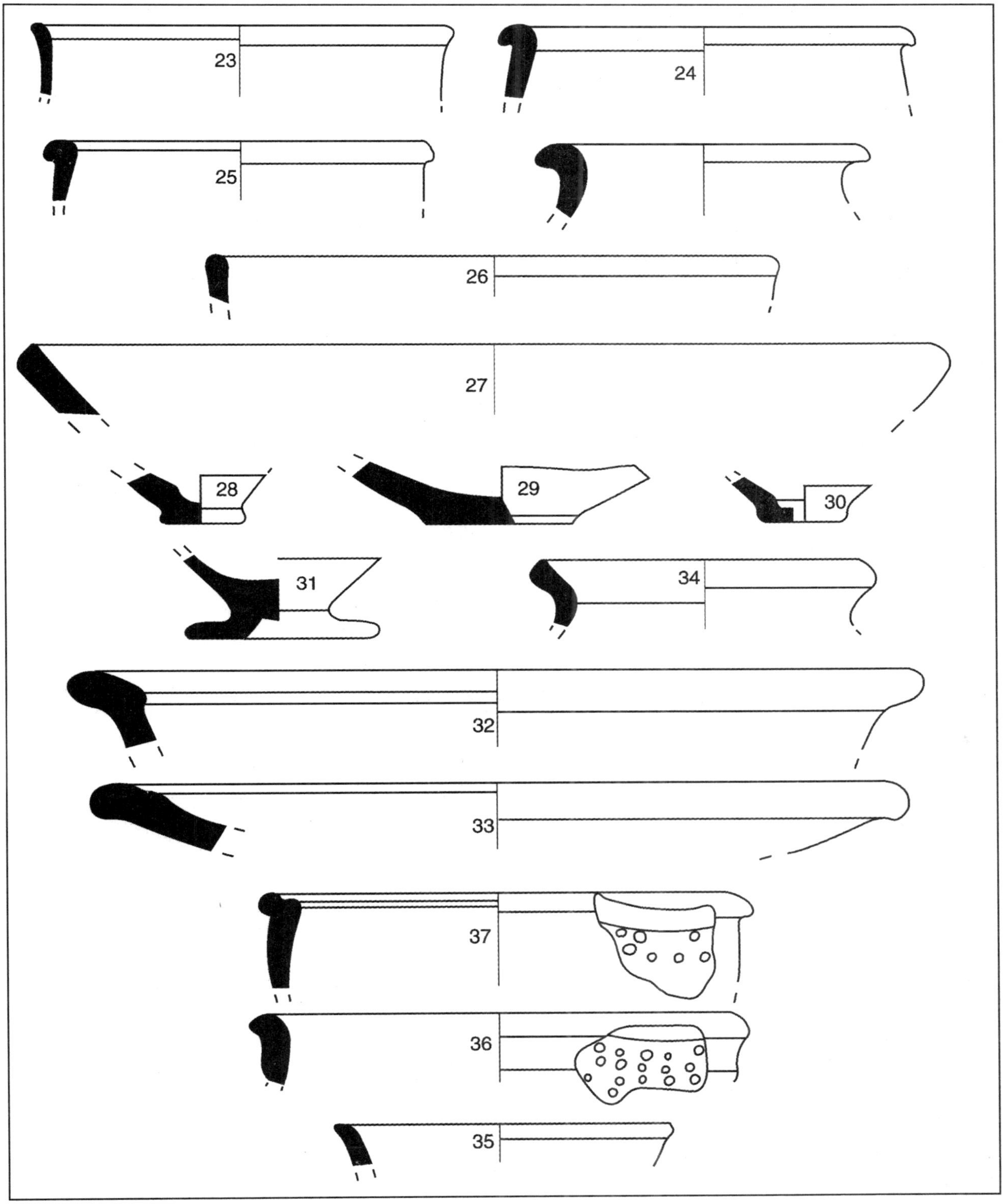

Fig. 25. Late Harappan pottery from BDK-VI.

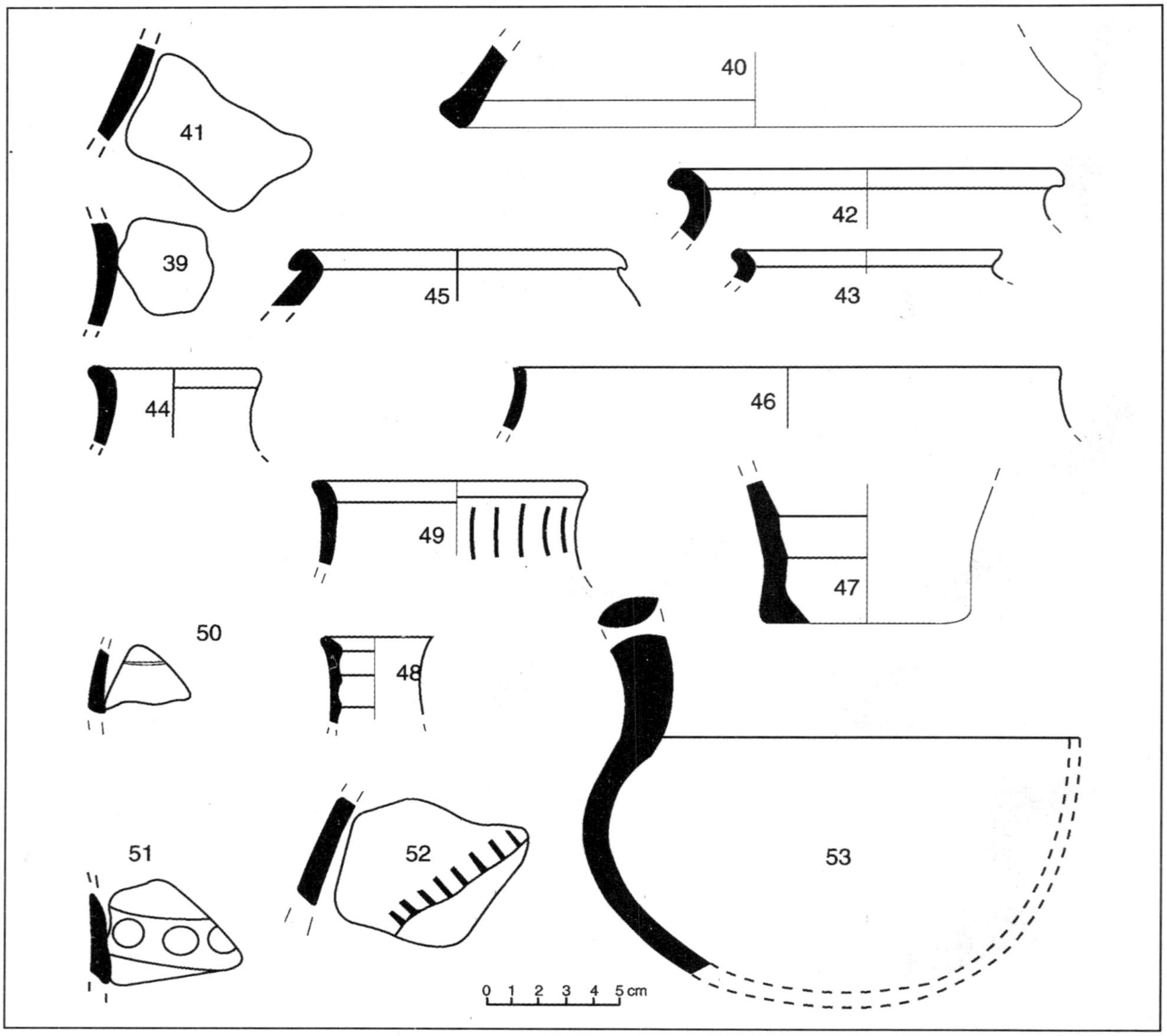

Fig. 26. Late Harappan pottery from BDK-VI.

were also recovered. During present excavations, all the above potsherds were noticed except perforated jars. Majority of the potsherds have a thick encrustation of salt, which makes difficult to trace the surface treatment like wash, slip and painting. The ceramic type indicates that they had contact with the Saurashtra of late Harappan community. Most of the shapes and type occuring at Bet Dwarka have close affinity to the characteristic feature of the Saurashtra late Harappan. The site is located on the eastern coast of the island, which is very well protected from high wave and tidal current. Presently, the height of the site from the high water line is about 3 m. The important types of ware of this period are mentioned below:

5.1.1 Red ware

The majority of pottery falls in this category. It is heavy and sturdy ware with red colour section and surface. It is made of fine, levigated clay, which is well-fired, resulting in a sturdy ware and emit a metallic sound when struck. Almost all the vessels have smooth surface. Majority of vessels are wheel-turned and treated with red slip of red wash. There are a few sherds of coarse fabric in red ware at Bet Dwarka. Clay used for these sherds is not well-levigated and a lot of micro-shells are noticed on the surface which resulted in the pitted surface.

5.1.2 Buff ware

This is generally associated with red ware in the late Harappan and post Harappan sites in Saurashtra. The vessel of this ware has a buff colour surface and section. Normally, the clay used is fine and the vessels are thin and sturdy. Similar buff ware potsherds have also been reported from Rangapur, Lothal and Nageshwar from Mature Harappan level. Perhaps this ware is the survival of Harappan influence on Bet Dwarka pottery. The important types are jars, miniature vessels and a bowl in Bet Dwarka. Sometimes, vessels are painted in thick brownish to red colour.

5.1.3 Black ware

Three jars and one basin are of black ware. The clay is not well-levigated and is ill-fired. They have a very coarse fabric and rough surface. This type of pottery is not reported from Harappan and late Harappan sites in Saurashtra.

5.1.4 Grey ware

A few sherds of grey ware were recovered during surface exploration. However, excavations did not reveal any sherds of this ware. It is noticed in Rangpur IIB-IIC, Kalibangan II (Rao, 1985) and Mohenjodaro (Mackay, 1953). Its grey colour, which occasionally deepens into black, is attributed to the use of carbonaceous matter. It may also be due to firing under reducing conditions. The texture of the vessels is homogenous and the surface is well-burnished. The only type in this category is a bowl. But at Nageshwar, it is represented by convex-sided bowls, pedestal base of a pot and a few non-descriptive sherds (Hegde *et al.*, 1990).

5.1.5 Painted potsherds

Three potsherds of red ware painted in black colour were recovered from here. The important design is roundels on the shoulder portion of a bowl, wavy lines on the shoulder and rim portion of a miniature vessel, and a horizontal thick band on the shoulder of a jar.

5.1.6 Slipped ware

Apart from red slip ware, a few other slip ware in small quantity were noticed, such as cream slipped, chocolate slipped and black slipped ware which are common at several Harappan and late Harappan sites in Saurashtra.

5.1.7 Pottery description (Fig. 23 to 26)

1. Large size jar with a flaring but slightly beaded rim and short-necked; bulged profile; treated with red wash; black core is noticed; coarse fabric and ill-fired. BDK-VI, 2001-02.
2. Medium size jar with a splayed-out, beaded rim and short-necked; treated with red wash; coarse fabric and ill-fired. BDK-VI, 2001-02.
3. Small size jar with a splayed-out beaded rim; dull red wash is noted; black core is present; coarse fabric and ill-fired. BDK-VI, 2001-02.

4. High-necked jar with splayed-out beaked rim; treated with red wash; coarse fabric and ill-fired. BDK-VI, 2001-02.
5. Short-necked jar with a squarish rim and bulbous body in dull red ware; fine fabric and well-fired. BDK-VI, 2001-02.
6. Jar with splayed-out, slightly beaked rim; medium fabric and well-fired. BDK-VI, 2001-02.
7. Jar with beaked and splayed-out rim in dull red ware; medium fabric and well-fired. BDK-VI, 2001-02.
8. Small-sized jar with a beaded rim; treated with red slip; coarse fabric and ill-fired. BDK-VI, 2001-02.
9. High-necked jar with externally projected beaked rim; exterior treated with chocolate colour slip; fine fabric and well-fired. BDK-VI, 2001-02.
10. Jar with a raised and externally projected triangular rim in dull red ware; medium fabric and well-fired. BDK-VI, 2001-02.
11. Miniature jar with a splayed-out and nail-headed rim; treated with red slip; very thin section; fine fabric and well-fired. BDK-VI, 2001-02.
12. Bowl with a sharpened featureless rim and convex-sided; internally treated with chocolate colour while the exterior is treated with a thick band of chocolate colour slip; the exterior has two grooves below the rim, running parallel along the rim. It is made of fine fabric and is well-fired. BDK-VI, 2001-02.
13. Bowl with a sharpened featureless rim and convex-sided; treated with dark brown colour slip on both sides; fine fabric and well-fired. BDK-VI, 2001-02.
14. Bowl with sharpened and featureless rim with straight sides; chocolate colour slip on both sides; smoky core noticed; it is a coarse fabric and is ill-fired. BDK-VI, 2001-02.
15. Bowl with sharpened and featureless rim with straight sides in dull red ware; fine fabric and well-fired. BDK-VI, 2001-02.
16. Bowl with sharpened and featureless rim and straight sides. Towards the base portion, it is convex-sided; sariation marks are also visible; it is of dull red ware; fine fabric and well-fired. BDK-VI, 2001-02.
17. Bowl with sharpened rim and thin section; convex-sided; fine fabric and well-fired. BDK-VI, 2001-02.
18. Bowl with sharpened, externally projecting rim in dull red ware; convex-sided; fine fabric and ill-fired. BDK-VI, 2001-02.
19. Bowl with sharpened, externally projected rim; dull red ware with straight sides; fine fabric and ill-fired. BDK-VI, 2001.
20. Bowl with externally projected beaked rim with convex sides. A band of red slip is noticed below the rim externally; medium fabric and well-fired. BDK-VI, 2001-02 (Pl. 26, no. 4).
21. Bowl with externally projected beaked rim and straight sides; externally treated with red slip; fine fabric and well-fired. BDK-VI, 2001-02.
22. Bowl with short, externally projected beaked rim and straight sides; external and rim portion treated with red slip; medium fabric and well-fired. BDK-VI, 2001-02.
23. Bowl with sharpened, externally projected rim in dull red ware; straight sides; fine fabric and ill-fired. BDK-VI, 2001-02 (Pl. 26, no.1).

24. Bowl with externally projected triangular type rim with convex sides; fine fabric and well-fired. BDK-VI, 2001-02.
25. Bowl with short, externally projected beaked rim; exterior and rim portion treated with chocolate colour slip; well-fired and of fine fabric. BDK-VI, 2001-02.
26. Bowl with an obliquely cut rim and convex sides; externally treated with black slip; well-fired and of medium fabric. BDK-VI, 2001-02.
27. Bowl with everted rim; treated with red slip on both sides; thick smoky core indicate deficiency in firing; coarse fabric. BDK-VI, 2001-02.
28. Bowl with pedestal base; thick section, fine fabric and well-fired. BDK-VI, 2001-02.
29. Bowl with contiguous flat base; it has a fine fabric and is well-fired. BDK-VI, 2001-02.
30. Bowl with pedestal base, corrugated profile; string mark noticed on the base; fine fabric and well-fired. BDK-VI, 2001-02.
31. Bowl-on-stand with short stem; fine fabric and well-fired. BDK-VI, 2001-02.
32. Dish with an outward projected rectangular rim, and a prominent carination is also noticed; thick walls; horizontal thick bands of chocolate colour on exterior and interior are present; fine fabric and well-fired. BDK-VI, 2001-02 (Pl. 26, no. 5).
33. Dish with an externally projected beaded rim; slip flaked off; thick wall; fine fabric and well-fired. BDK-VI, 2001-02.

Black Ware

34. Medium size jar with a nail-headed rim; bulbous body, ill-fired and coarse fabric. BDK-VI, 2001-02.
35. Small size jar with splayed-out and beaded rim; thin section, coarse fabric and ill-fired. BDK-VI, 2001-02.
36. Medium size jar with an outward projected, sharpened rim; bulbous body; design consists of two rows of dotted holes on the shoulder area which are not through. BDK-VI, 2001-02.
37. Basin with a flat-topped rim; design consists of deep holes in four rows; straight sides; coarse fabric and ill-fired. BDK-VI, 2001-02.

Black Slipped

38. Miniature vessel with a out-turned sharpened rim; treated with a thick light black slip on both sides; medium fabric and well-fired. BDK-VI, 2001-02.

Cream Slipped

39. Body portion of a jar; treated with a thick coat of cream slip on the exterior; smoky core, medium fabric and ill-fired. BDK-VI, 2001-02.

Chocolate Slipped

40. Base part of a dish-on-stand with a slightly raised, beaded rim; a thin coat of chocolate colour slip is applied on the exterior; medium fabric and well-fired. BDK-VI, 2001-02.
41. Sherd of an unidentified vessel with a thin coat of chocolate colour slip on the exterior; fine fabric and well-fired. BDK-VI, 2001-02.

Buff Ware

42. Small size jar with outward projected squarish rim; treated with buff slip on the exterior; fine fabric and ill-fired. BDK-VI, 2001-02.
43. Small size jar with an externally projected squarish rim; it is pinkish buff in colour; slip has been flaked off; medium fabric and well-fired. BDK-VI, 2001-02.
44. Miniature vessel with an outward projected sharpened rim; thin coat of buff slip on the exterior; fine fabric and well-fired. BDK-VI, 2001-02.
45. Miniature vessel with an out-turned splayed-out rim; treated with buff slip; exterior has a thick band of red colour; reddish section, fine fabric and well-fired. BDK-VI, 2001-02.
46. Vessel with a very thin section; fine fabric and well-fired. BDK-VI, 2001-02.
47. Goblet with a flat base; it has a smoky core and thick section; coarse fabric, ill-fired, thick section. BDK-VI, 2001-02.
48. Thin stem of a possible bowl-on-stand; hollow from inside; fine fabric and well-fired. BDK-VI, 2001-02.

Painted Sherds

49. Rim portion of a miniature vessel; outward projected sharpened rim; treated with red slip on the exterior and rim area internally; externally, it is painted with vertical lines while internally, a thick band of black colour is present on the rim area. BDK-VI, 2001-02.
50. Body portion of a miniature pot; black vertical lines on the shoulder area on red slipped pot; fine fabric and well-fired. BDK-VI, 2001-02.
51. Shoulder portion of a jar with roundless design between two lines running parallel; painting is done with chocolate colour over a red washed surface; medium fabric and well-fired.

Incised Design

52. Body portion of a jar; nail-headed design around the body portion; ill-fired and coarse fabric. BDK-VI, 2001-02.

Stud Handled Bowl

53. Handle portion of a stud handle bowl (Pl. 26, no. 2); top portion of the stud is broken; sharpened rim; it has a smoky core, coarse fabric and is ill-fired. BDK-VI, 2001-02.

5.2 PERIOD II

A thick deposit of this period has been noticed in BDK-I, II and III. The pottery comprises mainly of red ware and majority of them have been treated with thick red slip, and a few of them have a polish. Painted sherds are practically absent from this period. The clay used for these vessels are well-levigated. However, firing is indiscriminate as most of the vessels have unoxidised core, which suggest that they are not well-fired. The important characteristic features of different wares recovered during the excavation are given below:

5.2.1 Red Polished Ware

This ware is reported from a number of sites in India. The ware came to be recognised as one of the most important ceramic industries of the early historical period, and labelled as such

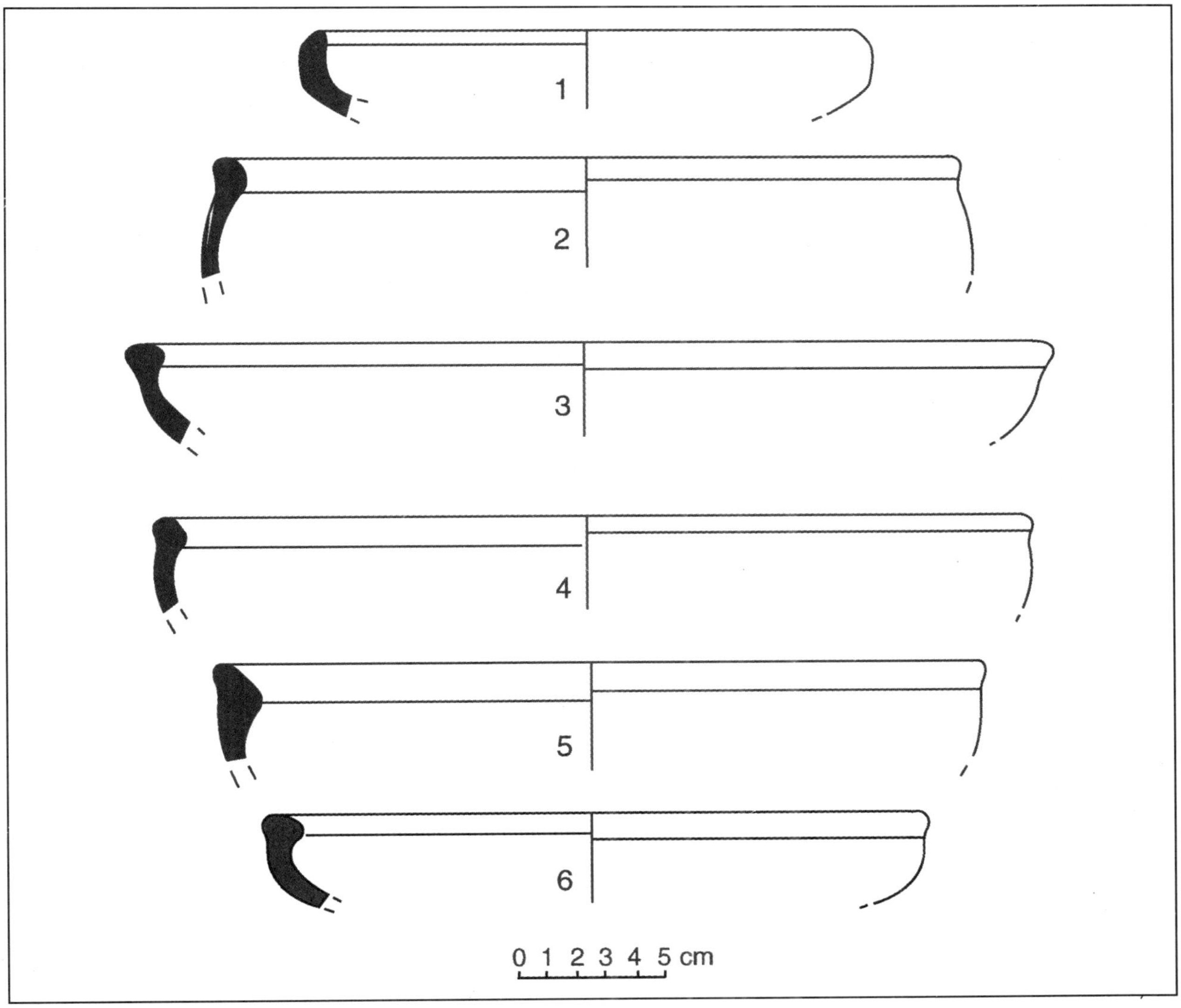

Fig. 27. Historical period pottery (dishes).

after the excavation at Amreli. The vessels are made of fine levigated clay, treated with a thick red slip, which is polished. Fired at high temperature, they are sturdy and produce a metallic sound when struck. The colour varies from dark red to pink. The nuclear region of the ware is Kathiyawad, with the largest number of types coming from Amreli. The ware, with varieties of shapes such as sprinkler and *surahi,* is widely distributed in India. Amongst others, commonly noticed shapes are jars with grooved rim, flaring neck, bulbous body and ring-footed base. The bowl with an in-curved beaded rim and carinated shoulder and the bowl with convex sides and thick, in-curved rim are some of the noteworthy features in Bet Dwarka pottery. The ware has been dated between 1st century BC and 5th century AD. Many leading archaeologists consider this ware as an imported one or at least an imitation of the Roman Samian ware (Subbarao, 1958: 46-7), but the nuclear region of the ware, its quantity, availability in large number with fundamental differences and a probable pre-Christian beginning, tend to point its indigenous origin. A sherd of bowl of this ware has the *brahmi* letter "A" inscribed on it. (Pl. 27).

5.2.2 Amphorae

It is thick gritty and compact in appearance and has a coarse fabric and surface. This ware was mainly used for exporting wine and olive oil from the Roman Empire. Since olive oil was in lesser demand in India and sherds have been found with dried resin mixture, it is most probable that all Indian finds are wine amphorae. The shape of this vessel is elongated with a pointed base, a narrow cylindrical neck and two handles attached to the rim and the shoulder. The shape could be understood at Nevasa, as sherds from different parts of the pots were found there.

5.2.3 Coarse Red Ware

In this category of ware, the surface is not at all treated either by way of a slip or burnishing. The clay used, technique of making, and method of firing them are similar to the slipped ware.

5.2.4 Burnished Ware

A few sherds of this ware have been found in the early level of Period II. The surfaces are burnished, while the clay used and the technique employed in shaping and firing is similar to that for slipped and coarse red wares.

5.2.5 Description of Pottery

Dishes (Fig. 27)

1. Dish with an in-turned featureless rim; convex-sided; it is devoid of any treatment; coarse fabric and ill-fired. BDK-III.
2. Dish with a slightly outward-turned and flat-topped rim; straight sides; internally treated with red slip; coarse fabric and ill-fired. BDK-III.
3. Dish with a flat, thickened rim and slightly in-turned; treated with black slip; medium fabric and well-fired. BDK-III.
4. Dish with an in-turned thickened rim; treated with red slip and polished; convex-sided; medium fabric and ill-fired. BDK-III.
5. Dish with an in-turned thickened rim; treated with red slip; medium fabric and ill-fired. BDK-III.
6. Dish with an outward projected rim; blunt carination; treated with black slip; medium fabric and well-fired. BDK-III.

Bowls (Fig. 28-30)

1. Bowl with a triangular thickened rim; on the exterior a ledge below the rim is present; convex-sided; treated with red slip; coarse fabric and ill-fired. BDK-III.
2. Bowl with a thickened rim and straight sides; treated with red slip; coarse fabric and ill-fired. BDK-III.
3. Bowl with a thickened rim and flat top; treated with red slip; straight sides; smoky core, coarse fabric and ill-fired. BDK-III.
4. Bowl with an oblique cut rim; convex-sided; it is devoid of any treatment; medium fabric and ill-fired. BDK-III.

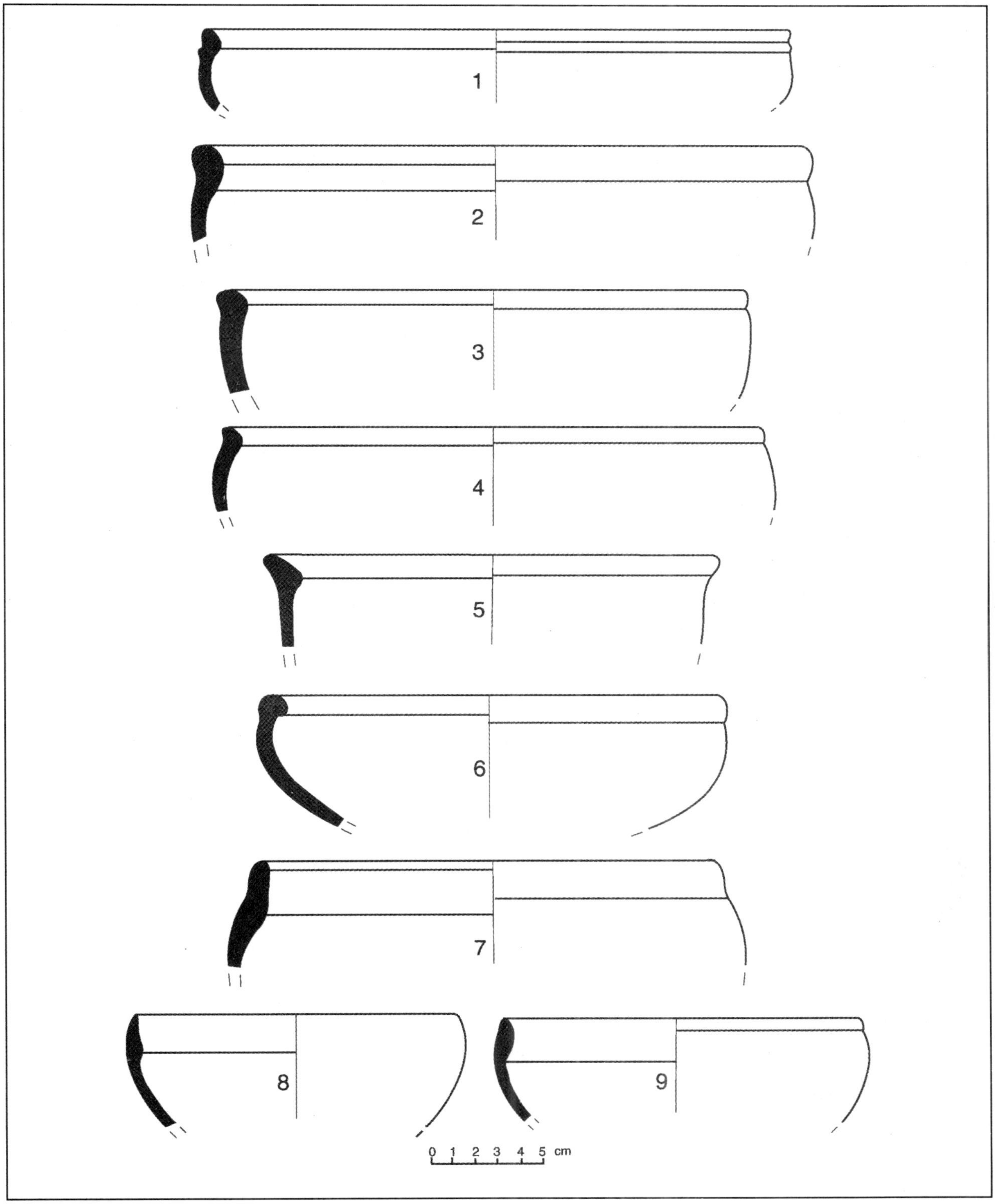

Fig. 28. Historical period pottery (bowls).

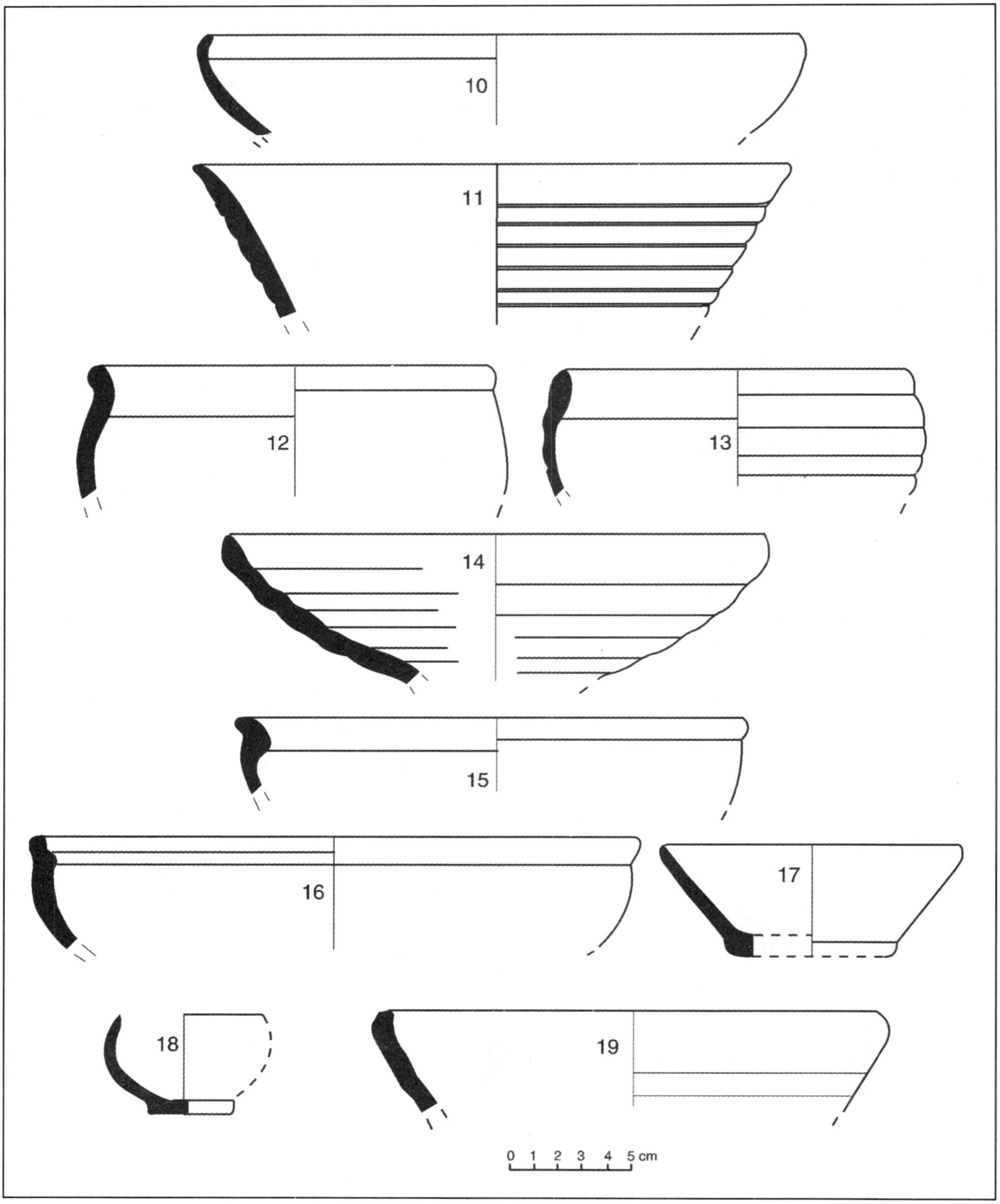

Fig. 29. Historical period pottery (bowls).

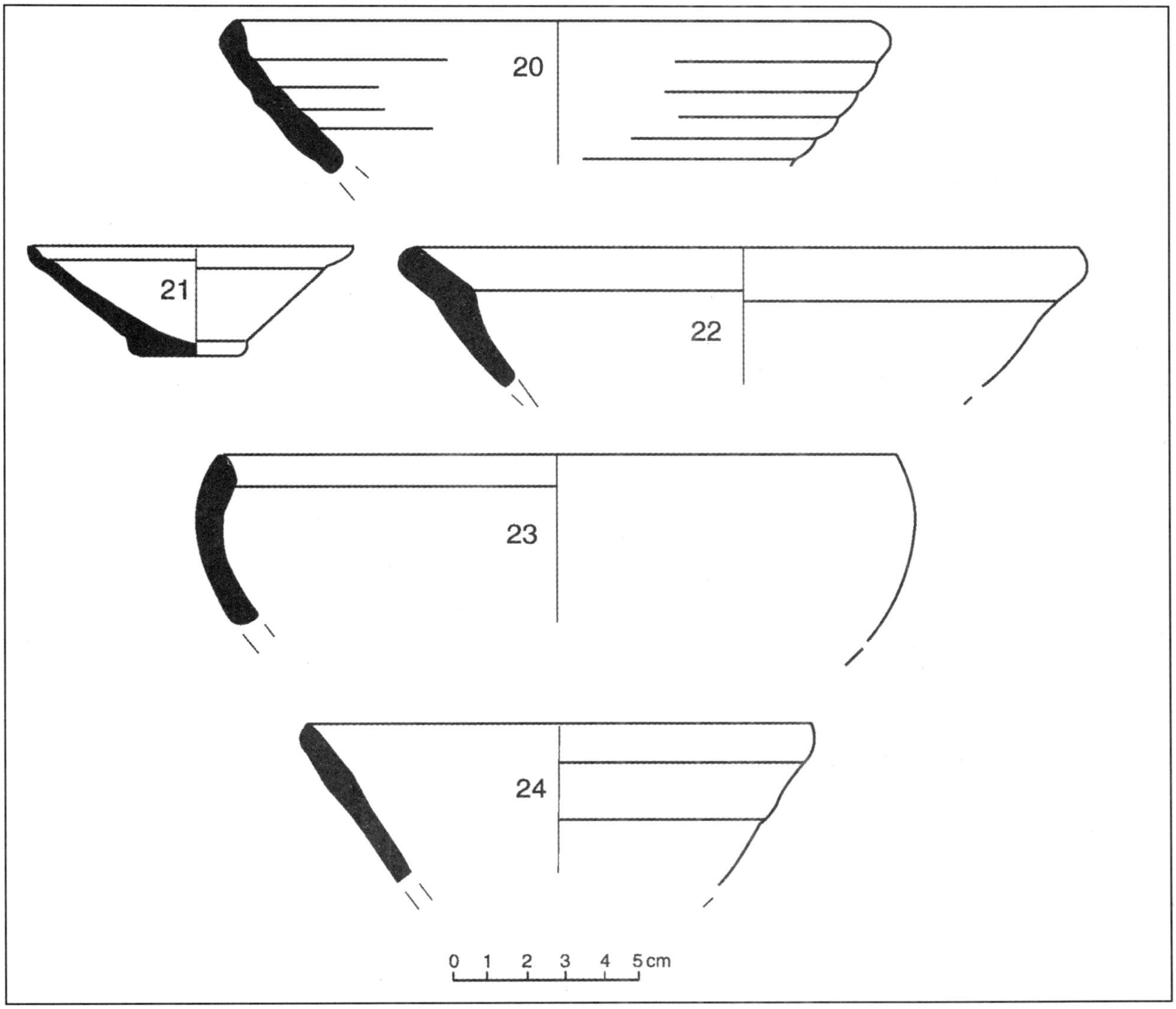

Fig. 30. Historical period pottery (bowls).

5. Bowl with a thickened rim; internally treated with red slip; medium fabric and ill-fired. BDK-III.
6. Bowl with a thickened rim; flat-topped; internally treated with red slip and on the exterior with red wash; medium fabric and well-fired. BDK-III.
7. Bowl with a featureless rim; internally, a raised band below the rim is present; straight sides; treated with red slip; medium fabric and ill-fired. BDK-III.
8. Bowl with a sharpened rim, thickening downwards; convex-sided; red slip; flaked off; coarse fabric and ill-fired. BDK-III.
9. Bowl with a featureless, sharpened rim; internally, a prominent rib below the rim is noticed; convex-sided; treated with red wash; medium fabric and ill-fired. BDK-III.
10. Bowl with an in-turned sharpened rim; treated with red wash; pitted surface and flaring sides; coarse fabric and ill-fired. BDK-III.

11. Bowl with a slightly out-turned sharpened rim; exterior grooved; treated with red wash; medium fabric and well-fired. BDK-III.
12. Bowl with a featureless and slightly out-turned rim; treated with red slip; convex-sided; coarse fabric and ill-fired. BDK-III.
13. Bowl with a sharpened rim; rim is slightly thickening downward; convex-sided; it has a corrugated profile; treated with red wash; medium fabric and ill-fired. BDK-II.
14. Bowl with an in-turned sharpened rim; corrugated profile; it is devoid of any treatment; medium fabric and ill-fired. BDK-II.
15. Bowl with an internally projected triangular type rim; straight sides; treated with red slip; medium fabric and well-fired. BDK-II.
16. Bowl with a sharpened rim; it is thick just below the rim; it is of red polished ware; convex-sided. BDK-II.
17. Small bowl with a featureless rim; coarse fabric and ill-fired. BDK-II.
18. Small-sized bowl with a featureless rim; convex-sided; it is devoid of any treatment; slightly pedestal base; coarse fabric and ill-fired. BDK-III.
19. Bowl with a slightly in-curved sharpened rim; corrugated profile; medium fabric and ill-fired; treated with red wash. BDK-I.
20. Bowl with slightly in-turned, sharpened rim; corrugated profile; coarse fabric and ill-fired. BDK-I.
21. Small bowl with a sharpened in-turned rim with flaring sides; pedestal base; coarse fabric and ill-fired. BDK-I.
22. Bowl with an out-played featureless rim; medium fabric and well-fired. BDK-I.
23. Bowl with thickened rim; convex sides; treated with red wash; smoky core; medium fabric and ill-fired. BDK-I.
24. Bowl with a sharpened edge; corrugated profile; coarse fabric and ill-fired. BDK-I.

Bases of bowls (Fig. 31)

1. Ring-footed base of a vessel; thick section; treated with red slip; smoky core; medium fabric and ill-fired. BDK-II.
2. Pedestal base of a black-and-red ware bowl and string-cut base; externally treated with black slip; thick section; medium fabric and well-fired. BDK-I.
3. Pedestal base of a bowl; medium fabric and ill-fired. BDK-II.
4. A ring-footed base of a vessel; exterior treated with red slip; fine fabric and well-fired. BDK-II.
5. Ring-footed base of a vessel; treated with red wash; medium fabric and ill-fired. BDK-III.
6. Large-sized bowl with a pedestal base; corrugated profile; treated with red wash; coarse fabric and ill-fired. BDK-III.
7. Bowl with a string-cut pedestal base; flaring sides; corrugated profile; coarse fabric and ill-fired. BDK-III.
8. Ring-footed base of a vessel; treated with red wash; medium fabric and ill-fired. BDK-III.
9. Bowl with a string-cut pedestal base; it is devoid of any treatment; medium fabric and well-fired. BDK-III.

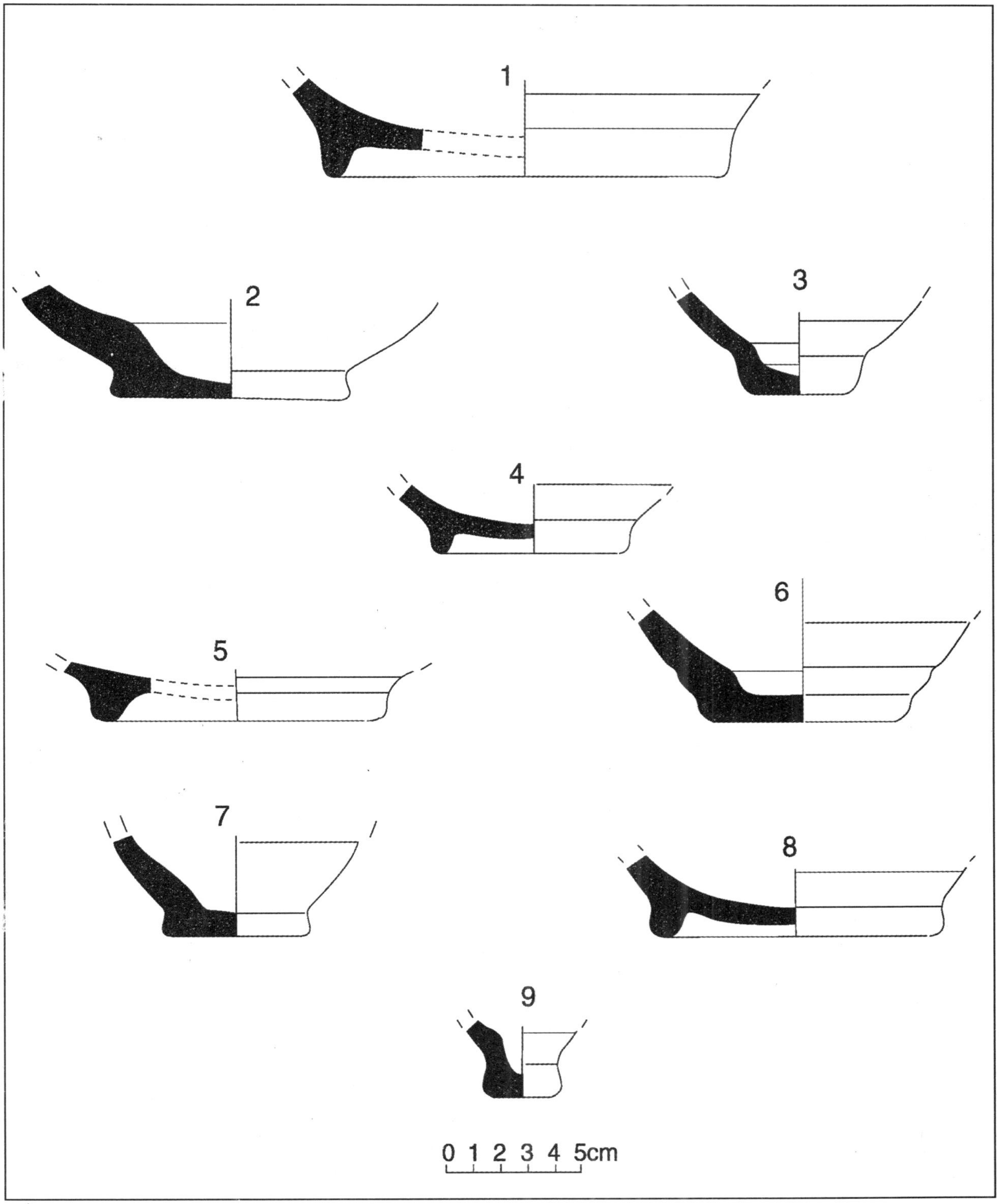

Fig. 31. Historical period pottery (bowls).

Jars (Fig. 32–36)

1. Jar with an out-turned beaked rim; treated with red wash; coarse fabric and ill-fired. BDK-III.
2. Jar with an outward projected rim; bulbous body; it is treated with red wash; a thick band of black colour on the top of rim is present; medium fabric and well-fired. BDK-III.
3. High-necked jar with an out-turned and under-cut rim; internally, treated with red wash; coarse fabric and ill-fired. BDK-III.
4. Jar with an outward projected, slightly under-cut sharpened rim; a number of thin grooves on the shoulder area have been observed; treated with red wash; coarse fabric and ill-fired. BDK-III.
5. Jar with an outward projected rim; a groove on the rim is present; three grooves on the shoulder area are noticed; treated with red slip; smoky core; coarse fabric and ill-fired. BDK-III.
6. Jar with an outward projected rim and short neck; three grooves on the exterior of the rim are noticed; bulbous body; coarse fabric and ill-fired. BDK-III.
7. Jar with an outward projected rim and short-necked and bulbous body; rim painted with black-over-red by vertical lines while shoulder with horizontal lines; treated with red slip; coarse fabric and ill-fired. BDK-III.
8. Large-sized jar with an outward projected collared rim; it is grooved internally; treated with red wash; medium fabric and ill-fired. BDK-III.
9. Jar with an outward projected featureless rim; groove on the inner side; short neck; treated with red wash; pitted surface; coarse fabric and ill-fired. BDK-III.
10. Small-sized jar with an out-turned thickened rim and it is grooved internally; concave neck; it is devoid of any treatment; medium fabric and ill-fired. BDK-III.
11. Jar with an outward-projected collared undercut and grooved rim; concave neck; treated with red wash; medium fabric and well-fired. BDK-III.
12. Jar with a raised neck and outward-projected squarish rim; concave neck; treated with red wash; medium fabric and ill-fired. BDK-III.
13. Jar with an outward projected grooved rim; concave neck; medium fabric and well-fired. BDK-III.
14. Jar with an outward projected rim; flat-topped; concave neck; it is devoid of any treatment; coarse fabric and ill-fired. BDK-III.
15. Jar with an out-turned, oval-collared rim, slightly under-cut from inside and a bulge profile; treated with red wash; coarse fabric and ill-fired. BDK-III.
16. Jar with a splayed-out projected rim; concave neck; treated with red wash; coarse fabric and ill-fired. BDK-III.
17. Jar with an outward projected squarish rim; it has a bulbous body; a few grooves on the exterior present; coarse fabric and ill-fired. BDK-III.
18. Jar with an outward projected squarish and grooved rim; slightly under-cut on the exterior; it is devoid of any treatment; coarse fabric and ill-fired. BDK-III.
19. Jar with an outward projected squarish and under-cut rim; flat-topped; coarse fabric and ill-fired. BDK-III.

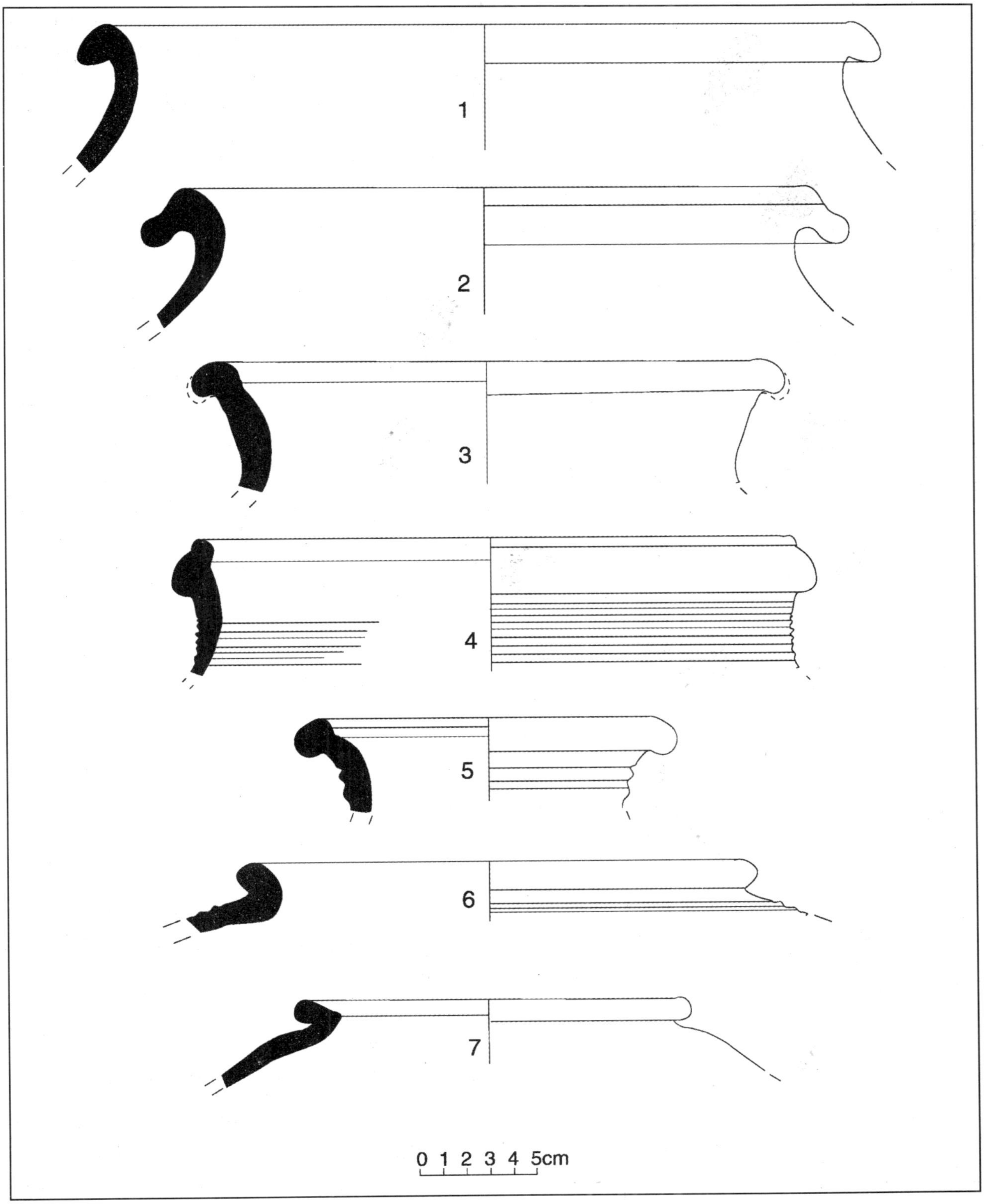

Fig. 32. Historical period pottery (jars).

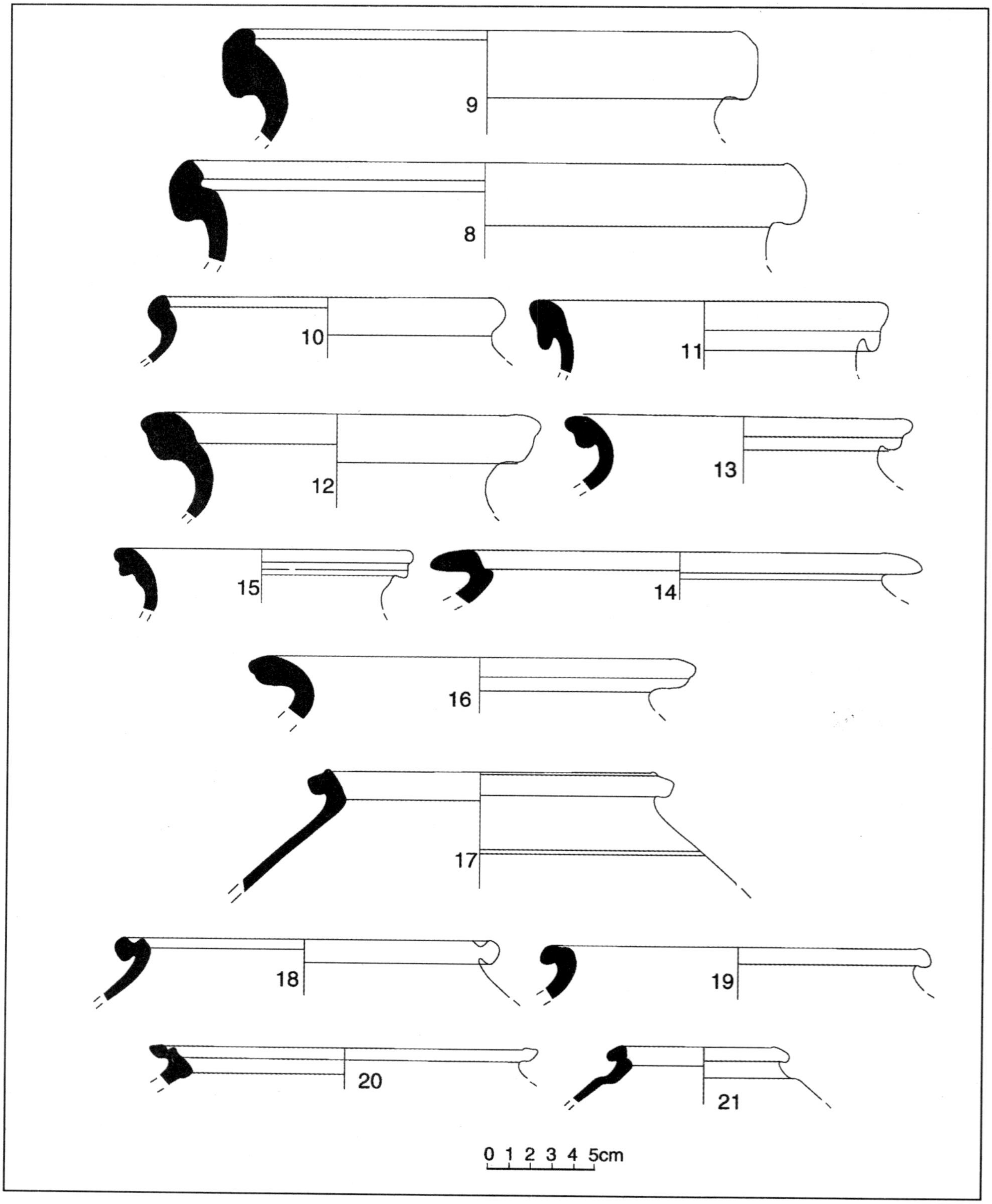

Fig. 33. Historical period pottery (jars).

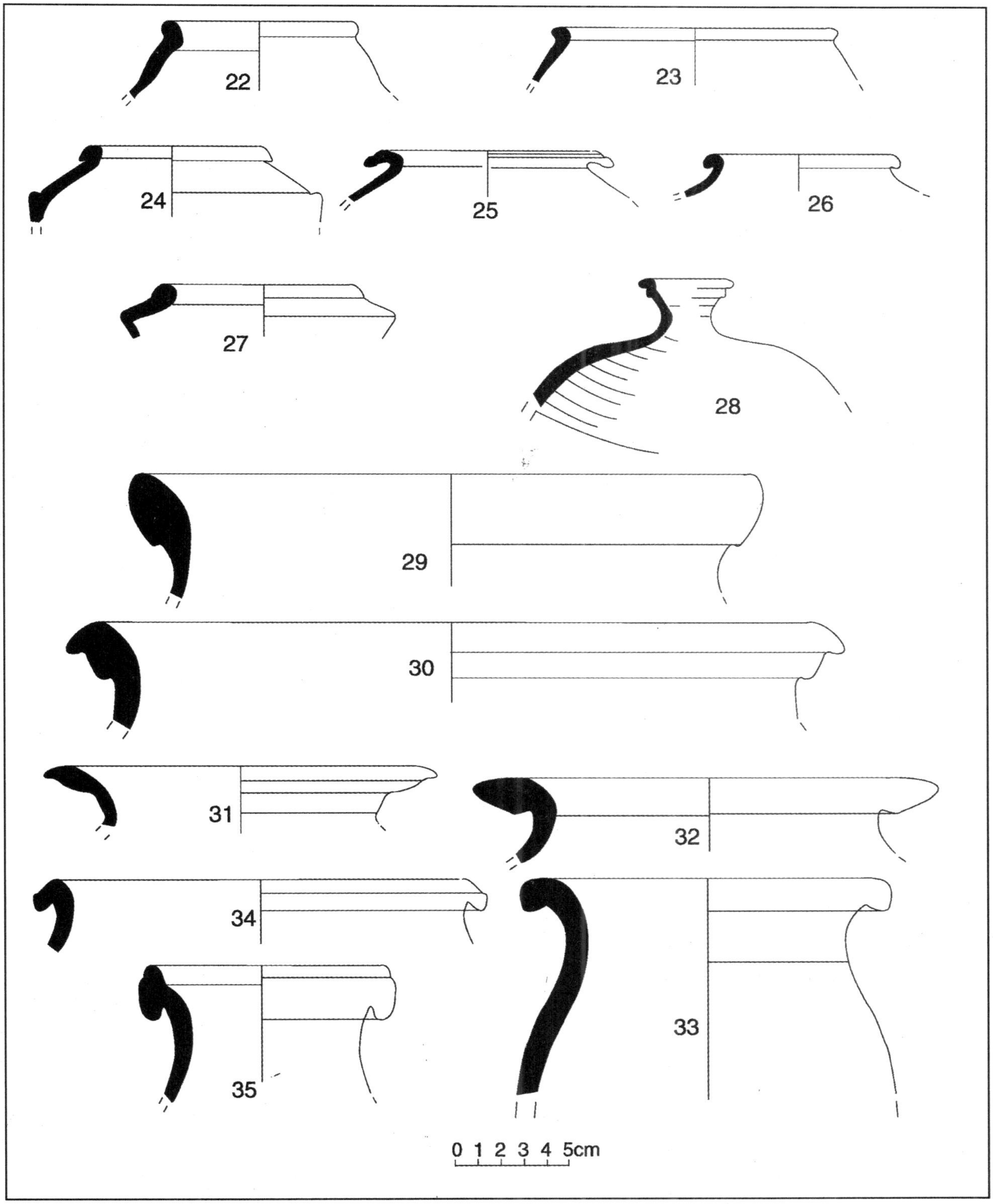

Fig. 34. Historical period pottery (jars).

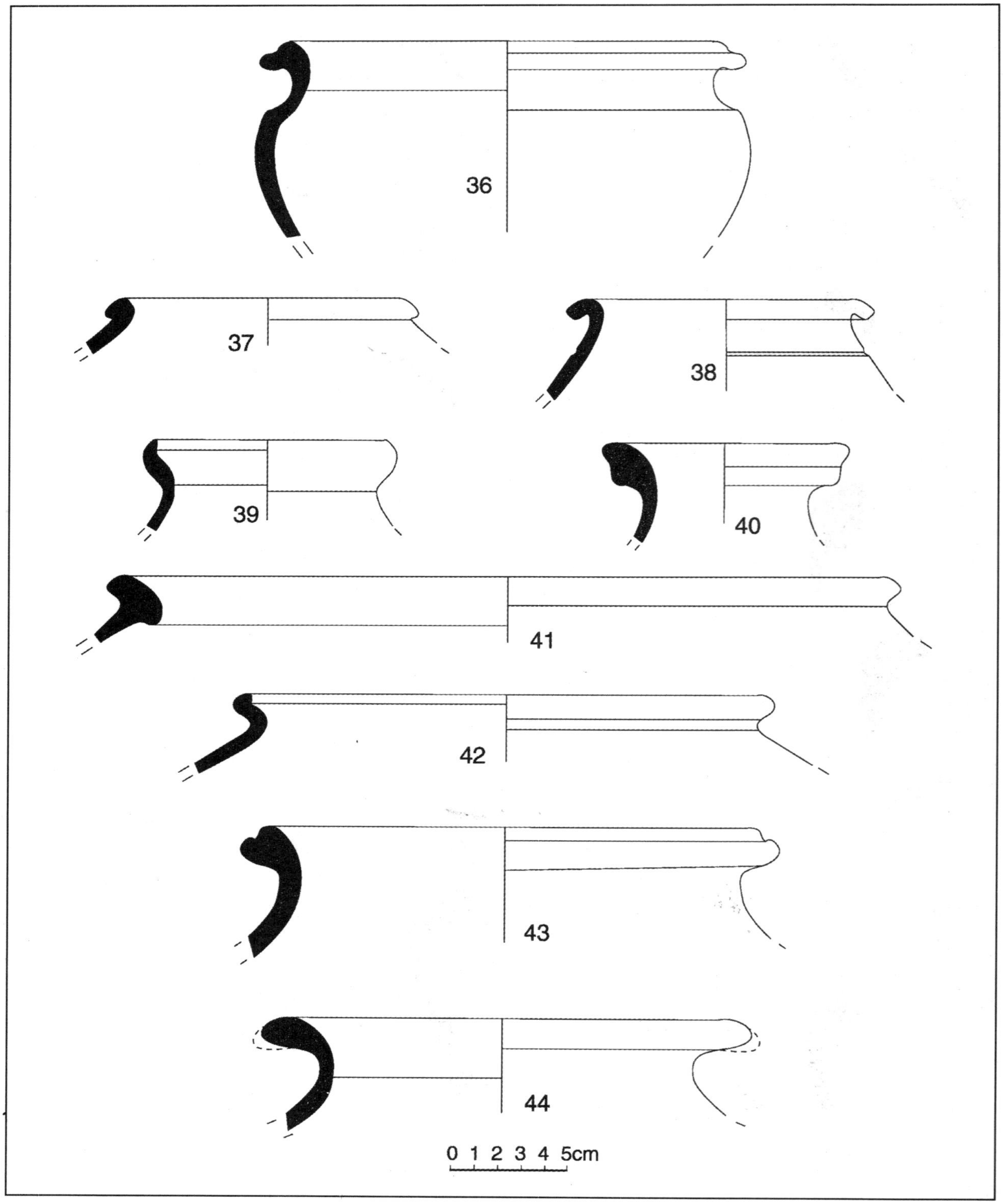

Fig. 35. Historical period pottery (jars).

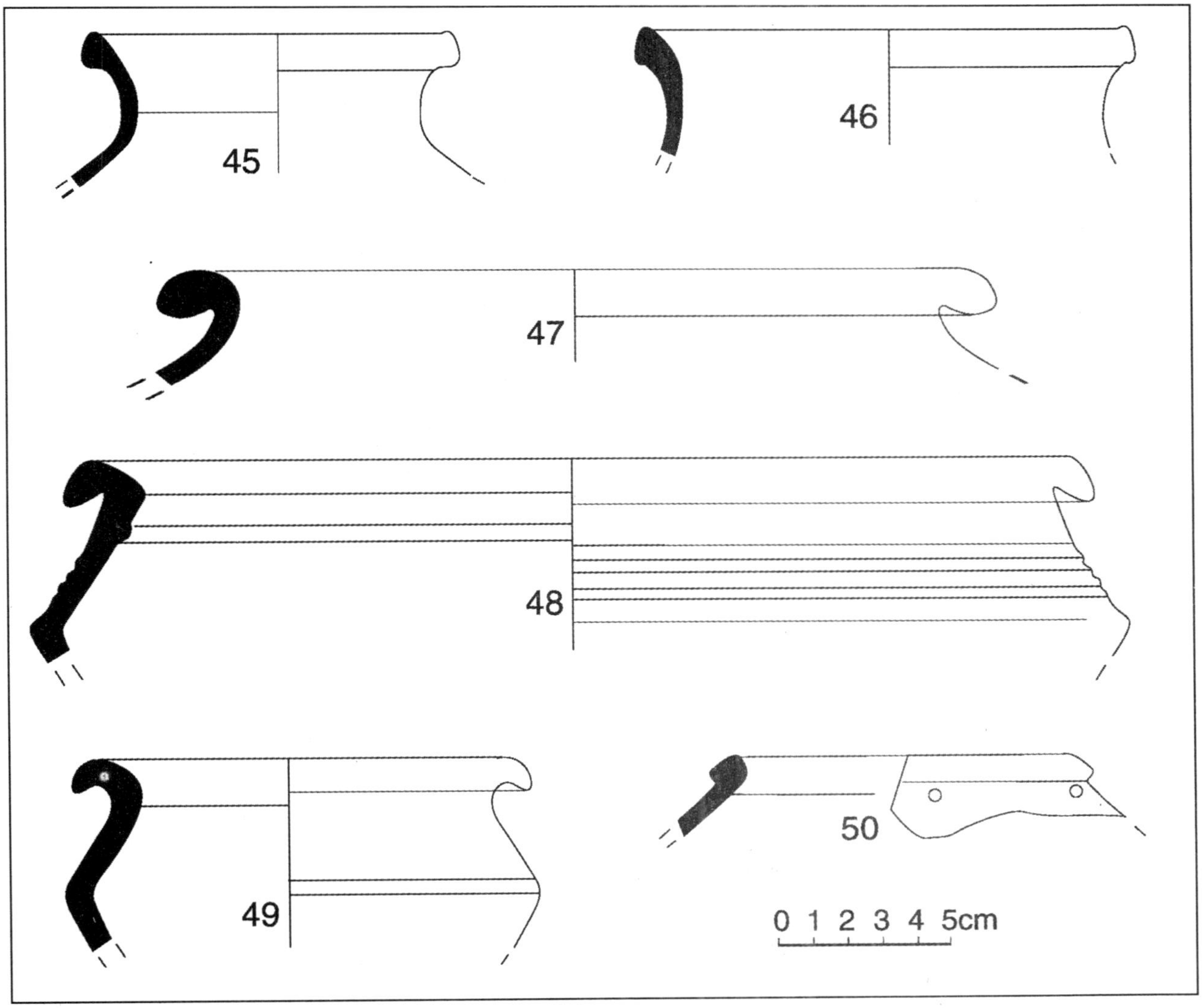

Fig. 36. Historical period pottery (jars).

20. Jar with an out-turned sharpened rim; it has two grooves on the rim; coarse fabric and ill-fired. BDK-III.
21. Outward projected rim of a miniature vessel and bulged body; treated with red slip; medium fabric and ill-fired. BDK-III. (Pl. 28)
22. Slightly out-turned rim of a miniature vessel; treated with red slip; medium fabric and ill-fired. BDK-III.
23. Miniature vessel with a slightly out-turned rim; treated with red slip; fine fabric and well-fired. BDK-III.
24. Miniature vessel with an out-turned beaked rim; bulged body; carinated shoulder; treated with red slip; fine fabric and well-fired. BDK-III.
25. Miniature jar with an out-turned rim, short neck and bulbous body; it is devoid of any treatment; medium fabric and ill-fired. BDK-III.

26. Miniature vessel with an out-turned beaked rim; bulged body; treated with red slip; medium fabric and ill-fired. BDK-III.
27. Miniature vessel with an outward projected rim; it has a short-necked and bulbous body; treated with red wash; medium fabric and ill-fired. BDK-III.
28. Miniature vessel with a splayed-out rim and bulbous body; treated with red slip and polished; medium fabric and ill-fired. BDK-III.
29. Jar with an oval-shaped collared rim and slightly under-cut on the exterior; coarse fabric and ill-fired. BDK-I.
30. Jar with a splayed-out, sharpened rim; a prominent under-cut ledge is also noticed on the exterior of the rim; concave neck; smoky core; coarse fabric and ill-fired. BDK-I.
31. Medium size jar with a splayed-out collared rim with slightly under-cut ledge; coarse fabric and ill-fired. BDK-I.
32. Jar with an outward-projected, nail-headed rim; flat-topped; smoky core; coarse fabric and ill-fired. BDK-I.
33. Jar with a splayed-out, looped and externally projected rim; coarse fabric and ill-fired. BDK-I.
34. Jar with a splayed-out, squarish under-cut rim; it has a raised neck and bulbous body; smoky core; coarse fabric and ill-fired. BDK-I.
35. Jar with a nail-headed, out-turned and under-cut rim; two grooves on the shoulder area; smoky core, medium fabric and ill-fired. BDK-I.
36. Outward projected featureless rim with a smoky core of a jar; externally, treated with red slip; interior has pitted surface; coarse fabric and ill-fired. BDK-I.
37. Small-sized jar with externally projected under-cut rim; it has a short neck and bulbous body; medium fabric and well-fired. BDK-I.
38. Jar with a splayed-out sharpened rim and outward projected; a groove on the exterior of the rim is present; raised neck; treated with red slip on the exterior; coarse fabric and ill-fired. BDK-I.
39. Jar with an out-turned, oval-collared rim; slightly under-cut from inside and a bulged profile; medium fabric and well-fired. BDK-I.
40. Jar with a splayed-out and grooved rim; concave neck; narrow-mouthed; treated with red slip; medium fabric and ill-fired. BDK-I.
41. Large-sized jar with a nail-headed rim and bulbous body; internally, treated with red wash; medium fabric and well-fired. BDK-II.
42. Jar with an outward projected, sharpened rim; a groove on the rim is present; it has a short neck and bulbous body; medium fabric and well-fired. BDK-II.
43. Jar with an outward projected, thickened rim; concave neck; treated with red wash; coarse fabric and ill-fired. BDK-II.
44. Jar with a splayed-out, outward projected sharpened rim; concave neck; bulbous body; exterior treated with red wash; coarse fabric and ill-fired. BDK-II.
45. Jar with an externally projected, triangular type rim; smoky core and treated with red wash; coarse fabric and ill-fired. BDK-II.

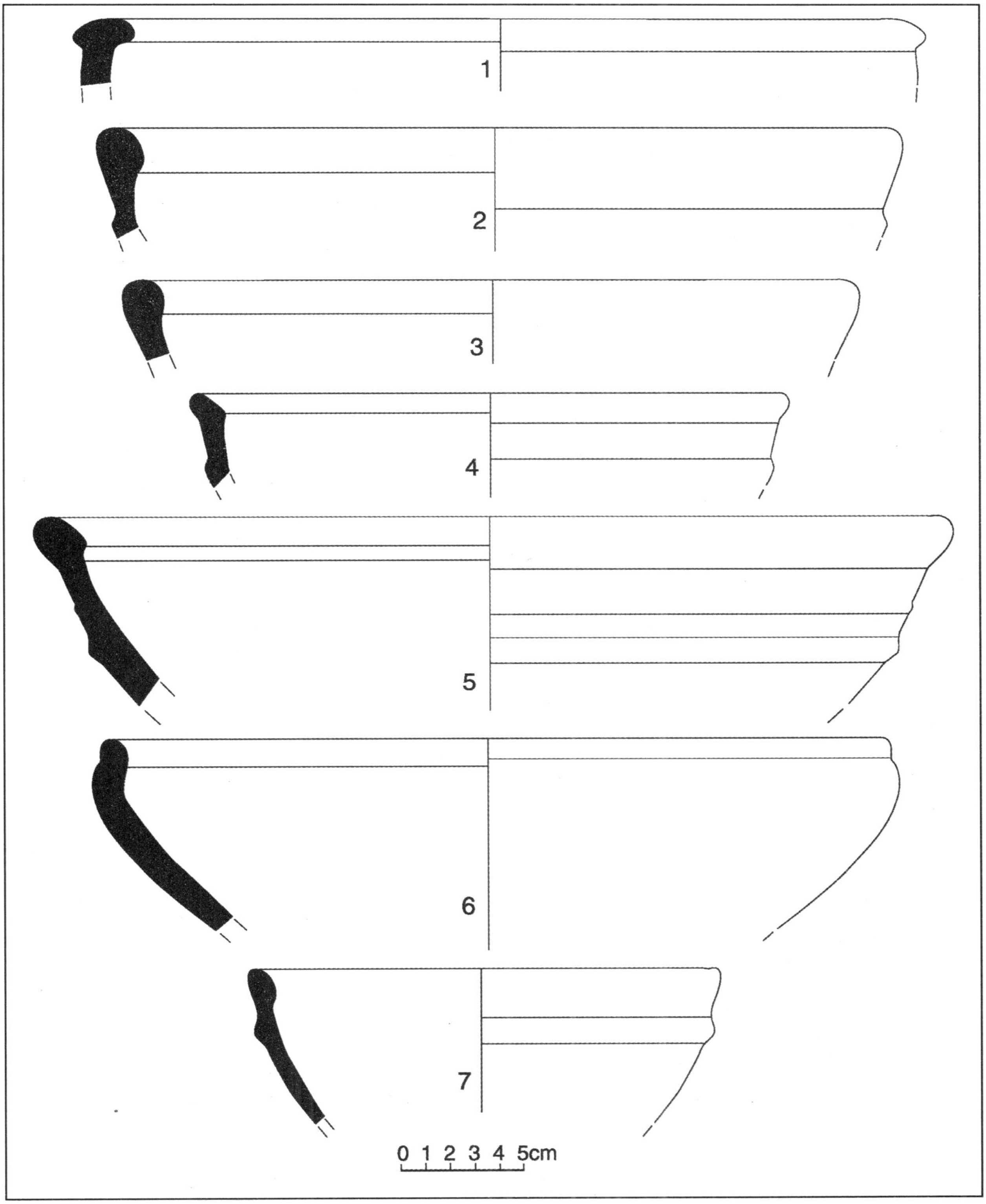

Fig. 37. Historical period pottery (basins).

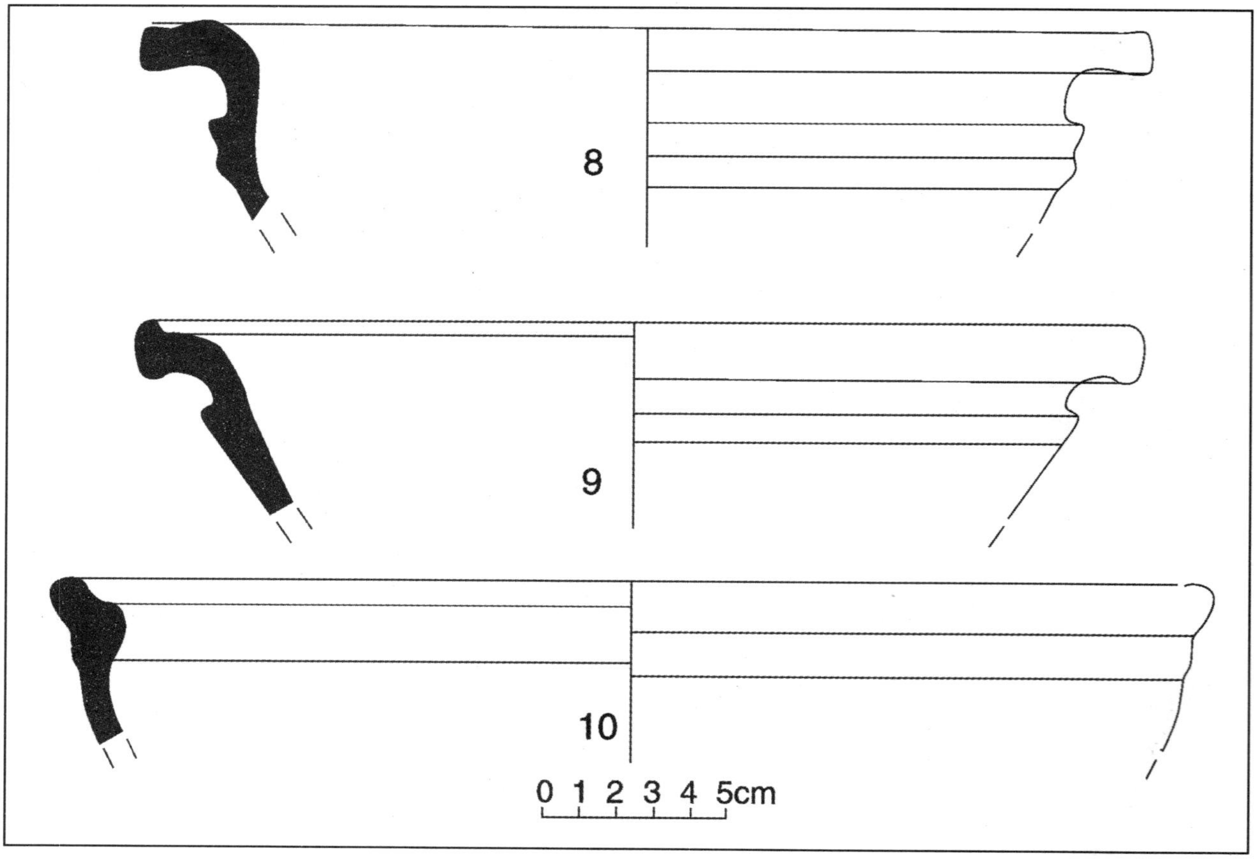

Fig. 38. Historical period pottery (basins).

46. Small-sized jar with an out-turned rim; concave neck; treated with red wash; coarse fabric and ill-fired. BDK-II.
47. Jar with an outward projected rim; narrow neck; bulbous body; it is devoid of any treatment; coarse fabric and ill-fired. BDK-II.
48. *Handi* with an out-turned sharpened rim; short neck; it has a carinated shoulder with several grooves; treated with black slip; coarse fabric and ill-fired. BDK-II.
49. *Handi* with an outward projected rim; carinated body; coarse fabric and ill-fired. BDK-II.

Black ware

50. Small-sized jar with a short neck, beaded rim and bulbous body; four holes around the neck, perhaps for hanging the jar; medium fabric and well-fired. BDK-II.

Basins (Fig. 37-38)

1. Basin with a nail-headed rim; thick section coarse fabric and ill-fired. BDK-III.
2. Basin with a thickened, beaded rim; treated with red slip and polished; a ledge on the exterior is noticed; coarse fabric and ill-fired. BDK-III.
3. Basin with a slightly in-turned beaded rim; treated with red slip; medium fabric and ill-fired. BDK-III.

4. Basin with a slightly out-turned and inward projected rim; a ledge on the exterior is present; treated with red wash; fine fabric and ill-fired. BDK-III.
5. Basin with an out-turned thickened rim; a prominent ledge on the exterior is present; medium fabric and well-fired. BDK-II.
6. Dish with a thickened rim; convex sides; a groove on the exterior, below the rim is noticed; treated with red slip; medium fabric and ill-fired. BDK-III.
7. Small-sized basin with beaded rim; red slipped medium fabric and ill-fired. BDK-I.
8. Basin with a splayed-out projected rim; carinated shoulder; treated with red wash; coarse fabric and ill-fired. BDK-III.
9. Basin with an out-turned squarish rim; carination appears from neck portion; treated with red wash; coarse fabric and ill-fired. BDK-III.
10. Basin with an out-turned, slightly inward projected, thickened rim; treated with red slip; smoky core; coarse fabric and ill-fired. BDK-II.

Lids (Fig. 39)

1. Lid with a banded rim and under-cut internally; it has corrugated profile on the exterior; medium fabric and well-fired. BDK-I.
2. Fragment of ink-pot type lid; internally, treated with red wash; medium fabric and ill-fired. BDK-I.
3. Ink-pot type lid with a slightly under-cut rim of dull red ware; coarse fabric and ill-fired. BDK-I (Pl. 29).
4. Lid with a sharpened rim; below the rim, a thick projection is present; two grooves on the exterior are present; treated externally with red wash; medium fabric and ill-fired. BDK-III.
5. Ink-pot type lid, which is treated with red wash; medium fabric and ill-fired. BDK-II.
6. Lid with a squarish, internally projected, under-cut rim; medium fabric and ill-fired. BDK-II.
7. Lid with an out-turned and grooved rim; slightly under-cut externally; a raised band on the exterior is noticed; treated with red wash; medium fabric and ill-fired. BDK-II.
8. Lid with an out-turned groove and under-cut rim; a rib around the knob on the exterior is present; treated with red wash; coarse fabric and ill-fired. BDK-II.
9. Lid with a beaded rim; a ledge on the exterior is noticed; treated with red slip; coarse fabric and ill-fired. BDK-III.
10. Lid with a conical knob; internally, treated with red wash; medium fabric and ill-fired. BDK-III.
11. Lid with a slightly out-turned, sharpened rim; thick section; treated with red wash; medium fabric and well-fired. BDK-III.
12. Ink-pot type lid with a rounded base; it is devoid of any treatment; medium fabric and ill-fired. BDK-III.

Pottery with Graffiti (Fig. 40)

1. Basin with an oval-shaped rim and a ledge on the exterior; between the ledge and rim, five graffiti marks are noticed.

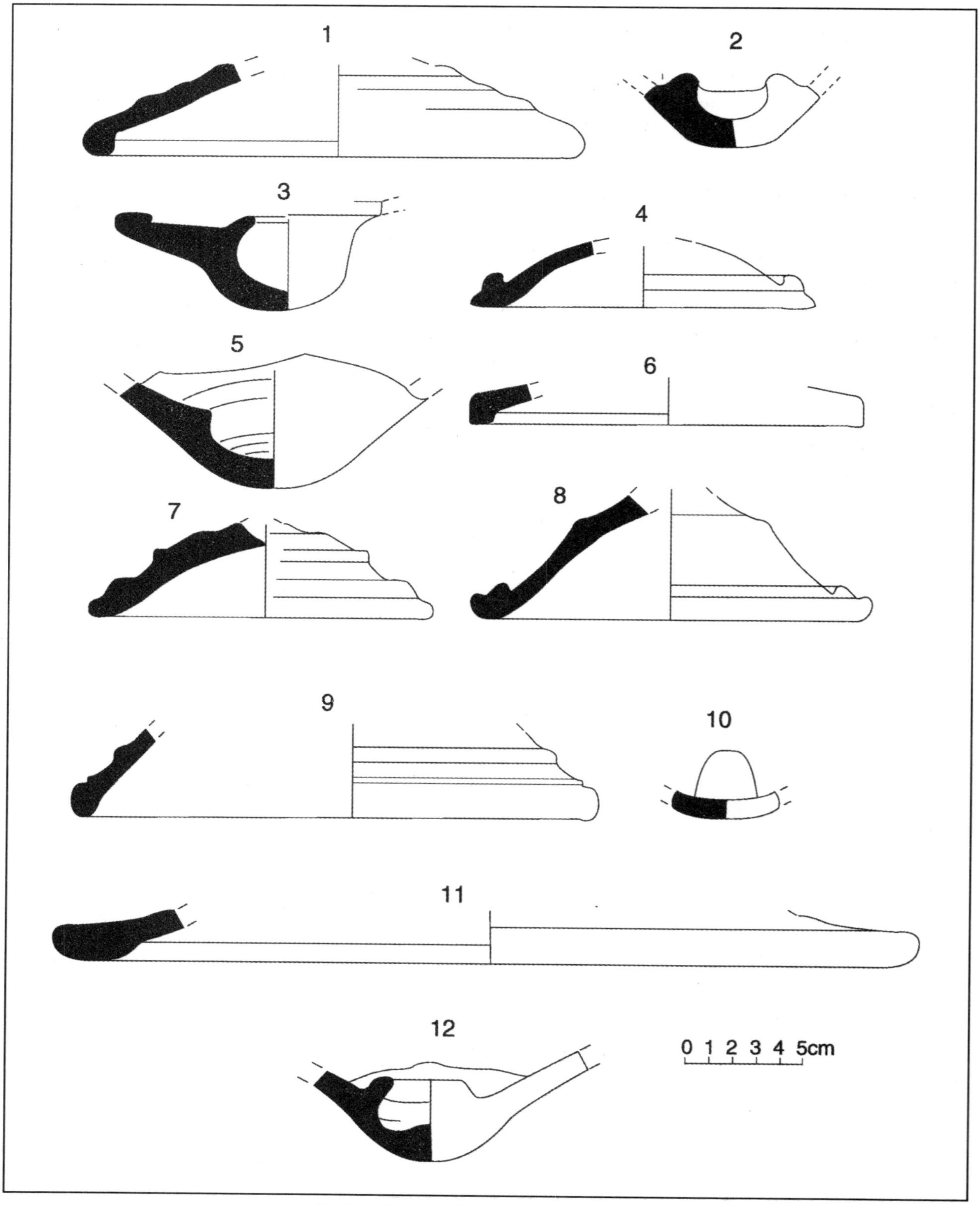

Fig. 39. Historical period pottery (lids).

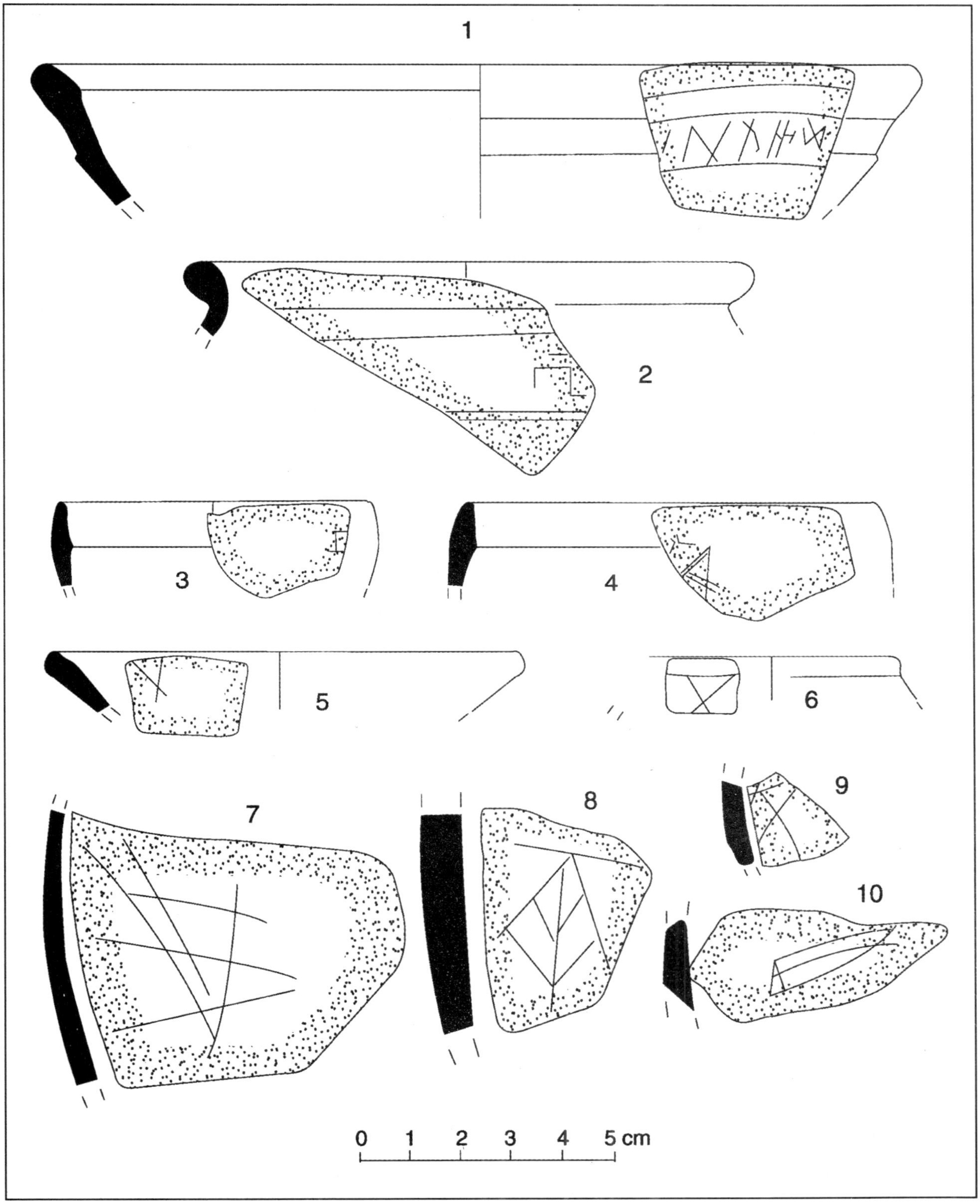

Fig. 40. Pottery with graffiti marks.

2. Rim of a jar with a Swastika symbol on the shoulder; a groove on the exterior is noticed; coarse fabric and ill-fired.
3. Bowl with a sharpened rim, convex-sided with a graffiti mark; a vertical line and two strokes on both ends on either sides are noticed; medium fabric and ill-fired.
4. Bowl with a featureless rim; a rib on the exterior with a graffiti mark is noticed; treated with red slip; medium fabric and ill-fired.
5. Bowl with slightly in-turned rim in grey ware; corrugated profile with a graffiti mark on the exterior; coarse fabric and ill-fired.
6. Miniature vessel with a slightly out-turned rim; treated with red wash; a graffiti mark on the exterior like a cross; coarse fabric and ill-fired.
7. Body part of a pot with a graffiti consisting of six lines – three lines are horizontal, one vertical cutting across the three and the other two slightly angled, cutting the horizontal lines.
8. Potsherd with a graffiti mark; treated with red wash; coarse fabric and ill-fired.
9. Small potsherd with graffiti marks like a cross.
10. Potsherd with a leaf-shaped graffiti mark; it has a thick section; medium fabric and ill-fired.

Chapter–6

Ancient Shell Industry at Bet Dwarka Island

6.1 INTRODUCTION

Shell fishing is one of the oldest professions practiced by man for survival. However, it has been recognised as a major industry during the proto-historic period in the Indian sub-continent. Many ancient trade routes have been identified by archaeologists on the basis of the sources of shells found during exploration. India has played a major role in developing Indian ocean trade. Several excavations have yielded the remains of different types of marine shells. The first systematic use of shells for various household purposes has been noticed during the Indus Civilization. Several sites, including Lothal (Rao, 1979), Nageshwar (Hegde *et al.*, 1990), Kuntasi (Dhavalikar *et al.*, 1996), Surkotada (Joshi, 1990), Mohenjodaro (Marshall, 1931), and many more sites have yielded rich antiquities on the various uses of shells.

After Nageshwar, Bet Dwarka is the second site in the Okhamandal region where a flourishing shell industry in archaeological context has been noticed. Earlier Nageshwar, a Mature Harappan site, was recognised as a major shell-working centre of the Harappan period (Hegde *et al.*, 1990) in Okhamandal region.

6.2 EXCAVATIONS

For the excavation, six places were identified on the Bet Dwarka island and at each location trenches were dug to the depth of virgin soil. These trenches were numbered as BDK-I, II, III, IV, V, and VI. Over 3000 shell remains have been noticed from these trenches so far. Significantly, the layer 6 and 7 of trench BDK-I, yielded exceptionally higher quantity of shell remains (Pl. 30). Varieties of shells have been noticed from each trench. Radiocarbon[14] dates from these shells varied from 3470±80 years BP to 1910±80 years BP (Table 2). The important shells recovered from Bet Dwarka excavations are the *Turbinella pyrum* (chank), *Chicoreus ramosus* and *Dentalium octangulatum*. The first two types of shells were generally used for the various purposes like making of beads, bangles, ladle, spoon, inlay work, seals and other shell artifacts, but the third variety was used for bead only, as it was naturally shaped in such a way that it did not require any re-working on it. During our stay at Bet Dwarka, we observed that a few people were still using a shell bead and after some enquiry they informed that these shells had medicinal property. There are a number of other varieties of shells (Table 7 to 10) from different trenches which may have been used for food, etc. The details of occurrence and habitat of some important shells are given below.

6.3 CHANK *(Turbinella pyrum)*

From the total number of shells noticed from the excavation, the largest number of shells are from this group. The important artifacts from this group are beads, bangles, apex and columella. The chank shell is ovate in shape, thick-walled and without any protuberance. The central columella is solid, spiraling and can be distinguished from that of outer large gastropods by the presence of 3 to 4 prominent ridges, to which major muscles are attached. An average length of shell can be upto 15 to 20 cm and width 10-15 cm (Hegde *et al.*, 1990: 125). This shell provides a unique structure for the manufacture of several bangles from a single shell. The organism living inside is also edible and very nutritious (Hegde, 1990). The colonies of these shells are noticed generally on sandy bottom or in sandy areas between coral reefs or rocky areas, but they are generally present in the shallow littoral zone, down to depths of 20 m (Mahadevan and Nayar, 1974).

Chank shell has a restricted distribution, occurring only in the protected bays of the sub-continent. At present, major concentrations of this shell has been observed at the southern tip of India, the Gulf of Mannar, all around Sri Lanka and as far north as the mouth of the river Godavari. On the western coast of the sub-continent, it is not so common but in the Gulf of Kachchh and along the coast of Sind and Baluchistan, West of Karachi, large deposits are found (Kenoyer, 1984). In the Gulf of Kachchh also they are found only along the west shore, occurring at depths ranging from 5 to 20 m. This shell generally rolls up with current from deeper water towards the coast during summer months and disperses back into deeper water during the cold winter months (Bhan and Kenoyer, 1984). Chank shells found in shallow waters near the coral reefs are often interlaced with bore holes by boring organism such as Cliona sponge. Hornell (1915) notes that these bore holes are not found on shell fished from deeper waters or regularly fished beds.

Gulf of Kachchh harbors rich gastropods fauna. So far, 72 species of gastropods have been recorded from this area (Menon *et al.*, 1961). Among these, sacred *Chank X. pyrum* holds a special position as this is the only species of gastropods of commercial importance. Most important beds of this type are known to occur in the inter-tidal zones off Okha, Aramda, Posithra, Azad, Wadinar, Bhaana, Salaya, Sikka, Pirotan island and Bedi on the southern bank of the Gulf (Nayar and Mahadevan, 1973).

Although the chanks are known to occur in depths of 10-20 m with sandy bottom (Hornell, 1951), along the Gujarat coast, they are found in the proximity of the coral reefs and are collected by hand-picking during low tide around Bet Dwarka island. In the excavation, the largest number of shell artifacts belongs to this shell (Table 11-13).

Pl. 30. Layer 6 of BDK-I containing shell remains.

Pl. 31. Dentalium shell.

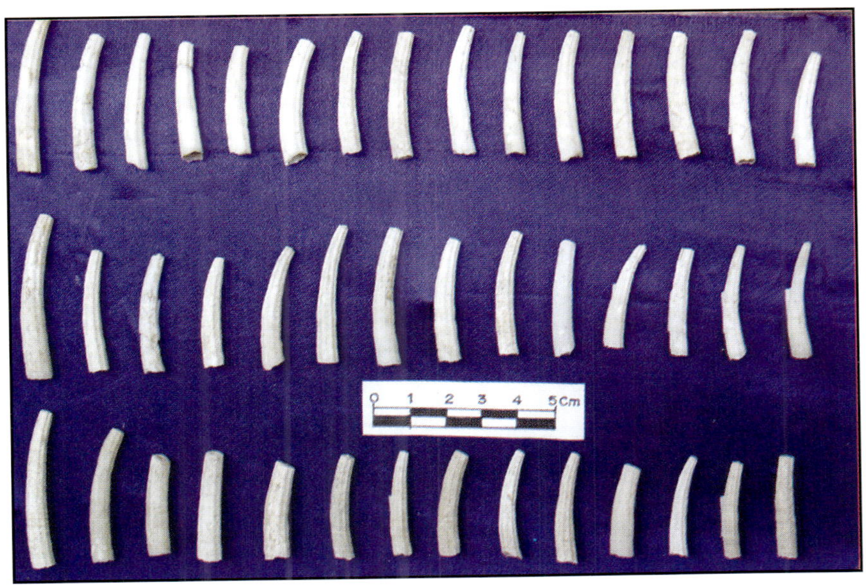

Pl. 32. Shell bangles.

Pl. 33. Apex portion of chank shell.

Pl. 34. Columella with saw marks.

Pl. 35. Unfinished ladle.

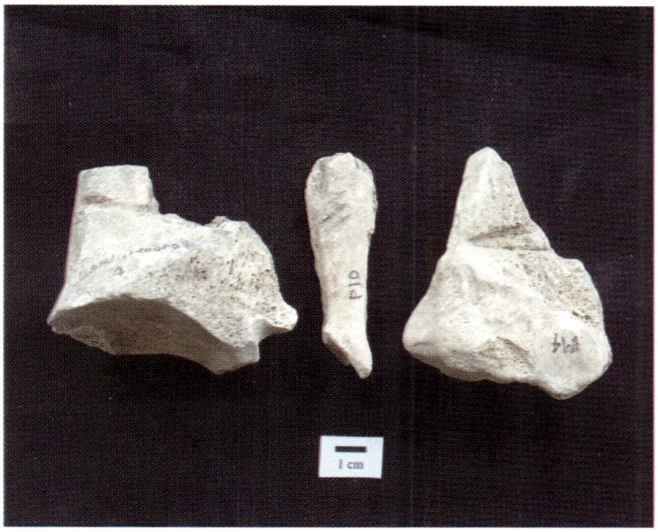

Pl. 36. Evidence of bone modifications.

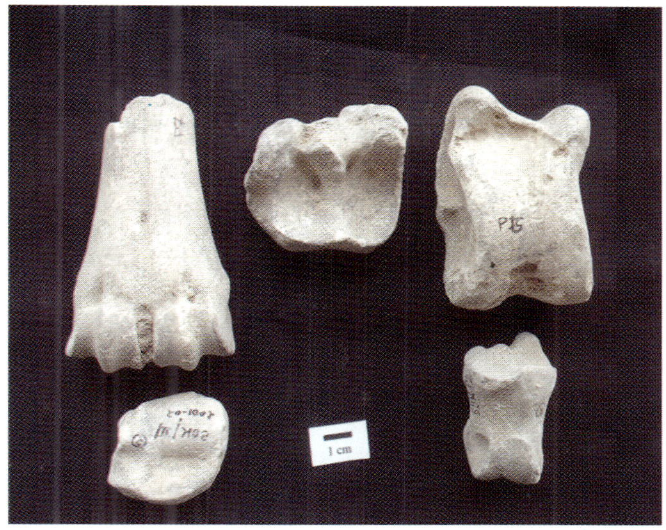

Pl. 37. Bone of *Bos indicus*.

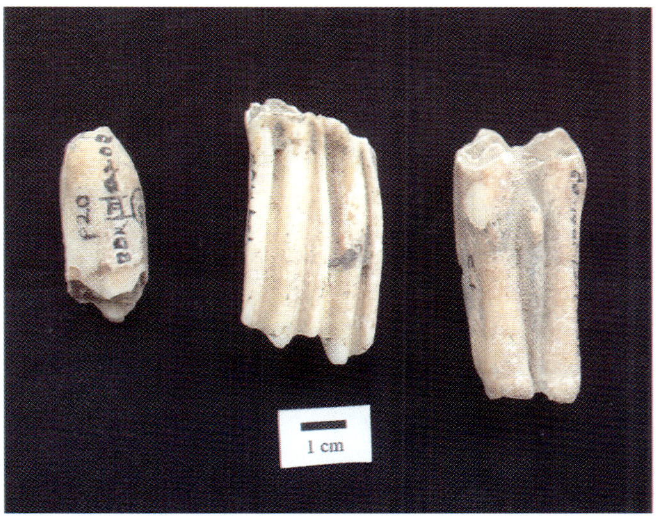

Pl. 38. Mandibular and maxillary teeth of *Bos indicus*.

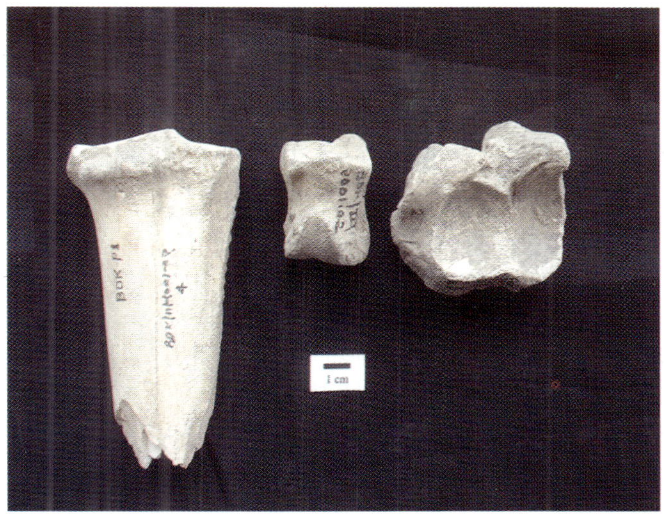

Pl. 39. Proximal portion of a metacarpal, second phalanx and centrotarsal bone of *Bubalus bubalis*.

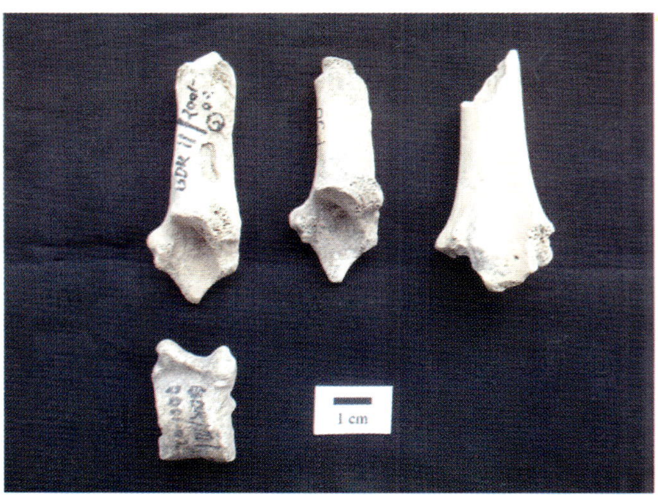

Pl. 40. Bone of *Capra hircus*.

Pl. 41. Unidentified bones of a sea mammal (?).

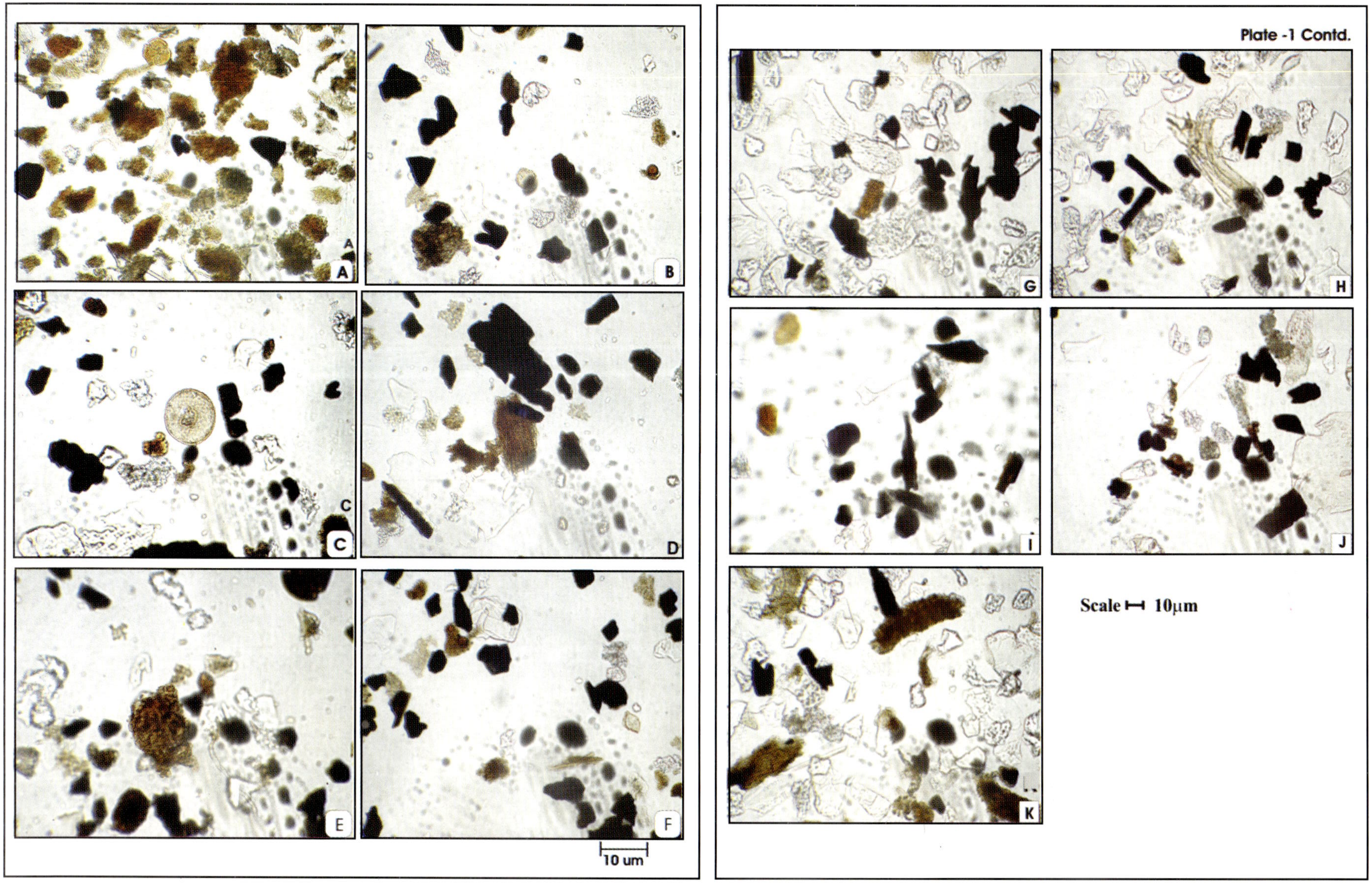

Pl. 42 A. Abundance of brown organic matter and colourless amorphous debris. Black opaque unidentified organic debris showing round edges are low in percentage. B. Increase in black opaque debris. Amorphous organic matter shows gelification in the centre. C. Protozoan cyst and black debris. D. Lath-shaped black opaque organic debris of larger size. Acid-resistant inorganic particles high and low amorphous organic matter. E & F. Black unidentified debris with round edges. Algal bodies and marine acritarchs. G to J. Woody lath-shaped unidentified opaque black phytoclasts. K. Larger particle size. Poorly sorted phytoclasts. Brown, identifiable tissue present. Amorphous organic matter, low in number. Acid-resistant inorganic particles in good number. (Colour)

6.4 *CHICOREUS RAMOSUS*

Another important shell used in Bet Dwarka is *Chicoreus ramosus,* which is amply found in the Gulf of Kachchh. The length of the shell ranges between 7 cm to 25 cm and width between 6 cm to 20 cm (Kenoyer, 1983). Structurally, this shell is large, inflated with hollow spiraling columella and numerous spines and nodes covering the entire body surface of it. The sutures are solidly joined, making it possible to produce large circlets from each shell, provided all the spines are first removed. Unlike *Turbinella pyrum,* it is not suitable for making solid objects from its columella. The flesh of this species is edible.

Generally, *Chicoreus ramosus* occur in the inter-tidal zone, especially in rocky or reef areas, to depths of 20 m. It preys upon oysters and other shellfish by perforating the hard calcium of the shell with an acidic secretion, and consuming the soft part of the organism (Kenoyer, 1983). Similar boring worms and sponges also attach this species, so that the apex and anterior parts of the shell are generally perforated by predator holes.

This species has a very wide distribution throughout the Indo-Pacific region, but its actual distribution along the coast of the sub-continent is somewhat limited. It is common in the shallow bays of South India and Sri Lanka, and again in the Gulf of Kachchh. However, it is not common further west, along the Sind and Makran Coast.

6.5 OTHER SHELLS

Besides the shells mentioned above, there are varieties of shells that have been identified (Table 7-10) which were perhaps used for food and decoration. The most important among them is Dentalium shell (Pl. 31, Fig. 41), which is available in large scale on the western shore of the Bet Dwarka island and used even today as bead by the local people.

6.6 BANGLES MANUFACTURING

A large number of shell fragments have been found during surface exploration and excavations. They are of various sizes and varieties such as plain surface with square or rectangular section, narrow bangles with a single ridge and triangular section, and thin bangles with a circular section (Fig. 42 and Pl. 32). A few bangles with 2-3 grooves on the outer surface were also noticed.

Chank shell has been used extensively for manufacturing shell bangles. Another gastropod, *Chicoreus ramosus*, has also been used for making bangles. Primarily, the outer body of the shell is used to fashion the bangle. Initially, the apex portion (Pl. 33) is chopped off and then bangles of required thickness can be sawn from the body portion. The saw marks are noticed on the columella of many shells (Pl. 34); the marks indicate the thickness of saw (which may be of steel or copper) as 1.0 to 1.5 mm. The shell bangle manufacture technology is similar to that noticed during the Harappan period at various sites like Nageshwar (Hegde *et al.,* 1990), Shahr-I-Sokhta (Durante, 1979) and Mohenjodaro (Kenoyer, 1985). This tradition continued during the Late Harappan at Bet Dwarka and, later on, during the historical period. Interestingly, the initial method described for Nageshwar (Hegde *et al.,* 1990) shell bangle manufacturing is different from that of Bet Dwarka. At Bet Dwarka, they have chopped the apex with saw, as one can notice the saw marks. However, the rest of the method is same for obtaining the bangles.

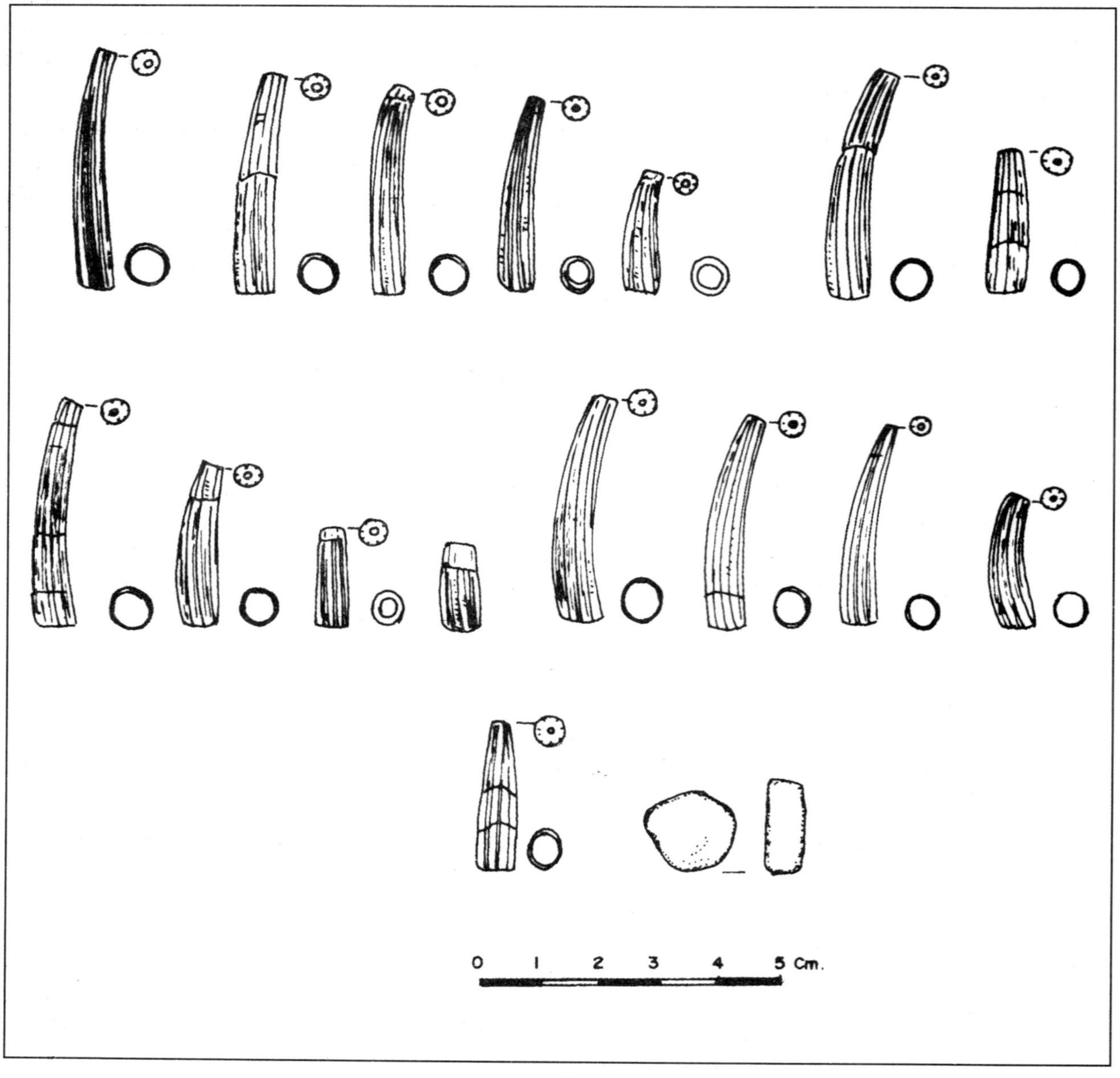

Fig. 41. Dentalium shells.

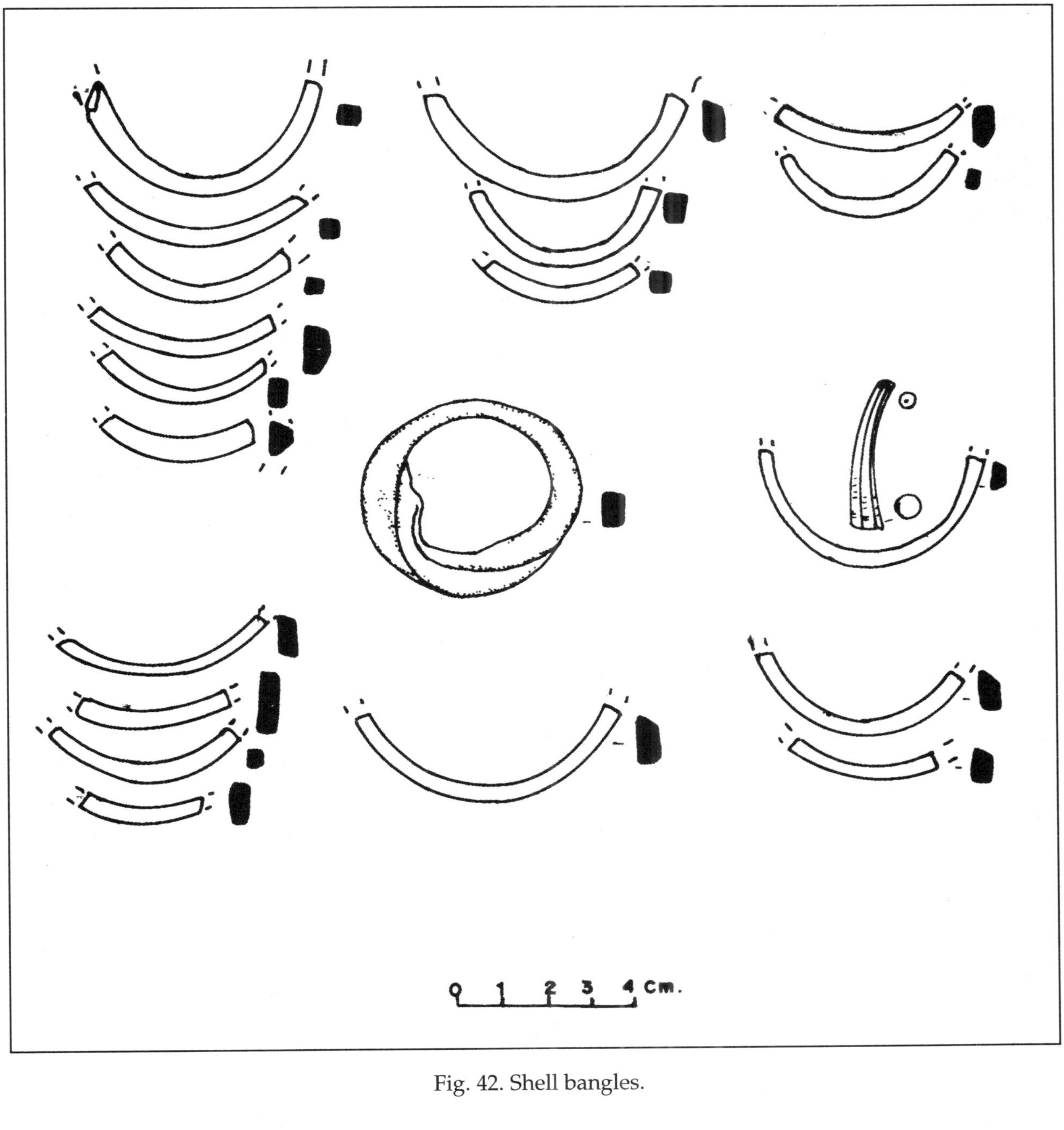

Fig. 42. Shell bangles.

6.7 BEAD MANUFACTURING

Six shell beads have been recovered from the exploration, and four of them are circular in shape with an axial hole. The fifth is a long one with square section and perforation in the middle. With all probability, these beads have been made from the columella part of *Turbinella pyrum* as they are similar to those found from Harappan period sites across the sub-continent. Besides this, a large number of dentalium shell beads were also recovered from the excavation.

6.8 LADLE

Ladles were made from *Chicoreus ramosus*. Before the body of shell could be cut, all the exterior spines were first sawn or chipped-off. Then a diagonal cut was made from the top of the main whorl extending around both sides of the shell, and eventually reaching the narrow anterior end of the shell. A handle was formed by making two parallel longitudinal cuts from the anterior tip towards the main body whorl. In this manner, a rough ladle was detached from the shell and by repeating the process on the remaining half of the shell, a second, but smaller, ladle could also be produced. Though we could not find any complete and prepared ladle from the limited excavations at Bet Dwarka, there was found and unfinished ladle (Pl. 35), and presence of a large number of waste of *Chicoreus ramosus* suggests that ladle were manufactured and must have been exported to other contemporary sites in Saurashtra and Kachchh regions.

6.9 ABSOLUTE DATES FROM SHELLS FOR ARCHAEOLOGICAL SITE AT BET DWARKA

Absolute dating from marine shell is a very common practice and every event of marine geological history has been dated from the shells. In archaeology, many pre-historic sites have been dated using marine shell. However, dating from shells belonging to the proto-historic and historical periods has not received enough attention. From Bet Dwarka, seven shell samples have been dated with conventional C^{14} method (Table 2). The dates of Bet Dwarka archaeological sites range between 3470±80 (cal. 3830-3640) years BP and 1910±80 (cal. 1950-1730) years BP. They are in agreement with the archaeological findings. The oldest date came from a late Harappan site (BDK-VI), which is generally dated between 19th and 14th century BC. Similarly, historical period sites on the southern coast of the island are dated from 5th century BC to 4th century AD, which corresponds to archaeological context. Historical period dates have also been reaffirmed by the AMS method from charcoal and thermoluminescence method from potsherds. The C^{14} dates from the shells of Bet Dwarka island have opened up another dimension in the field of absolute dating of an archaeological site, particularly of recent times.

6.10 CONCLUSION

The widespread use of shell objects on many sites in ancient India is well-known. The shell bangle industry from West Bengal, particularly from Dacca (now in Bangladesh), is famous even to this day. Archaeological findings from Bet Dwarka indicated that marine resources, specifically shell, attracted early settlers (late Harappan) on the island, which later became a major industry of the island. Perhaps this was one of the biggest shell industries during the historical period. The products from shell must have been traded within and outside the country. Shells have been used very effectively as suggested by C^{14} dating material, which have provided very useful timeframe for Bet Dwarka settlement, dating back to proto-historic period to historical period.

Table 7. Shells from BDK-I.

Name of species	*Layers*									
	1	*2*	*3*	*4*	*5*	*6*	*7*	*8*	*9*	*10*
*Babylonia spirata**						1				
Arabica arabica					1	1				
Conus aroneosus										
Erosaria inocellata				1	1	1				
Turbo coronatus	8			6	3					
Turbinella pyrum	1	3	8	4	2	46	505	15	1	
*Turbo brunneus**	5			2				5	1	
Cypraea annulus			1							
Chicoreus ramosus			4	1			3			
Cardium flavum				1		1				
Monetaria moneta				3	29					
Hemifusus cochlidium			1				1	1		
Anadara ehrenbergi					1					
Nerita polita					1					
Laevicardium papyraceum		1								
Dentalium sp	3			5	4	31	193	30	5	
Trochus stellatus					1					
Electroma alacorvi									1	
Astraea stellata						1				
Total	**17**	**4**	**14**	**23**	**43**	**82**	**702**	**51**	**8**	

Table 8. Shells from BDK-II.

Name of species	*Layers*									
	1	*2*	*3*	*4*	*5*	*6*	*7*	*8*	*9*	*10*
Babylonia spirata	1	1		1	2	3	1			
Arabica arabica		1								
Erosaria inocellata				1						
Cypraea tigris				1						1
Thais mutabilis	1				1					
Hyotissa numisma							1			1
Turbo coronatus	4	3	5	1		4				4
Turbinella pyrum	10	6	9	9	10	3	4		5	5
Turbo brunneus	8	2	6	1	5	5	3			15
Circenita callipyga				1	1					
Cypraea annulus		1		1		1				
Cardita bicolor					1					
Chicoreus ramosus	4	3	5		7	1	5		4	5
Cardium flavum	1		1	1						1

Monetaria moneta						1				
Anadara ehrenbergi		1				1			1	1
Nerita polita			3	3						
Laevicardium papyraceum	1									1
Dentalium sp.	19	2	1	3		7	5	9		
Trochus stellatus						1				
Murex brunneus	3			1	3	2	2		3	1
Clavus crassa		1								
Adusta onyx			1							
Turbo ramosus								4		
Turritella terebra									1	
Paphia malabarica										1
Potamides cignulatus										1
Total	**52**	**21**	**31**	**24**	**30**	**29**	**21**	**13**	**14**	**37**

Table 9. Shells from BDK-III.

Name of species	*Layers*									
	1	*2*	*3*	*4*	*5*	*6*	*7*	*8*	*9*	*10*
Babylonia spirata	5				4	4	5			
Arabica arabica				2			2			
Conus aroneosus							1			
Erosaria inocellata	2			1	1		1			
Cypraea tigris							1			
Thais mutabilis							1			
Hyotissa numisma							1			
Turbo coronatus							1		4	
Turbinella pyrum	10	5	8	17	14	37	28	5	3	1
Turbo brunneus				5	7	6	8			
Circenita callipyga									1	
Cypraea annulus									2	
Erosaria turdus									2	
Tonna galea								1	2	
Cardita bicolor									1	
Thais carnifera				2				1		
Chicoreus ramosus	2		1	2	1	1	2	5	1	1
Cardium flavum	1				1					
Monetaria moneta	4			5	7					
Hemifusus cochlidium					1					1
Anadara ehrenbergi					1					
Nerita polita	2									
Dentalium sp.	18	6	6	14	20	4	2	1		
Total	**44**	**11**	**15**	**48**	**57**	**42**	**53**	**13**	**16**	**3**

Table 10. Shells from BDK-VI.

Name of the species	*Layers*	
	1	2
Arabica arabica	1	
Turbinella pyrum	1	1
Hemifusus cochlidium	1	
Tonna cepa	1	1
	1	

Table 11. Layer-wise distribution of artifacts of *Turbinella Pyrum* from BDK-I.

Layers	Bangles	Apex portion	Columella	Waste
1	1	1		1
2		3		1
3		8		2
4	5	4	4	3
5	5	2		5
6	24	46	1	16
7	>100	392	566	178
8	8	9	15	8
9	1		1	3
Total	**>150**	**465**	**587**	**217**

Table 12. Layer-wise distribution of artifacts of *Turbinella Pyrum* from BDK-II.

Layers	Bangles	Apex portion	Columella	Waste
1	12	9	10	3
2	5	6	4	1
3		8	9	5
4	6	6	6	9
5	5	7	10	5
6	3	3		
7	6	2	4	2
8				
9	10		4	3
10	2	3	5	
11	1			
Total	**50**	**44**	**52**	**14**

Table 13. Layer-wise distribution of artifacts of *Turbinella Pyrum* from BDK-III.

Layers	Bangles	Apex portion	Columella	Waste
1	33	8	10	13
2	22	5	4	1
3	12	5	6	8
4	13	5	9	17
5	24	8	12	14
6	18	12	37	10
7	7	25	28	9
8		1	5	2
9	2	3	3	1
10			1	1
Total	**131**	**72**	**115**	**76**

* Chapter is contributed by A.S. Gaur, Sundaresh and Vardhan Patankar.

Annexure A

Report of Animal Bones Collected from Bet Dwarka Island, Gujarat

P.P. Joglekar

INTRODUCTION

This report is based on animal remains collected during the excavations in the 2001-2002 field season at the Bet Dwarka island, in the Gulf of Kachchh, Gujarat (Gaur and Sundaresh, 2003). Standard archaeozoological methods used during this work include a routine protocol of the laboratory analysis, data storage and quantitative analysis developed at the archaeozoological laboratory at Deccan College (Joglekar, 1991; Thomas and Joglekar, 1995). Bone fragments broken during the recovery and transport were mended. Identification of the skeletal elements up to the species level was carried out with the help of standard reference skeletons available at the Deccan College. In case of a few closely related species such as the sheep and the goat, identification keys were employed (eg Schmid, 1972; Joglekar *et al.*, 1994; Pawankar and Thomas, 2001). Even after careful examination, some fragments could not be identified. These were grouped into broad classes such as *Bos/Bubalus* (cattle or buffalo) and *Capra/Ovis* (goat or sheep).

NATURE OF THE FAUNAL MATERIAL

The faunal material from both trenches (BDK-II and III) is well-preserved. A total of 72 (1676 g) fragments were examined, of which 68 (94.44 %) were identifiable. In general, the condition of the fragments indicates that the animal bones after their deposition did not undergo any physical movement. A few bones showed evidence of bone modification (Table 14). Only two fragments found from BDK-II showed marks of butchering/carcass processing. One of these is a thoracic vertebra of cattle/buffalo (BDKP10) found from layer 2. A cattle calacaneum found from layer 4 (BDKP06) showed a mark of charring, besides the marks of butchering/carcass processing. Only one fragment (cattle/buffalo rib) found from BDK-III (layer 8) showed marks of butchering/ carcass processing. A single fragment (black buck calacaneum: BDKP31) found from BDK-III (layer 7) showed that it was charred.

Table 14. Bone modifications seen at BDK-II and BDK-III (Pl. 36).

Trench	**BDK-II**						**BDK-III**				
Type of modification/layer	1	2	3	4	5	Total	6	7	8	9	Total
Charred	0	0	0	0	0	0	0	1	0	0	1
Cut mark	1	1	2	1	1	6	1	1	2	1	5
Butchering mark	0	1	0	0	0	1	0	0	0	0	0
Charred and butchering mark	0	0	0	1	0	1	0	0	0	0	0
Total	1	2	2	2	1	8	1	2	2	1	6

Six fragments clearly showed cut marks. These include a tibial fragment (BDKP12) of goat (layer 1), a fragment of the radius of cattle (layer 2), and a fragment of the radius of buffalo (layer 3). Five fragments found from BDK-III showed that these were cut. These include one cattle metacarpal (BDKP21), one cattle calacaneum (BDKP27), and a single buffalo femur fragment found from layer 9.

As far as bone breakage is concerned, in most of the cases ancient breaks occurred when the fragments were in fresh condition. In some cases such broken/cut pieces of the bone were found together. For example, in BDK-II, a right side mandible of cattle was broken near the symphysis portion, and both these pieces are found together from layer 4. Similarly, two ancient fragments of a proximal metacarpal bone of goat/sheep were found from layer 8 of BDK-IIII.

ANIMALS FOUND AT BET DWARKA

The species identified from trench BDK-II and BDK-III (Table 15-16) mainly consists of domestic mammals, with the sole exception of a single wild mammalian species (black buck). The bones of *Bos indicus* (cattle) out-number the other species in both the trenches (Pl. 37-38). The distribution of skeletal elements indicates that both meat-bearing and non-meat-bearing parts of these animals are found.

Table 15. Species identified from trench BDK-II.

Species/layer	1	2	3	4	5	6	Total	Weight (g)
Bos indicus (cattle)	2	3	1	5	3	1	15	538
Bos/Bubalus	0	2	1	1	0	0	4	64
Bubalus bubalis (buffalo)	0	1	2	1	0	0	4	358
Capra hircus (goat)	1	1	1	0	0	0	3	30
Capra/Ovis	0	0	0	0	0	0	0	0
Antilope cervicapra	0	0	1	0	0	0	1	10
Total	3	7	6	8	3	1	27	1000

Only six buffalo bones were found together in BDK-II and III, all of which are of adult animals (Pl. 39). The bones from BDK-II include an isolated molar, a single second phalanx, metacarpal proximal portion, and a radius fragment. The radius fragment belong to a large male buffalo and it bears a cut mark. The bones from BDK-III include a centrotarsal from layer 8 and a fragment of femur from layer 9.

The bones of goat and sheep are only nine of which it was not possible to determine in three cases whether these belonged to sheep or goats (Pl. 40). Three fragments each from BDK-II and III belonged to goats. One of the three bones (a calcaneum from layer 7) found from BDK-III, belonged to the young one, whereas all the three specimens from BDK-II were of adult animals.

Table 16. Species identified from trench BDK-III.

Species/layer	2	3	4	6	7	8	9	10	Total	Weight (g)
Bos indicus (cattle)	1	2	0	3	5	4	0	0	15	340
Bos/Bubalus	0	0	0	3	5	8	0	1	17	192
Bubalus bubalis (buffalo)	0	0	0	0	0	1	1	0	2	82
Capra hircus (goat)	0	0	0	1	2	0	0	0	3	16
Capra/Ovis	0	0	1	0	0	2	0	0	3	10
Antilope cervicapra	0	0	0	0	1	0	0	0	1	8
Total	1	2	1	7	13	15	1	1	41	648

Layer 10 has four unidentified fragments (28 g).

The black buck is the sole wild mammal found in this faunal assemblage. Only two bones of this animal are found. These include a distal fragment of an adult tibia (BDKP17) found from layer 3 in trench II, and a calacaneum of a sub-adult found from layer 7 in trench III (BDKP31).

Among the skeletal elements that could not be identified, a special mention of two such fragments must be made (Pl. 41). These fragments most probably belong to the cranium of a sea mammal, but it is not possible to identify the species due to lack of comparative material.

BONE MEASUREMENTS

It was possible to measure several skeletal elements using the standard archaeozoological method of measuring the bones (Driesch, 1976). Tables 17-18 provide measurements of bones wherever it was possible to measure. Bone measurements do provide valuable information about animal sizes, and are useful for both intra-site and inter-site comparison (Joglekar, 2000-2001). A single astragalus (BDKP15) measurement of cattle indicated that this animal was of 119.3 cm at the withers. Three measurements of goat are available to comment on the height at the withers of goats kept at Dwarka. These estimates are 70.98 cm (based on astragalus BDKP32), 70.68 cm (based on calacaneum BDKP11), and 62.40 cm (based on calacaneum BDKP30). At present, it is not possible to compare these measurements for want of information from other sites in Gujarat, except the site of Padri (Joglekar, 1993-94, 1996-97). The cattle and goats reared at Dwarka are not very different in sizes than those found in the early historic contexts at Padri. All the measurements tabulated in this report could be used for such comparisons in future.

Table 17. Measurements of animal bones found at BDK-II and III.

Bone	Astragalus	Astragalus	
Reg. no.	BDKP32	BDKP15	
Context	BDK-III (7)	BDK-II (4)	
Species	*Capra hircus*	*Bos indicus*	
Lateral length	31.30	71.00	
Medial length	29.71	65.10	
Maximum distal width	19.12	47.20	
Maximum lateral thickness	14.00	36.72	
Maximum medial thickness	14.35	37.81	
Bone	Calcaneum	Calcaneum	Calcaneum
Reg. no.	BDKP11	BDKP30	BDKP31
Context	BDK-II (2)	BDK-III (7)	BDK-III (7)
Species	*Capra hircus*	*Capra hircus*	*A. cervicapra*
Maximum length	62.00	56.35	61.94
Maximum width	18.00	18.30	18.36
Maximum height	22.00	21.82	22.20
Bone	Centrotarsal	Centrotarsal	Centrotarsal
Reg. no.	BDKP09	BDKP23	BDKP08
Context	BDK-II (4)	BDK-III (8)	BDK-II (2)
Species	*Bos indicus*	*B. bubalis*	*Bos indicus*
Maximum length	——	——	36.65
Maximum width	51.93	62.48	35.12
Maximum thickness	——	——	18.34
Bone	First Phalanx	First Phalanx	
Reg. no.	BDKP18	BDKP25	
Context	BDK-II (1)	BDK-III (8)	
Species	*Bos indicus*	*Bos indicus*	
Maximum length	68.64	62.27	
Maximum proximal width	31.40	27.31	
Proximal thickness	38.15	28.36	
Maximum distal width	——	25.95	
Bone	Second Phalanx	Second Phalanx	Second Phalanx
Reg. no.	BDKP02	BDKP24	BDKP16
Context	BDK-II (2)	BDK-III (8)	BDK-II (3)
Species	*Bos indicus*	*Bos indicus*	*B. bubalis*
Maximum length	49.19	——	46.14
Maximum proximal width	30.14	——	32.24
Proximal thickness	32.56	——	33.11
Maximum distal width	25.32	25.87	31.00

Table 18. Measurements of animal bones found at BDK-II and III.

Bone	Maxillary PM2	Maxillary Molar
Reg. no.	BDKP20	BDKP05
Context	BDK-II (3)	BDK-II (3)
Species	*Bos indicus*	*Bos indicus*
Maximum length	16.72	28.42
Maximum width	17.59	18.60

Bone	Maxillary Molar	Maxillary Molar	Maxillary Molar3
Reg. no.	BDKP04	BDKP28	BDKP03
Context	BDK-II (6)	BDK-III (7)	BDK-II (2)
Species	*Bos indicus*	*Bos indicus*	*B. bubalis*
Maximum length	27.50	25.95	31.47
Maximum width	(22.43)	21.80	22.53

Annexure B

Palynological Study of Sedimentary Soil Sequences from Bet Dwarka Island

Anjum Farooqui

INTRODUCTION

The climate and sea level fluctuations largely influence the coastal geomorphology and vegetation. Palynostratigraphical succession in a sedimentary soil sequence reflects the magnitude, direction and duration of the fluctuating biophysical factors such as geomorphology, soil and water quality, tidal influence and even the coastal microtopography (Ellison, 1989). Mangroves play an important role to preserve the imprint of coastal dynamics.

According to Tyson (1995), the organic residue in the sediment includes mainly phytoclasts, palynomorphs and zooclasts. The phytoclasts include cellular organization, structured botanical tissue-type and amorphous (cell-filling) organic particles. The palynomorphs include all types of pollen or spores. Remains of zooplankton include body parts of arthropods, crustaceans, copepod eggs, protozoan cysts, etc.

The objective of the present study is to record Middle to Late Holocene sea level trends in the Bet Dwarka island, and also to know the reasons for the decline in historical human settlement (Vora *et al.,* 2002, Gaur and Vora, 1999). This is attempted through palynological analysis of coastal sedimentary soil sequence, using mangrove pollen, marine planktons and clastic terrestrial land pollens as indicators.

METHODOLOGY

The organic debris and palynomorphs have been isolated following Erdtman (1943) and studied under light microscope. Organic residue was identified/classified following Tyson (1995). It includes total acid resistant organic residue. The analysis helps to determine the depositional environment, vegetation and the supporting ecosystem in the past. Photo plates 42 and 43 show the nature of phytoclasts throughout the soil sequence. Photo plates 44-48 are the palynomorphs, mostly recorded from surface or sub-surface sediment or as mentioned in the results.

RESULTS

Palynostratigraphical succession was carried out in sedimentary soil sequence from Bet Dwarka island. Phases of depositional environment and sea level fluctuation have been identified in sediments on the basis of phytoclasts, palynomorphs and zooplankton remains. The age of the sediment has been discussed in detail by Vora *et al.* (2002). The same sedimentary soil sequence has been analysed in the present work for the palynological evidences. On the basis of the evidence of 2nd century AD coins at 80 cm depth, the depositional time-period of 2.15 m (BDK-I) sedimentary soil sequence is extrapolated and, therefore, should be Middle Holocene (around 4000 yrs. BP). Another 95 cm of sedimentary soil sequence (BDK-VI) from Bet Dwarka island was deposited since 3760 +/− yrs. BP (Vora *et al.*, 2002).

BDK-I (2.15 m SEDIMENTARY SEQUENCE)

Phase- I

The surface and sub-surface sediment show a good percentage of the variety of phytoclasts (Pl. 42). Black unidentifiable opaque particles are less in number. Amorphous organic residue is also in good percentage. Identifiable margins and gelified central phytoclasts were also observed indicating bacterial degradation. The fibrous tissue constituting elongated cellular structure, typical of monocots, were also observed. Algal and fungal spores (Pl. 46-47) were also present. Oxidized woody trachieds of plant origin (Pl. 48) were common. Presence of *Pinus, Acacia* and *Polyalthia* show its anthropogenic introduction in the area. Few marine acritarchs (Pl. 45) were recorded. Resinous debris (Pl. 48) were also recorded from this phase, indicating a warmer climatic condition.

Results indicate dysoxic to anoxic, shallow, stabilised near- shore depositional environment. The energy of water flow was low. Mangroves and marine forms were perhaps transported through sea-water during high tides.

Phase II

The organic residue is poorly sorted. Black unidentifiable opaque debris are in abundance (Pl. 42). Low-to-nil amorphous organic matter was recorded. Phytoclasts show structured outer rim with middle gelification (Pl. 48). Few blade-shaped particles were observed which are uniformly opaque and structureless. Protozoan cysts (Pl. 47), fungal spores and algal bodies were rare. Only *Poaceae*, and *Chenopodiaceae* members were recorded in few number. No mangroves or its associates and other arboreal land plants were recorded in this phase.

Results suggest of oxic depositional environment. Terrestrial clastic influx was weak during this phase. This indicates that the sea-water thrust was landwards. The water flow was of high energy, shifting the shoreline landwards. Consequently, the island was inundated to a large extent. During this period, the freshwater thrust was weak that could be attributed to either weak climate or the hydro-isostatic adjustment that may have taken place subsequent to tectonic activity in the area. It may be noted that local micro-geomorphological changes inducing hydro-isostatic adjustments may not match the regional climatic or relative sea level fluctuations.

Phase III

The surface soil sample (up to 15 cm depth) comprises of fairly good percentage of organic debris that include variety of phytoclasts and palynomorphs. The size of the particles and preservation is variable. These are orange-brown or dark brown structured and structureless material of irregular shape. Besides this, translucent cuticles, membranous tissues, the structured phytoclast lacking obvious biostructure were also observed. The overall phytoclasts indicate partial oxidation at the time of deposition. Few black unidentifiable clastic particles with round edges were recorded, indicating its distant transportation (Pl. 42A-B).

The allochthonous fraction includes terrestrial palynomorphs such as *Pinus*, *Schefflera* (a tree that generally grows along the river), *Polyalthia, Hopea spp.* and other terrestrial land plants (Pl. 44). Trilete and monolete spores are present. Algal and fungal detritus are abundant (Pl. 45-46). Saprophytic fungal spore such as *Tetraploa* were recorded. The autochthonous fraction include acritarchs, marine green algae (*Siphonocladales*) and a low percentage of mangroves and its associates.

Results indicate oxic to dysoxic shallow depositional near-shore environment showing similarity with Phase I . Low percentage of mangroves and acritarchs indicate that the nearness of the shoreline and the mangrove palynomorphs would have drifted through sea-water during high tides.

BDK-VI (SURFACE TO 95 cm DEPTH):-

Two phases were demarkated from this trench. These are:

Phase I

The preservation of the phytoclasts (Pl. 43) show similarity with the BDK-I trench. Palynomorphs were poorly preserved in this phase (surface and at 15 cm depth). Except for poaceae and few chenopodiaceae pollen, no other pollen taxa were recorded. Few algal and fungal spores were recorded. Poorly sorted, black unidentified opaque debris with almost round edges were common, indicating oxic depositional environment and high water energy. No signs of marine incursion were recorded.

Phase II

The surface soil sample shows abundance of fungal spores and gelified phytoclasts with their margins cellular and irregular. Larger black opaque debris were recorded from this phase. The terrestrial land pollen includes mainly exotics such as *Acacia* and *Casuarina.* The pollen grains of *Polyalthi, Schefflera,* etc were also recorded. Stray record of rhizophoraceae pollen and its associates, along with the acritarchs, indicate nearness of shoreline and associated patchy mangrove fringes.

DISCUSSION

Examples from archaeological sites belonging to the Harappan Period such as Lothal, Padri, Bet Dwarka and others have been cited (Gaur and Vora, 1999) to indicate shoreline movement in relation to the last 4500 yrs. BP. In Bet Dwarka, the archaeological material spread in the present inter-tidal zone suggests the human settlement of 2nd century BC that was destroyed by the sea (Ansari and Mate, 1966). These help us to assume that Bet Dwarka was established at the beginning of the 2nd millennium BC. Evidences of infilling and episodes uplifts during the recent past have also been reported (Shakhawala and Shringarpure, 1990). The interpretations from the present palynological study in Bet Dwarka sediments reveal three ecological phases, and its associated vegetation indicate the coastal dynamics during Middle and Late Holocene

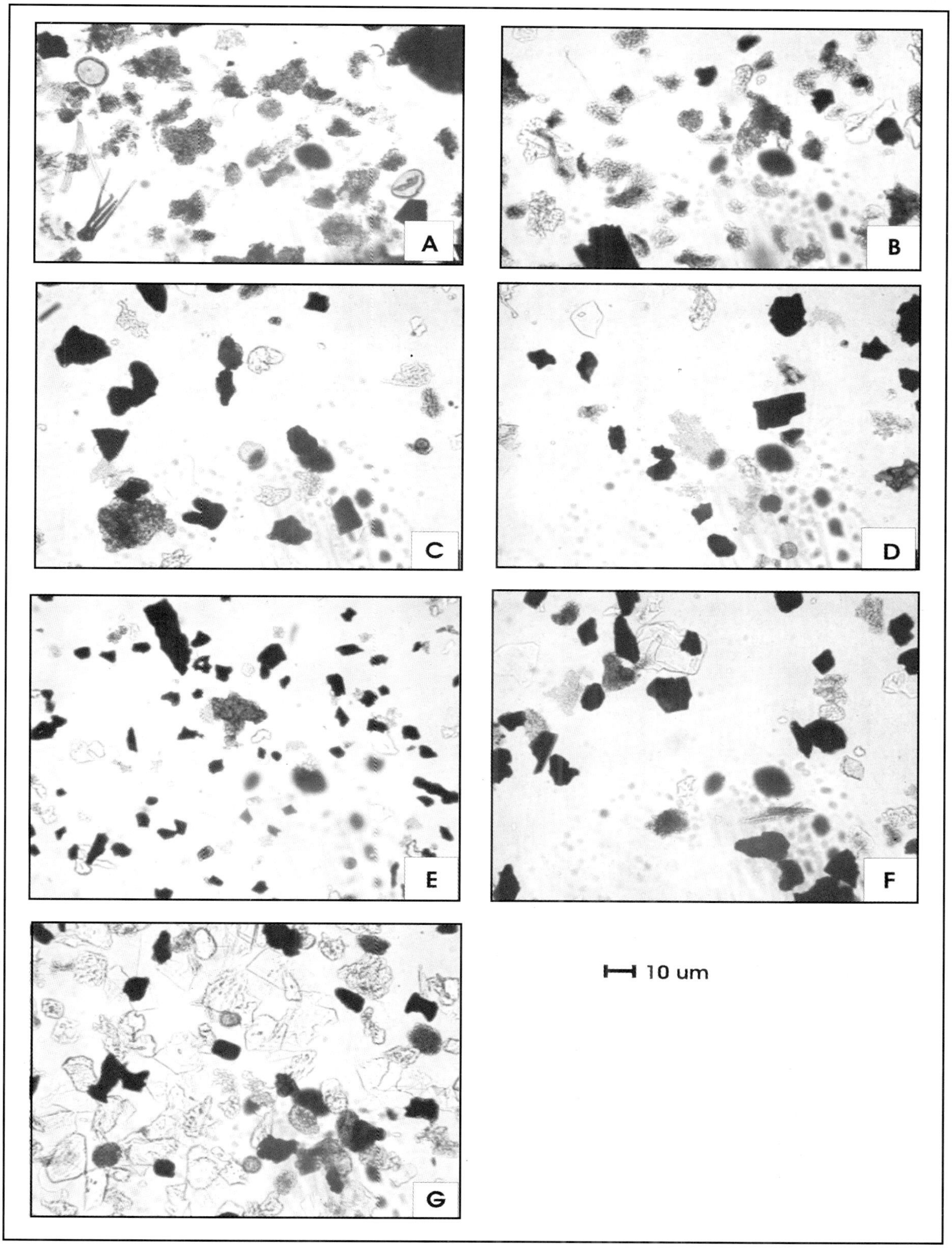

Pl. 43 A. Opaque, black unidentified debris are less in number followed by amorphous organic matter. Few gelified tissues, filamentous debris and fungal fruiting body. Large size particles. B & C. Black unidentified debris increase in percentage. Amorphous debris decrease in size. Poorly sorted debris with round edges. D. Small size particles. Black unidentified opaque particles, more in number. Few elongated lath-shaped debris, also present. Algal bodies present. E. Brown to black organic matter. Amorphous debris low in number. Photomicrographs of palynomorphs and zooplanktons from Bet Dwarka island recovered mostly from surface (10 cm) and below 100 cm in BDK-I and at 95 cm in BDK-VI sedimentary soil sequence.

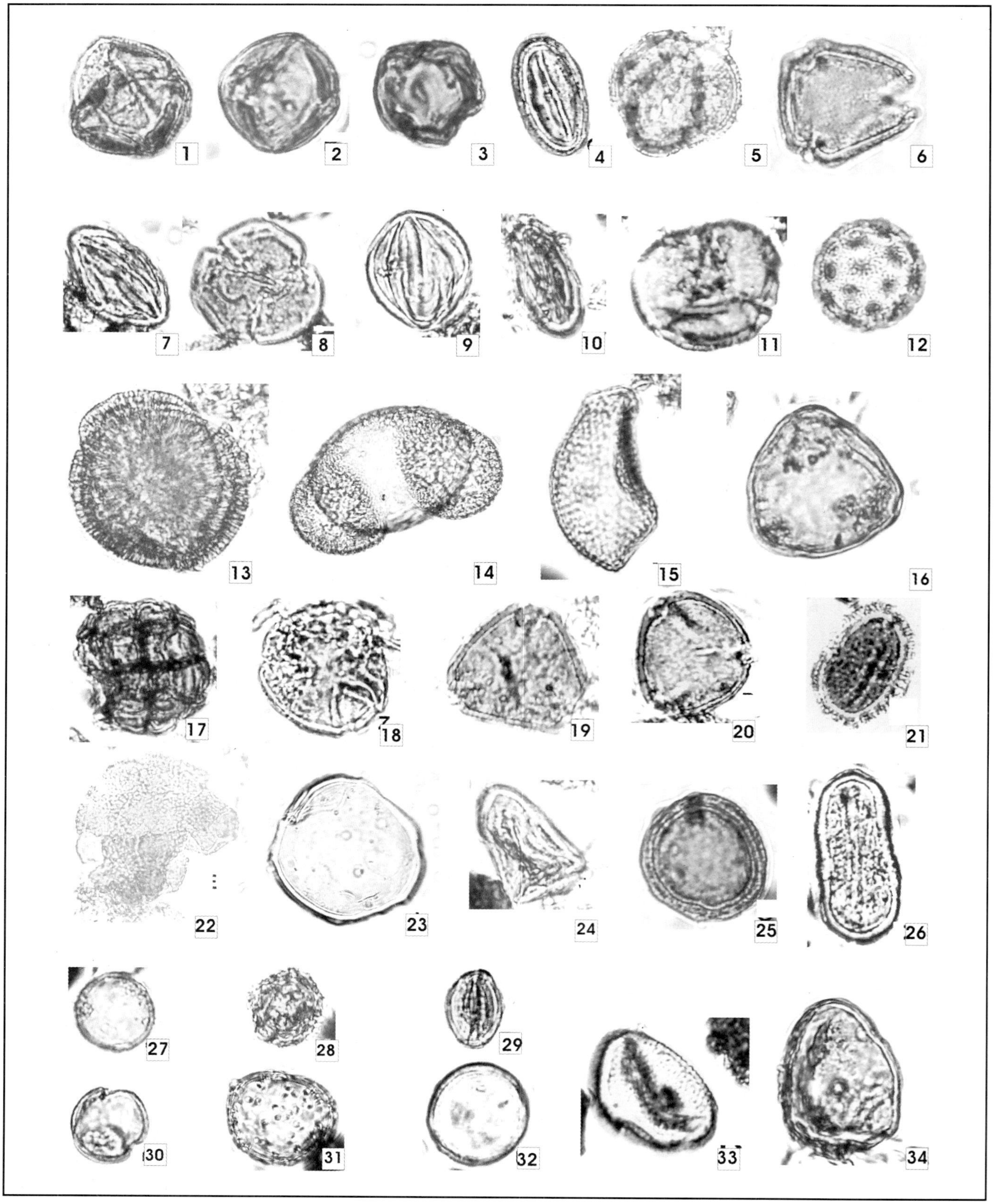

Pl. 44. *Rhizophoraceae* 1 to 3; *Aegiceras* 4; *Excoecaria* 5; *Duranta* 6; *Aegiceras* 7; *Meliaceae* 8; *Anacardeaceae* 9; *Heritiera* 10; *Schefflera* 11; *Chenopodiaceae* 12; *Euphorbiaceae* 13; *Pinus* 14; *Aquatic pollen* 15; *Casuarina* 16; *Acacia* 17; *Hopea* 18; *Myrtaceae* 19; *Heritiera* 20; *Oleaceae* 21; *Chrozophora* 22; *Poaceae* 23; *Cyperaceae* 24; *Caryophyllaceae* 25; *Umbelliferae* 26; *Urticaceae* 27; *Asteraceae* 28; *Elaeocarpus* 29, 30; *Polyalthia* 31; *Aquatic pollen* 32; *Poaceae* 33-34.

in the area. Evidences of Middle Holocene sea level highstand has been recorded from the east coast of India (Banerjee, 2000; Vaz and Banerjee, 1996; Farooqui and Vaz, 2000). Accordingly, the sea level rose until around 7000 years and then gradually receded until around 4000 yrs. BP. During this period, mangrove line too followed the shoreline but declined/reduced from most of the part of the east coast. The west coast of India, too, experienced similar sea level highstand (Merh, 1992; Patel, 1991).

The Phase I in the present study suggests of a receding shoreline during the latter-half of the Middle-Holocene (perhaps around 4000 yrs. BP). Mangroves existed in the area during this time-period. The depositional environment suggested of low energy and shallow near-shore environment that would have been conducive for human settlement. However, Phase II shows two cycles, each of low and high sea level for shorter duration and low magnitude. During this period, the sea-water invaded the island to destabilise the vegetation and the proto-historic human settlement. The sea level then lowered in the end of the Christian era, enabling the settlement again, which was subsequently destabilised with the rise in sea-water. The end of Phase II and the Phase III in BDK-I at Bet Dwarka shoreline shows stability again, enabling the human settlement that continues till today. Mangroves existed in the recent past but the deterioration in its diversity must have started a decade or two back. The relative sea level rise and fall during the early part of Late Holocene in Bet Dwarka is in conformation with the records from east coast of India (Vaz and Banerjee, 1998). However, the shoreline shifting in Bet Dwarka island could also be attributed to tectonically induced hydro-isostatic adjustments. The Phase I in BDK-VI represents higher water level comparable to Phase II of BDK-I. The Phase III of BDK-I is comparable to Phase II of BDK-VI.

CONCLUSION

Based on phytoclasts and palynomorph succession in a sedimentary soil sequence, it is interpreted that the sea-water revisited land during the latter half of the Middle Holocene and early Late Holocene. The magnitude and extend of invasion was low as compared to the previous transgressive phase in early Middle Holocene. But, the intermittent rise and fall could not stabilise the coastal vegetation and historical habitation. The sea level was close to its present level some 4000 to 3500 years ago. The present position of the shoreline should have reached sometime during the 'Little Ice Age' Period.

Annexure C

Late Harappan Copper Fishhook: Evidence on the Advance Fishing Technology in Ancient India

A.S. Gaur and Sundaresh

INTRODUCTION

There are numerous evidences of the exploitation of marine resources such as fishing by pre-historic man along the Indian coast. Hora (1954) has rightly observed that,

> pre-historic man in several parts of the world have gathered sufficient knowledge about fish through observation and made use of it in catching fish for food by the use of hook and line.

People of Indus Valley Civilization were great seafarers and perhaps established their colonies overseas in Gulf countries (Ratnagar, 1981; Gaur, 2000). While studying painting of fish on the pottery of Harappan Period, Hora (1954) concluded that the fish painted on pottery are of marine type. Perhaps, baskets or traps were in use for catching fish, as a fisherman carrying two such baskets is painted on a potsherd. These records indicate that Harappans were more familiar with marine fishing. The distribution of shell bangles and other shell artifacts in each and every Harappan site is also indicative of a well-organised marine fishing activity. There are several fishhooks from Mohenjodaro (Marshall, 1931), Harappa, Chanhudaro (Majumdar, 1934), Lothal (Rao, 1979), Padri and many other sites located on the coastal belt of Gujarat. Sarkar (1953) has suggested great similarity between fishhooks of Indus valley sites and modern ones, and he believes that this feature is suggestive of continuity of cultural trait.

The sanskrit word *badisha* has been used for fishhook in ancient Indian literature, including *Mahabharata*. A 12th century AD Indian text, *Manasollasa*, written by the Chalukya king, Someswara, mentioned a chapter entitled *Matsyavinod* (pastime of fishing), mentioning how a king can derive pleasure out of angling (Hora, 1954).

An onshore excavation was undertaken in the Bet Dwarka island to obtain the cultural sequence and to understand the man and sea relation. A large number of pottery, beads of stone, shell and terracotta were found, besides copper artifacts. The recovered copper artifacts are coins, ring and earrings and a well-preserved fishhook. The present paper deals with a copper fishhook, which was discovered from trench BDK-VI, located on the northern part of the island. A detailed discussion of its dating and comparative study has been made here.

DESCRIPTION OF FISHHOOK

The fishhook has been found about 50 cm below the surface in layer 2. It is well-preserved and is one of the bigger hooks of the Harappan Period reported so far. It is 7 cm long and weighs 9 grams. The diameter of the shank is 0.3 cm. A layer of thick encrustation over the hook was removed by chemical treatment. It has a sharp, barbed point, straight sank without forming any curve or eye. However, the top is beaten up and made wide and thin, perhaps for holding thread (Pl. 49, Fig. 19). Some of the Mesopotamian sites, like Ur, have yielded similar type of fishhooks. Several Harappan sites have yielded fishhooks, which are barbed and range in length from 1.25 to 7 cm (Sarkar, 1953). Fishhook from Bet Dwarka is one of the big and well-preserved fishhooks from the Late Harappan sites. However, the biggest copper fishhook has been reported from Padri – another Harappan site on the southern Saurashtra coast (Shinde and Thomus, 1993).

HARAPPAN FISHHOOK TYPES

Copper fishhooks from Harappan sites can be broadly divided into two categories, ie, barbed and un-barbed. Shinde and Thomus (1993) have suggested that barbed fishhooks are generally used to catch large marine fish, whereas the un-barbed variety is used for catching small riverine fish. A number of barbed fishhooks have been reported from Mohenjodaro. Un-barbed fishhooks are mainly from Chanhudaro and Harappa. A number of sites in Gujarat like Kuntasi, Rojdi, Dholavira and Lothal have yielded copper fishhooks of both varieties. The fishhooks reported from Lothal contain tiny barbs and the loops touch the shaft of the hook (Rao, 1979).

Fishhooks have been divided into three varieties based on shanks: i) hooks consisting of a straight shank without forming any curve or eye; ii) hooks with straight shanks but turned outward, the bent loop does not touch the shanks; and iii) hooks consisting of a straight shank but curved out to form a small eye, which is either connected with the shank or only slightly separated from it. The fishhook under discussion here falls into the first category. Many sites of Mesopotamia, like Ur, have yielded the specimens similar to the Bet Dwarka one. The best metallic fishhooks were probably developed by the Harappans, and were certainly superior to those from contemporary sites in Egypt and Mesopotamia (Shinde and Thomus, 1993).

It is well-known that the Harappan Period witnessed a significant development in copper metallurgy. It is believed that the copper requirement of Harappans of Punjab, Haryana, Rajasthan and Gujarat was met by Sikar-Jhunjhunu area of the Khetri belt (Thapar, 1991). Archaeological evidence also suggests that Ganeshwar, located roughly 75 km away from the Khetri copper mines and dated to century 3000-2000 BC, was the main supplier of copper during the Harappan Period (Agrawal, 1984).

DATING

Earlier explorations and excavations near this site indicated the site to be of Late Harappan Period, based on archaeological finds which has been confirmed during the present excavation by scientific methods. TL dating of potsherds collected during surface exploration (Vora *et al.*, 2002) suggested a date ranging from the 16th to 14th century BC. Two worked shell samples from stratified layer 1 and 2 were collected during the present excavation, and the same were dated by Birbal Sahni Institute for Palaeobotany, Lucknow. It has provided a time-bracket for Bet Dwarka late Harappan settlement between 18th and 14th century BC. The fishhook was recovered from layer 2, therefore, a precise time-bracket for this layer is 18th to 16th century BC (Table 2).

CONCLUSION

The excavation at Bet Dwarka island has confirmed the oldest settlement dating back to the Late Harappan Period. They have exploited marine resources available around the island. They had extraordinary technology for fishing, which has continued for thousands of years. The discovery of copper fishhook in the context of the Late Harappan Period suggest that the large-scale fishing activity continued in Bet Dwarka island even after the Harappan Period. Chronology has been verified with the findings from Saurashtra as well as with absolute dating method.

Annexure D

The Signature of Seismic Activity During Early Historical Period in Bet Dwarka

C.P. Rajendran and Kusala Rajendran

INTRODUCTION

Seismicity of northwestern India is perhaps unique because it has generated two major earthquakes during a short span of less than 200 years (Fig. 43). Among the past events, the 1819 earthquake (M>7.5) is well-known and quoted as a classic example for co-seismic ground deformation (Oldham, 1926; Rajendran and Rajendran, 2001). The recent earthquake near Bhuj (January 26, 2001) has further focused attention on the threat from future earthquakes in this region (Bendick *et al.*, 2001; Rajendran *et al.*, 2001). There may be two or three specific issues that must be considered in assessing the seismic hazard of regions like Kachchh that fall in the ancient rift system. One, that the rift may host many structures capable of generating large earthquakes, but due to long recurrence intervals, they may appear inactive today. Two, many structures formed as part of rifting may be hidden and in the absence of sufficient sub-surface data, these sources may remain elusive. Three, the seismic source zones may be characterised by varying recurrence rates, thereby requiring an independent evaluation.

Each of these issues needs to be considered in the regional hazard evaluation, and in this paper we address the question of isolating seismic sources and developing their histories. Although the traditional approach has been to use the historical database to assess a region's past history, it is generally known that a few hundred years of data is insufficient to assess its earthquake potential. This is especially true for regions where the recurrence interval of large earthquakes is much longer than their documented histories. In recent years, archaeoseismology and paleo-seismology have evolved as useful tools for reconstructing a region's past earthquake history (Stiros and Jones, 1996; McCalpin, 1996). Identifying seismically-induced liquefaction features, deducing their stratigraphic context, and dating the various horizons to constrain the age of the earthquake is the technique followed in paleo-seismology (eg Obermeier, 1995). Archaeoseismology, on the other hand, uses the disruptions caused by earthquakes, to cultural settlements and the combined use of both these techniques offer much more reliable age constraints

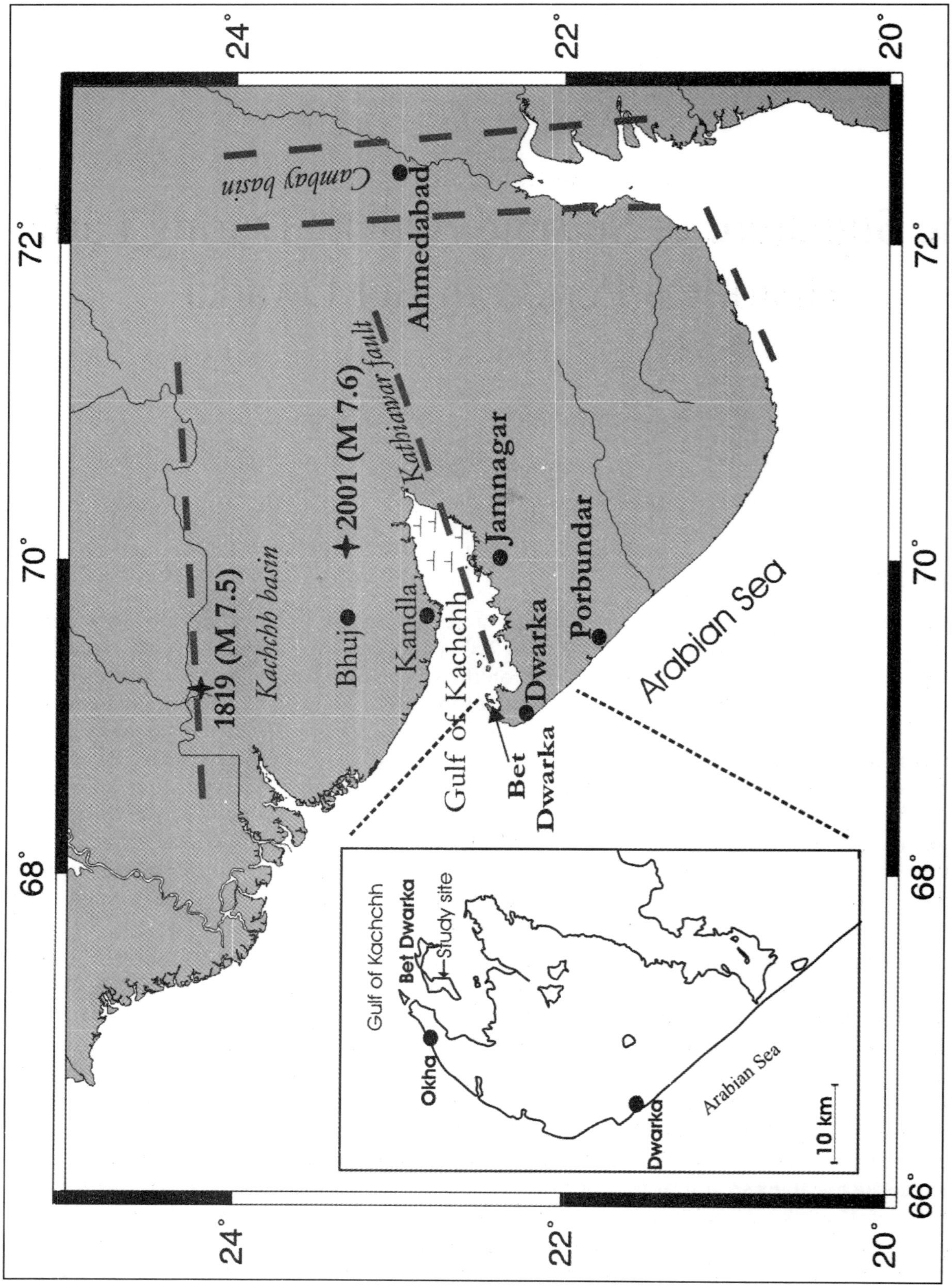

Fig. 43. Map of Gujarat with faults and earthquake centres.

(Tuttle *et al.*, 1996). Disruptions to occupation levels are particularly useful because they often contain datable materials like pottery, bones and organic matter (charcoal, peat, etc).

Our exploration in the Kachchh region began with the primary objective of identifying the penultimate earthquake in the 1819 source. Our studies led us to the evidence for an ancient earthquake that occurred about 1000 years ago (Rajendran and Rajendran, 2001). The success of deciphering the earthquake history in the Rann of Kachchh owed much to the identification of earthquake-induced liquefaction features. The rich historic data offered corroborative evidence to ascertain the timing of the penultimate earthquake in the 1819 source (Rajendran and Rajendran, 2002). With the occurrence of the 2001 Bhuj earthquake, it became evident that there are other seismic sources in the Kachchh-Saurashtra region. Investigations in the areas affected by the Bhuj earthquake have not so far revealed evidence for any past activities of comparable size associated with this source (Rajendran *et al.*, 2001). However, some recent investigations near Dholka, in Ahmedabad, suggested the possibility for an earthquake around 3000 years BP, its source remaining to be confirmed (Rajendran *et al.*, 2002). Thus, the available data, although scanty, point to the possibility for multiple sources in the Kachchh region, and they are probably characterised by varying recurrence rates.

If indeed there are multiple seismic sources in the Kachchh-Saurashtra region, it is important to conduct a systematic search for possible paleoliquefaction features in areas of suspected activity. We believe that the sites of ancient cultures are excellent locations to start this search and we began from Dwarka, an ancient cultural centre that flourished in Gujarat since Harappan times (~3000 years BP), (Vora *et al.*, 2002). Being a coastal town, Dwarka is well located to preserve the impact of storm surges, cyclones and sea level changes, and such climatic phenomena that would have affected ancient human settlements. It could also preserve effects of nearby or distant earthquakes that may have produced disruption of strata, venting of sand, etc that are generally associated with large earthquakes in this region (Rajendran *et al.*, 2001). This question is particularly significant in the case of Dwarka because of its close proximity to an old rift (Fig. 43; Biswas, 1982; Talwani and Gangopadhyay, 2001). It should, however, be mentioned that no significant seismic activity has been reported from here, except for a reported occurrence of a tremor on 12th May 1962 near Dwarka, which, according to local information, lasted for 48 seconds (Pushkar Gokani, personal communication).

We have a rich tradition of oral history, anecdotal accounts and mythology centred on this temple-city, with occasional references to natural disasters. Therefore, this area offers many challenges and opportunities in applying scientific methods to authenticate these anecdotal references. Towards the end of 2001, National Institute of Oceanography (NIO) took up some excavations in Bet Dwarka to identify and date the cultural levels (change). We took this as an opportunity to examine whether any of the cultural strata showed signs of earthquake effects. This paper discusses our preliminary observations in this trench and reports on a soft-sediment deformation feature, which appears to be seismically induced. Rather unrelated to other known earthquakes in the Kachchh-Saurashtra region, the timing and location of this ancient earthquake may have many implications on the seismic hazard of this region.

BACKGROUND

Bet Dwarka, a narrow strip of island in the Gulf of Kachchh, is located 5 km north of the mainland of Okhamandal, the locale of the temple-city of Dwarka. The island and temple-city of Dwarka and the surrounding coastal waters have been the loci of archaeological excavations led by several groups (eg Ansari and Mate, 1966; IAR-Indian Archaeology, 1969; Rao, 1987; Vora *et al.*, 2002). The archaeological findings at Bet Dwarka indicate that it had been an active port in the proto-historic times (4000 years BP) and continued to host human inhabitations during the historical period, the age of the oldest occupation level in the trenches being about 3800 years (Vora *et al.*, 2002). A similar proto-historic site is located at Nageshwar on the northwestern coast of Saurashtra, 17 km northeast of Dwarka (Ratnagar, 2001). The artifacts recovered from this site include shells and pieces of gastropods, probably mined from shallow bays off the coast and apparently used for bangle-making. The terrain at Bet Dwarka presently supports only scanty vegetation, which reflects dry conditions and a low ground water table. The cliff sections in the island are dominated by grey-and-yellow coloured clay with intercalations of brownish sandy clay (eg Bhatt, 2000). The trenches at Bet Dwarka exposed a thick section containing yellowish loamy soil with artifacts of potsherds, shells, bones and specks of carbon. The layers containing pottery sherds and shells have been categorised tentatively into different occupation levels on the basis of archaeological evidence (for a discussion, see Vora *et al.*, 2002). The occupation level at the bottom-most (oldest) part of the trench is designated as level 11 (Pl. 50), (Vora *et al.*, 2002; internal report, NIO). The levels are identified on the basis of preliminary observations and further resolution of this tentative classification is awaited (Vora *et al.*, 2002; internal report, NIO).

CHARACTERISTICS OF THE DEFORMATIONAL STRUCTURES AT BET DWARKA

The NIO team excavated several trenches, but we had the opportunity to examine only three of them. Two of the three trenches were shallow (~2 m) and did not reveal any features that could be related to earthquake-induced deformation, but one of the deeper trenches exposed some interesting structures. We focused our geological studies in this trench (BDK-2), located on the top of the cliff (5 m above msl) on the eastern side of Bet Dwarka. This 3.3-m-deep trench, excavated in a north-south direction, bottomed on the yellowish clay layer, which constitute the base for the earliest habitation. Several occupational levels could be identified within this trench, but only the deepest level (numbered 11) appears to be disturbed by an anomalous sedimentary layer (numbered as level 10). This wedge-shaped layer of laminated silty sand with pottery, and shells with smattering of bones and charcoal had a maximum thickness of about 20 cm in the western corner of the trench, and its lateral extension was traceable for more than 2 m eastward before it got tapered off. The presence of this layer at the top of level 11 suggests that deposition of this layer postdates the lower-most occupation horizon in this trench.

The general profile of the sediment layer followed the eastward slope of the land. In the middle part of the section, however, the layer seemed to have bent downward, possibly due to the weight of the overlying material containing an assorted assemblage of stones, bricks and other artifacts (Pl. 50A and B). Judging from the shape and implied continuity of this layer into the western side of the trench with increased thickness, it is inferred that what was exposed on the northern wall could only be a partial view of a larger feature. Thus, we hypothesise that the exposure on the northern wall probably constitutes only the tail-end (distal part) of the sand body, with much of its proximal part remaining unexposed (Pl. 50A). The very shape of this wedge, with its restricted lateral continuity and out-of-sequence character, suggests that the sand body could be a product of a short-lived flow of transported material. Graded layering and internal lamination suggest that this layer could have formed due to re-mobilisation of sand mixed with water, probably emplaced from a deeper source. The internal structures such as lamination and graded bedding are typical of the processes related to laminar flow and re-sedimentation, generally classified as water-escape structures (eg Lowe, 1975). Clasts of clay that appear to have been mobilised during the sand-water intrusion were seen embedded within this layer (Pl. 50A).

Another feature that shares characteristics typical of sand-vents occur on the opposite wall of this trench (Pl. 51). This bowl-shaped structure with a maximum width of 1 m occurs at the same level as that of the main feature. Internally, it showed characteristic graded bedding with an overall fining upward sequence with a basal clast-bearing stratum. Although spatially separated, the characteristics of both of these features are suggestive of common origin. As in the case of sand-blow exposed on the northern wall, the southern wall of the trench has revealed only a part of the sand-vent's actual three-dimensional form. The structural integrity of such features could either be partially destroyed during the excavation and/or they may remain concealed within the unexcavated part of the sedimentary section. Techniques like 'incremental trenching' that employ progressive excavation of the feature (McCalpin, 1966), can be used to trace the three-dimensional shapes of such intrusive bodies. However, due to the reconnaissance nature of our work, we did not attempt this method. Besides, this style of trenching would have affected the on-going archaeological work.

WHAT CAUSED LIQUEFACTION IN BET DWARKA?

To arrive at a reasonable conclusion on the cause of the ancient liquefaction at Bet Dwarka, we need to assess all the possible scenarios. Among non-seismic causes, high tides and wave pounding may be considered, because this site is located near the sea. These possibilities can be ruled out, primarily because this feature is associated with human settlements with a continuity of thousands of years, which are generally not sited in areas subjected to occasional or seasonal high tides and wave pounding. Moreover, the site is located on an elevated terrace, and the surrounding sea itself is characterised by low energy conditions. Another possibility includes fluidization due to high pore-pressure associated with deep-seated confined aquifers. This is also rejected because the level at which this feature occurs is relatively shallow and the terrain conditions do not suggest the development of confined aquifers. A third reason could be landslides, but we do not have any evidence of favourable conditions at or near the study site, and judging from the low gradient topography, it is difficult to imagine such conditions could have existed ever in the past. None of the alternative causes of liquefaction conform to the field conditions, nor do they fully explain the sedimentological or stratigraphic characteristics of the Bet Dwarka features. This fact compels us to search for an alternate origin for the feature under discussion.

We have observed similar features that are preserved in the sedimentary sections near the source zone of the 1819 earthquake, in the Rann of Kachcch (Rajendran and Rajendran, 2001); the characteristics of those seismically-produced liquefaction features are comparable with the exposures at Bet Dwarka. With the occurrence of the Bhuj earthquake, we also had the opportunity to observe the mechanics of seismically-induced liquefaction (Rajendran *et al.*, 2001). The comparison is discussed in detail later in this paper. Liquefaction induced by earthquakes has been studied in many sites and the process is well-understood. The process is initiated when earthquake-induced shear stresses propagate through loose sands, generating volumetric straining of the sediment structure and forcing the sediment grains to enter into tighter packing, which inhibit the pore water from escaping. This leads to the rapid increase in pore water pressure weakening the grain-to-grain contact. If the pore water pressure increases to a certain threshold, the sand loses its strength and behaves as a liquid (Seed and Idriss, 1983). The escaping sediment-laden water forms sand-dikes, sand-sills and sand-blows, depending upon the local pressure gradient and lithological characteristics. The ability of sandy deposits to liquefy depends on the water content, sediment density, and the intensity and duration of shaking. It also depends on the sediment properties like grain size and sorting. If liquefaction features are to be considered as earthquake-induced, Obermeier (1995) suggests (1) they should show evidence for an upward-directed strong hydraulic force that was suddenly applied and was of short duration; (2) they should resemble liquefaction features generated by earthquakes in similar settings; (3) they should not be located in areas where other phenomena, notably artesian discharge, might produce similar features; (4) where evidence of age is present, it should support the interpretation that features formed in one or more discrete, short episodes that individually affected a large area; these episodes should be separated by long time-periods. Let us now assess each one of these criteria with reference to the Bet Dwarka feature.

The Bet Dwarka feature fully meets the first three criteria. Presence of clasts of the host sediments, and assorted mix of bricks, pottery and bones within the sand body suggests a violent ejection of sediment and water, which scraped the crater walls that moved laterally up to several metres, spilling out on the pre-earthquake surface (ie, before the establishment of succeeding settlement, numbered as 10). The forceful ejection of the sand is also implied by the flow bands that represent the transition from the turbulent violent eruption very shortly after initial venting to the final ebbing flow to the ground surface (Pl. 52). The characteristics discussed here are typical of sand-blow deposition. Although not fully represented, the sketchy outline of the companion feature exposed on the opposite wall, at the same level, can be considered as supporting evidence for venting, commonly associated with seismically-induced liquefaction.

The extent of 'fossilization' of earthquake-induced features could vary in ancient sediments, and what is exposed at Bet Dwarka could only be a partial view of the originally extensive feature. However, the fortuitous preservation of part of its diagnostic characteristics has enabled a comparison with modern analogs. These characteristics of the emplaced sand layer observed in the trench at Bet Dwarka are comparable to those produced by the 2001 Bhuj earthquake. Presence of a sand-vent, a sharp contact with the host sediments, clast inclusions, flow structures with graded sequences and progressive tapering of the sand apron were observed in these fresh sand-blows. In fact, it is clearly demonstrative of how the ubiquitous presence of multiple fining upward units, representing pulses of sediment and water, can be taken to be a typical characteristic of seismically-induced liquefaction feature, as suggested by Sims and Garvin (1995). Although of lesser clarity, the feature exposed at the Bet Dwarka shows evidence of sand-venting and internal stratification, inclusive of rip-up clasts, compelling us to classify this as earthquake-induced. A tentative model of formation of sand-blow at Bet Dwarka is shown in figure 5.

AGE CONSTRAINTS

We collected charcoal samples from within and immediately outside the emplaced sand layer, which were analysed by Accelerator Mass Spectroscopy (Table 3). Charcoal from the sediment

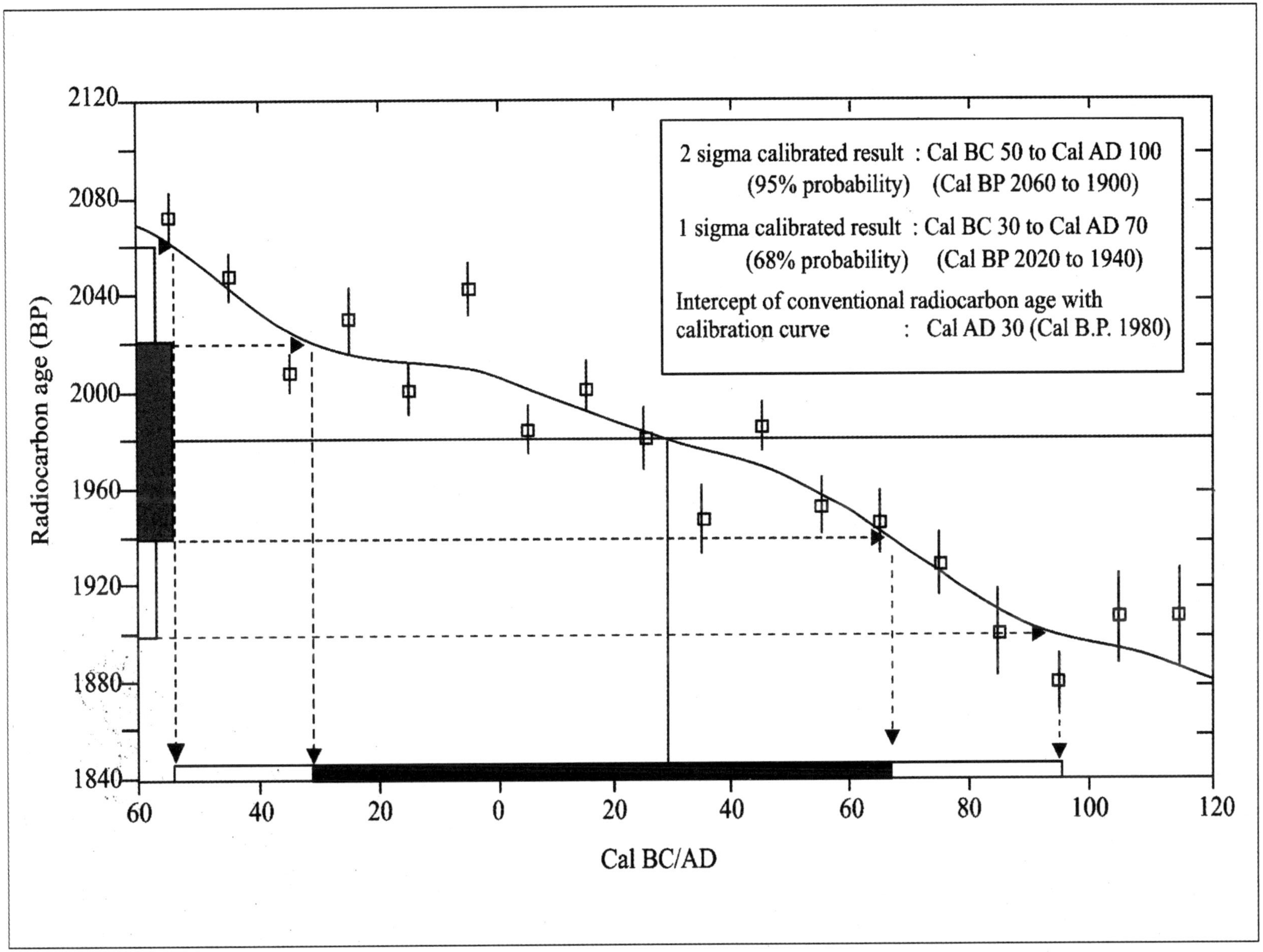

Fig. 44. Calibration curve for sample BDK-II showing age probability distribution with 1 and 2 sigma thresholds.

immediately overlying the sand-blow yielded a radiocarbon age of 1980±40 yr BP (cal. AD 25-AD 328; Fig. 44), whereas the sample obtained from the sand body yielded a slightly younger age of 1859±60 yr BP (cal. 50 BC-AD 100). The reversal of age is somewhat anomalous, but not wholly inexplicable. Inversion of ages – a situation where overlying stratum yields an older age in comparison to the subjacent older sediment horizon – can occur due to the remobilisation of sediments (Stanley, 2001). One possibility is that during the ejection and upward movement of sediments, older charcoal pieces from lower levels can be transported to the younger, overlying strata. Another possibility is that the older piece of charcoal may have been transported laterally down the slope, immediately after the event. Assuming that both the charcoal samples are associated with the deposition of the sand-blow, these dates are not treated here strictly as the contemporary age of the liquefaction event. Moreover, there is always an intrinsic element of uncertainty with regard to the dates derived from such samples, because of the time-gap between its origin and subsequent deposition. This is particularly a serious problem in fluvial or deltaic deposition, but the site of Bet Dwarka does not belong to such a dynamic environment. Therefore, large-scale displacement or long-distance transport of charcoals from their location of origin can be ruled out for the Bet Dwarka site. Since both the ages are somewhat identical, it is reasonable to believe that the liquefaction event may have occurred close to these dates, approximately at the beginning of the Christian Era. Combined average of multiple mean-and-standard-deviation estimates (Pinter, 1996) work out to be 1944 years BP. This combined mean age is closer to the date of the sample BDK-2-T (1980±40 yr BP), and it has a much smaller error margin compared to that of BDK-2-L.

This 2000-year-old feature has not shown any evidence of being disturbed afterwards. If this had happened, we would expect to find more than one distinct cross-cutting layer and dikes representing temporally separated liquefaction events – a feature typical of reactivated sand-dikes (Obermeier *et al.*, 1985; Talwani and Schaeffer, 2001; Tuttle *et al.*, 1990; Sims and Garvin, 1995; Rajendran and Rajendran, 2002). The lack of re-working of the sand-blow by later earthquakes indicates that no liquefaction events of this dimension could have affected this since the single episode that occurred ~2000 years ago. Furthermore, younger sequences succeeding the anomalous sand body, or the adjacent shallow trenches did not reveal any subsequently deposited sandy layers of similar characteristics. Alternately, it may also mean that hydro-geological conditions changed to such an extent that the subsequent earthquakes, including those that occured in 1819 and 2001, did not cause liquefaction in this area.

DISCUSSION

The presence of a possible sand-blow in the trench at Bet Dwarka can be accounted for by two possible scenarios: 1) it is an outlying feature generated from distant sources (eg 1819 and 2001), and 2) it is related to a nearby source. In the following section we will evaluate each one of these factors.

First, let us consider the question whether the ~2000-year-old sand-blow is related to earthquakes from the 1819 or the 2001 source. This, of course, means that what we observed at Bet Dwarka could only be a distant effect of a large earthquake. Till date, no evidence of an earthquake dating to ~2000 years has been observed in the epicentral areas of the 1819 and 2001 earthquakes. It should also be noted that the feature at Bet Dwarka is 'stand-alone' without being cross-cut or re-mobilised by any of these later events in the Rann of Kachchh. However, before ruling out the possibility for other liquefaction features, we must consider the temporal changes in hydro-geological conditions. Judging from the pattern of sea level variation over much of the study area, it appears that the sea level was higher than at present during the last several thousands years (Gaur and Vora, 1999), and, therefore, the ground water level at this location must have also been higher. Consequently, the hydrological conditions during a transgressive phase combined with wetter climatic regime must have increased the potential for liquefaction of sediments. We do not have enough site-specific data to suggest if the postulated higher sea level had any role in selectively increasing the liquefaction potential, but we do have some evidence to indicate that favourable site characteristics alone could not have generated the feature at Bet Dwarka.

It should be noted that the recent 2001 event whose epicentre is more than 200 km away from Bet Dwarka, did not generate any noticeable liquefaction; not even in the low-lying areas of Dwarka, although some minor damages to some buildings have been reported. This suggests that the ground shaking from a similar magnitude earthquake from the same source could not have produced liquefaction near Dwarka. There are no reports of liquefaction related to the 1819 earthquake from these areas; nor are there any evidence in the limited trench exposures. The historical accounts of the 1819 earthquake, however, indicate bubbling of water and small-scale liquefaction near the seashore at Porbundar, a port city located about 100 km south of Bet Dwarka (Oldham, 1926). For the sake of argument, let us assume that minor liquefaction effects could have indeed occurred in the low-lying inter-tidal areas of Dwarka. Even by the above standards, the ancient sand-blow at Bet Dwarka that measures more than 20 cm in thickness with a vent measuring up to 1 m, cannot be explained as due to large historical earthquakes from any of the afore-mentioned distant sources. We have evidence for a historical earthquake that occurred during AD 893 near or at the source of the 1819 event (Rajendran and Rajendran, 2002), and this could be another potential factor. However, this event does not seem to have produced any notable liquefaction near Bet Dwarka, an observation we made from the lack of cross-cutting relations. Further constraints come from the age data, which suggests that the causative event must have occurred between cal. 50 BC and AD 328 (see Table 3).

It may be mentioned here that excavations by H.D. Sankalia in 1963 near Dwarkadish temple (Dwarka temple in the mainland) revealed thick intervening deposits of clean sand and rolled potsherds between successive occupation horizons (see Ansari and Mate, 1966 for details). The excavations indicated that the earliest occupation level at Dwarka (~2000 yr BP) lies buried under 6 m of sand, possibly because of the sea encroachment. In the report by Ansari and Mate (1966), it is, however, stated that this sand deposition is local phenomena and not extended beyond 1 km. It is interesting to note that the timing (beginning of the Christian Era) of sand deposition somewhat coincides with the age of the liquefaction event. But with sketchy details, we are not in a position to speculate on the cause of this sand deposition and to find out any relation with the earthquake that may have induced liquefaction in the region. We are presently constrained by the lack of sufficient comparative database.

What is remarkable about the Bet Dwarka feature is its proximity to an eastwest trending rift boundary fault under the Gulf of Kachchh. We do not know whether this or any of the associated subsidiary thrusts under the Gulf of Kachchh or in the onshore part has been active. The occurrence of a moderately large 2000-year-old sand-blow near Dwarka, which we believe is seismically induced, raises the important question whether any part of this boundary fault could have generated a large earthquake in the past. These observations point to the possibility for a third seismic source, in the northwest coastal Gujarat, in addition to the two known sources of the 1819 and the 2001 earthquakes.

We admit that the mere presence of an isolated paleo-liquefaction feature itself does not constitute the proof for an independent source near Dwarka. A systematic survey of the area has not been made yet, to search for more of these structures from the nearby areas. Therefore, validity of our postulation of an independent large seismic source, either in the Gulf of Kachchh or onshore Dwarka, is contingent upon the discovery of more number of coeval liquefaction features of comparable dimensions, at least within the 30-50 km radius of Dwarka. On the other hand, if the trend in frequency and size of contemporary features shows an increase away from this location, it would argue for a different source. Presence of a seismic source, which apparently produced an earthquake 2000 years ago, has serious implications on the regional seismic hazard. This paper, therefore, emphasises the need to conduct more seismological and geological studies to define this seismic source and expand its earthquake history.

Calendar ages were estimated following Stuiver *et al.*, 1998.

Annexure E

Sea Level Changes During Last 2000 Years Around Bet Dwarka Island

A.S. Gaur, K.H. Vora and Sundaresh

INTRODUCTION

The sea level fluctuation has played a very dominant role in the emergence and devolution of the cultures during Pleistocene and Holocene periods. Several workers updated sea level studies along the west coast of India (Chatterjee, 1962, Agarwal *et al.*, 1973, Nair, 1971 and 1974, Gupta, 1977, Bruckner, 1989, Rao *et al.*, 2003). There are well-defined observational data on quaternary sea level oscillation. However, the above researches are based on the geological proxies like study of corals, limestone, foraminifera and other marine organisms. Also, these studies focus on large time-frame and high degree of error due to paucity of data, with varied methods in measurement of date due to various factors.

Study of the ancient human settlement on the shallow submarine zones and migration via the land bridges between continents has been continuing for over 50 years. Nevertheless, a few significant sites have been found on the continental shelves to date (Flemming, 1984). One of the primary reason for the absence of human settlement is that the continental shelves are dynamic areas of sedimentation and erosion. There tends to be both destructive erosional elements as well as deposional elements that might preserve site, both going on at the same time (Kraft *et al.*, 1984). Many archaeological sites with evidence of maritime activities either from the excavation or from literary reference, were important port towns during their heyday. In the course of time, they got either submerged or are now land-locked due to siltation, though sea level changes and tectonic activity also may be important factors at times. Such sites provide vital clues with dates to infer the shoreline changes in recent past. The present paper, therefore, deals with the sea level changes around Bet Dwarka island in the Gulf of Kachchh during the historical period (Late Holocene), based on archaeological evidences.

The history of maritime activities in Gujarat dates back to the 3rd millennium BC and evidence of the exploitation of marine resources like shells, salt and fishes has been recorded

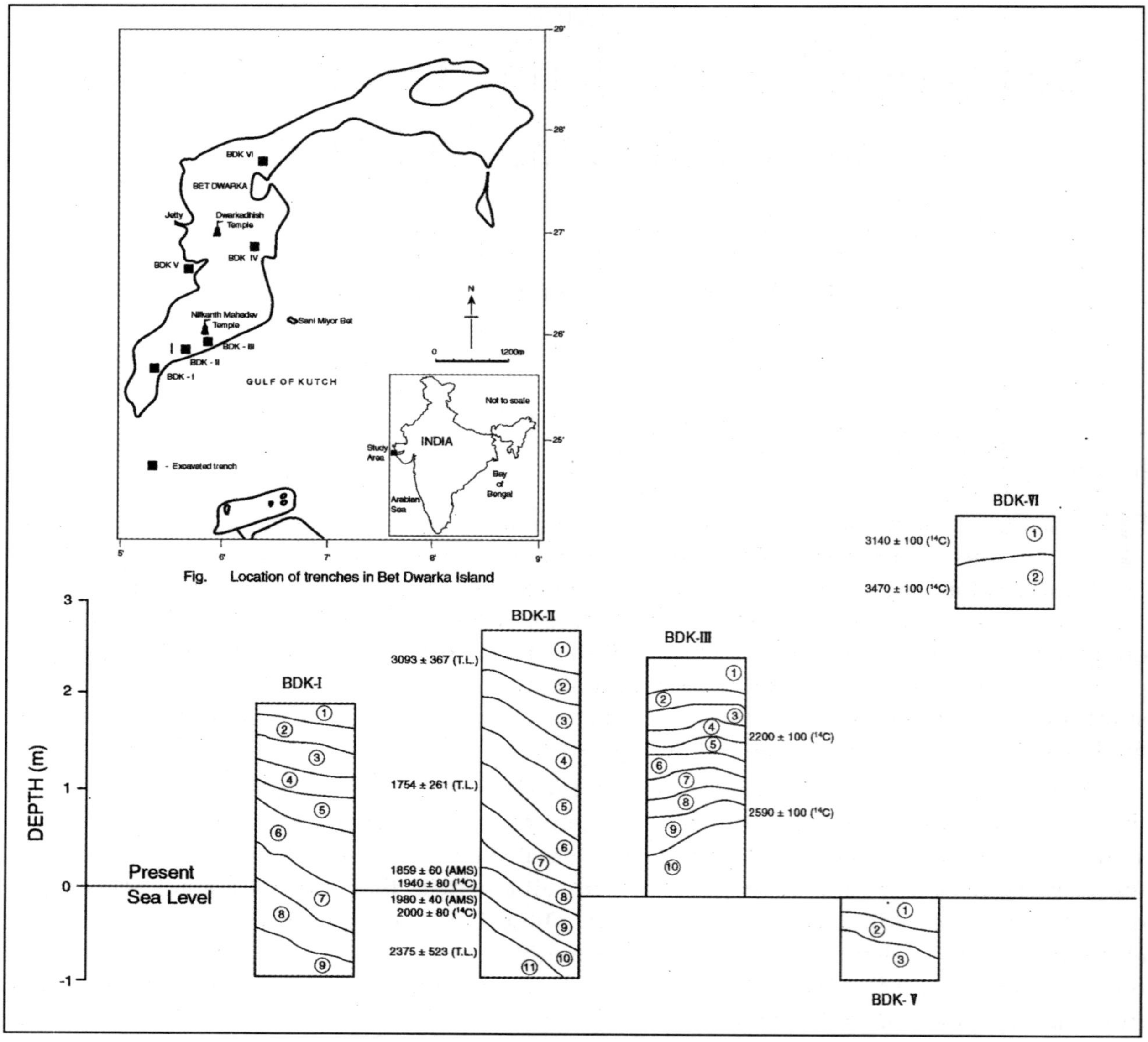

Fig. 45. Location of trench reference to the present shoreline.

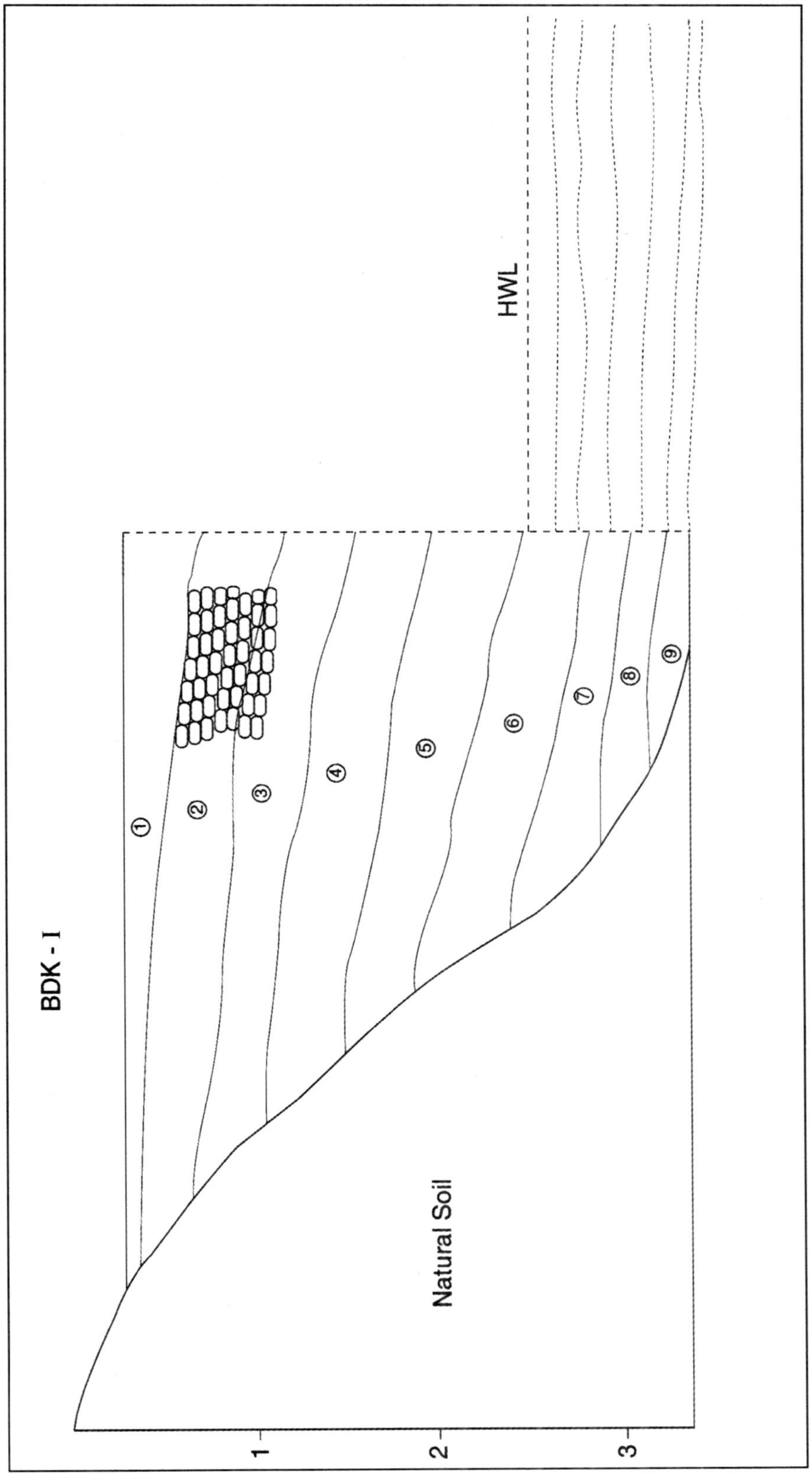

Fig. 46. Section of BDK-I in relation with the present shoreline.

from many coastal sites. Bet Dwarka island is situated at the entrance of the Gulf of Kachchh and it acted as a transit point between the northwest (Kachchh and Sind) and the southeast (Saurashtra and mainland Gujarat) for trade and commerce since the later phase of Indus civilization. Archaeological explorations suggest that the availability of marine resources around this island attracted early settlers and, later on, the island became an international trade centre since early historical period (Sundaresh *et al.*, 2002). Onshore explorations since 1983 revealed a large number of habitational remains of historical period in the inter-tidal zone, a proxy evidence on the shoreline change and sea level variation. To understand the stratigraphy of human habitation and man and sea relation, a few trenches were laid on the coastal area of the Bet Dwarka island for the excavations. While exposing the trenches, it was observed that the oldest habitational level in the three trenches are below the present high water line. It was then considered that this may provide some clues on sea level changes.

METHODOLOGY

A few trenches were laid, specially on the southeastern coastal area of the island and one trench each on the northeastern and western coasts. The excavation was continued till the occupational remains were recovered above the virgin soil bed. Layer-wise archaeological artifacts were recorded and samples were collected and dated by Radiocarbon, AMS and TL methods. Subsequently, the differences in level between depth of present high water line and occupational deposits in the three trenches namely, BDK-I, II and III, were measured (Pl. 53). Samples were dated by the radiocarbon method by Birbal Sahni Institute of Paeleobotany, Lucknow, and two samples from trench BDK-II were analysed by Accelerator Mass Spectroscopy (AMS) method by Beta Analytic, Miami, USA and Rafter Radiocarbon Lab Welington, New Zealand. Three samples were analysed by thermoluminsence by Prof. A.K. Singhvi of PRL, Ahmedabad.

RESULTS

For the excavation, six places were identified on the Bet Dwarka island and at each location trenches were dug. These trenches were numbered as BDK-I, II, III, IV, V and VI. The findings and total archaeological deposits of each trench (Fig. 45) are described below to understand the nature of habitation and difference between present-day high water line and the oldest deposit in each trench.

BDK-I

A trench measuring 5 × 5 m was laid in the southwestern coast of the island. A total deposit of 2.75 m was excavated with nine layers. Initial habitation took place at the foot of the hill extending towards sea. At a later phase, the habitation was extended towards the land (Fig. 46). The major part of the early habitation has been washed away by the sea and presently a high cliff section with archaeological remains facing sea has been noticed (Pl. 54). From layer 6, two copper coins of the Kushana Period (1st-2nd century AD) were recovered, and there is no habitational break-up from the lower strata. Interestingly, the lowest habitation of this trench was traced 65 cm below the present-day high water line.

BDK-II

A trench measuring 2.5 × 5 m was laid on the eastern side of the earlier trench on a high-terraced mound. A total deposit of 3.35 m was traced with 11 layers. The initial habitation was on a sloppy area extending towards the sea and gradually habitation extended landward also. The major portion of the early habitation has been washed away and a high cliff section with archaeological remains was observed. There are two AMS (Table 3), two Radiocarbon (Table 2) and three thermoluminescence (Table 6) dates suggesting that the oldest habitation was 2040 years BP and the youngest 1716 years BP. A potsherd with a graffiti mark (*Brahmi* letter "A") datable to the 3rd century AD was recovered from layer 4. The lowest habitation of this trench was traced up to 75 cm below the present-day high water line. It is pertinent to note that Rajendran *et al.* (2003) have traced liquefied material a proxy of the past earthquake which he dates to 1st- 2nd century AD.

BDK-III

A trench measuring 2.5 × 5 m was laid on the eastern side of the BDK-II near the present water pump house. A total deposit of 2.75 m with 10 layers was traced. The initial habitation was noticed on an even soil bed and the habitation was concentrated on the coastal area. There are three carbon^{14} dates available from this trench. The oldest deposit is dated to 6th century BC and is older than the earlier habitation above the two trenches. The lowest deposit is lying just above by a few centimeters of the present-day high water line.

BDK-IV

No archaeological finds were recorded below 10 cm from the surface.

BDK-V

A small trench measuring 1 × 1 m was laid in the inter-tidal zone near Khuda-Dost-Dargah during low tide. A total deposit of 65 cm was traced with three layers. The archaeological material indicates a possible date of the site in the beginning of the Christian Era. The site submerged during high tide.

BDK-VI

A trench measuring 2.5 × 2.5 m was laid in a presently cultivated land in the northeastern coast of the island. A total deposit of 95 cm was traced with two layers. Archaeological findings and two C^{14} dates of the worked shells suggest a date for the oldest habitation to 16th century BC. The oldest habitation is situated about 4 m above the present high water line.

DISCUSSION

The glacio-eustatic sea level reached the present level around 6000 yrs BP (Fairbridge, 1960; Gupta, 1974; Rao, 2003). However, minor sea level fluctuations have played a significant role in the evolution and devolution of many habitational sites situated along the coast. It is believed that after 6000 yrs BP, the sea level fluctuated between 2 m and 6 m above the present level at various places. Recent studies in northern Europe suggest three phases of rapid regression during the last 3000 years; they are 2600, 1500 and 950 BP (Morner, 1999). A sea level curved for North Konkan proposed by Ghate (1988), suggest a lower sea level around the Christian Era, which corresponds very well with the evidence from Bet Dwarka.

1. Absolute dates and early settlement at Bet Dwarka.

Carbon^{14} dates from Bet Dwarka island suggest that the oldest habitation is dated back to 3470± 80 years BP (layer 2); a late phase of Harappan civilization and habitation lasted up to 3140±100 years BP (layer 1). Settlement was concentrated on the northeastern (BDK-I) part of the island, about 3 m above the present high water line. The archaeological material is similar to those found at Rangpur and many other late Harappan sites of Saurashtra (Rao, 1965). After a long hitus, the island was habitated during the early historical period and remains were noticed at BDK-I, II and III. The oldest Carbon[14] dates came from BDK-III, which are 2590+100 BP (layer 9) and 2200+100 BP (layer 4). The material from this trench corresponds to those with early historical period sites of Saurashtra (Ghosh, 1989) and Deccan (Thapar, 1985). The lowest habitation of BDK-III is situated almost to the present high water line. Carbon[14] dates of BDK-II are 2000±80 BP (layer 10) and 1940±80 BP (layer 8); AMS dates from the same trench are 1980±40 BP (layer 10) and 1859±60 BP (layer 9). Two TL dates from the trench are 2375±523 years BP (layer 11) and 1754±261 BP (layer 6). The absolute dates are in agreement with the cultural deposit and verified by the discovery of coins and pottery. Early habitation of three sites, namely BDK-I, II and V are situated about a meter below the present high water line.

2. Possible sea level fluctuation around Bet Dwarka.

As evident from above that the lowest habitation in BDK-I and II are lying below the present high water line by about 70 cm, is an indication of a rise in sea level after the settlement at the island. Similarly, the site BDK-V near Khuda-Dost-Dargah also flooded during the high tide. And these (BDK-I, II and V) sites have a time-bracket between 2nd century BC to 4th century AD. It is during the early phase of the historical period settlement when habitation was extended towards offshore and gradually extended landwards during the later phase. However, the remains of the later phase were also destroyed by the sea which suggest that up to 4th century AD, sea level was lower than the present level. These evidences are in agreement with many other archaeological sites situated along the Indian coasts such as Poompuhar (Gaur and Sundaresh, 1998), Mahabalipuram (NIO, technical report) and Arikamedu (Wheeler *et al.*, 1946).

While hypothesizing the shoreline changes in the Gulf of Kachchh, it should be remembered that the area has been subjected to the tectonic disturbances which may have affected the sea level in one or other way. However, based on archaeological records of the region, following the sequence of episodic sea level changes is suggested for the area.

a. Sea level reached higher than the present level around 6000 years BP and continued till 3500 years BP, as a large number of Harappan port towns, which existed earlier along the coast, are now located far in hinterland away and higher than the present sea level in Gujarat and Pakistan. Similarly, a late Harappan site, datable to 3800 years BP in Bet Dwarka (BDK-VI), is located about 3 m above the high water line. This very well corresponds with the geological findings of the area.
b. Sea level continued at present level upto 2300 yrs BP, as an early historical period site (BDK-III) datable to 2600 to 2300 yrs BP is situated a little higher than the present high water line. Similarly, a well-known early historical period port town at Sopara, north of Mumbai (Ghate, 1988), was a very active port and had international trade relations.
c. Sea level fell after 2300 yrs BP and then lowered by 2 m to 3 m along the Bet Dwarka coast and perhaps 4 m to 7 m on the east coast as lots of habitation took place in the coastal areas which are now under water.

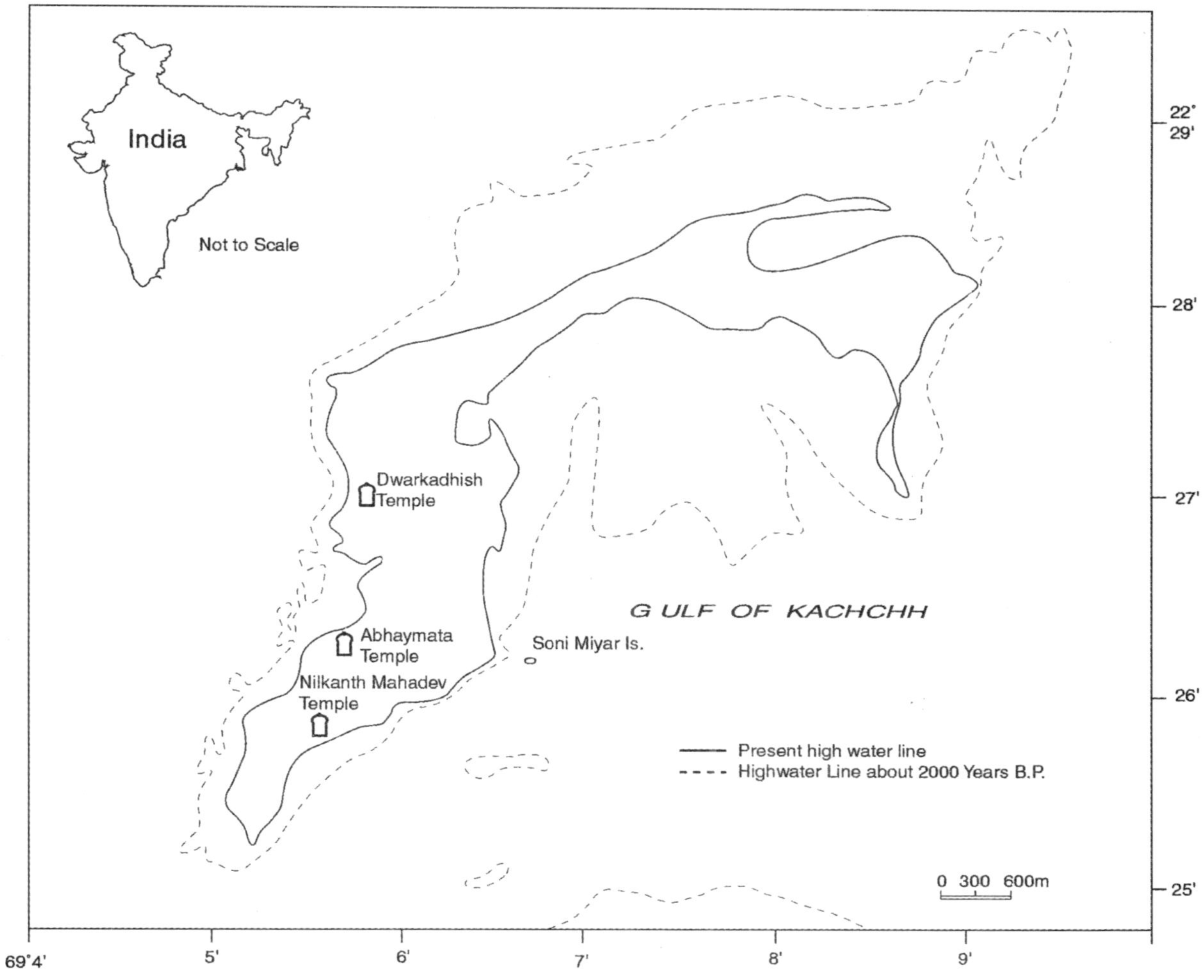

Fig. 47. A possible shape of the island about 2000 years before.

3. Likely shape of the Bet Dwarka island during the early historic period.

As discussed that the sea level was lowered around Bet Dwarka by 2-3 m, a vast area would have been exposed towards the northern and eastern parts of the island and a land bridge would have functioned during low tide towards the eastern side of the island, which is close to the mainland and even presently its depth is very shallow. A large area would have exposed even on the southern part where early historical period habitation took place. A large number of archaeological artifacts can be collected during low tide as far as 500 m from high water line. Figure 47 suggests that Bet Dwarka has a larger exposure towards the northeastern side and followed by southern side, while on the western side there may not be much differences as depth contour suggest a steep depth and even high cliffs on this side can be seen.

Causes of Shoreline Changes

There are various reasons for the changes of shoreline in past such as tectonic disturbances, coastal erosion, sea level fluctuation, etc.

1. It is well-known that Gujarat peninsula is very sensitive to tectonic disturbances. The evidences from archaeological sites like Dholavira (Joshi and Bisht, 1994) and Bet Dwarka (Rajendran *et al.*, 2003) have been recorded. Several earthquakes have affected land mass in various parts of Gujarat (Rajendran and Rajendran, 2002).
2. Coastal erosion is one of the prime cause of shoreline changes along the Indian coast and it has affected the coastal monuments (Sundaresh *et al.*, 1997). The studies have indicated that Bet Dwarka and Dwarka have been prone to coastal erosion during the last couple of centuries (Hashimi and Nair, 1988).
3. Sea level fluctuation is one of the important factors responsible for shoreline changes in the past. As stated earlier, minor sea level changes during the last 3000 years (Morner, 1999 and Ghate, 1988) have affected human settlement on the coastal area.

CONCLUSIONS

Archaeological evidences have been used successfully to determine the changes in shoreline during the past 2000 years. Human artifacts and radiocarbon samples from Bet Dwarka island have given some very interesting conclusion on the sea level shoreline changes along the Bet Dwarka island.

1. The sea level was lower than the present one by more than a meter between 2040 and 1820 years BP.
2. During the above period, a large area on the northern part of the island would have been exposed and the island could have been connected with the mainland towards the eastern side during low tide.
3. Sea level rose almost to the present level at around 1000 BP as most of the coastal sites of early historical period got submerged in the sea. Archaeological evidences from Mahabalipuram, Poompuhar, and Tranquebar in Tamil Nadu coast show similar trend.
4. Above inferences are very well corresponding to many other sites along the Indian coast. However, in contrast, many sites situated along the coastal area during the historical period are now situated far hinterland, perhaps due to siltation as most of them were located on the estuaries area.

Annexure F

Underwater Investigations in Bet Dwarka Island

A.S. Gaur and Sundaresh

INTRODUCTION

Bet Dwarka island is situated on the extreme west of the Indian territory in the Jamnagar district of Gujarat. The area has been mentioned by the author of *Periplus of Erythraean Sea*, who remarked that,

> ...[in] the Gulf of Baraca, which contains seven islands, the sea-bed is in some places abrupt, and in others rocky and sharp, so that the anchors lying there are parted, some being quickly cut off, and others chafing on the bottom (Schoff, 1974: 38).

Onshore explorations have revealed that Bet Dwarka island was inhabited by the late Harappan settlers for the exploitation of marine resources, especially for chank shell which is abundantly available in this region. There are frequent references as this area was famous for the chank shell industry during the early historic period (Chandra, 1977). An important aspect that may be noted here is that Bet Dwarka island was under occupation from Harappan to modern times. This indicates the importance of this island which, perhaps, is the only site in Saurashtra where a continuous habitation for more than 3500 years existed.

Under water, the most preserved remains of ancient maritime activity could be the stone anchors of different types, as every boat requires an anchor to halt in mid-sea. Being of little value, these anchors could be dispensed with when they were trapped in the rocks or thrown into the sea to reduce excess weight on board. The types and sizes of anchors indicate the kind of boats that visited the port (Frost, 1991), and with the help of these anchors it is possible to trace the authenticity of literary references about the trade route and the identification of a particular port.

Recent marine archaeological explorations by the Marine Archaeology Centre of National Institute of Oceanography, Goa, in the Okhamandal area of Gujarat coast, specially at Dwarka and Bet Dwarka, revealed a number of stone anchors of different shapes and sizes made out of locally-available rocks (Sundaresh *et al.*, 1999; Gaur *et al.*, 2001). The data presented here were

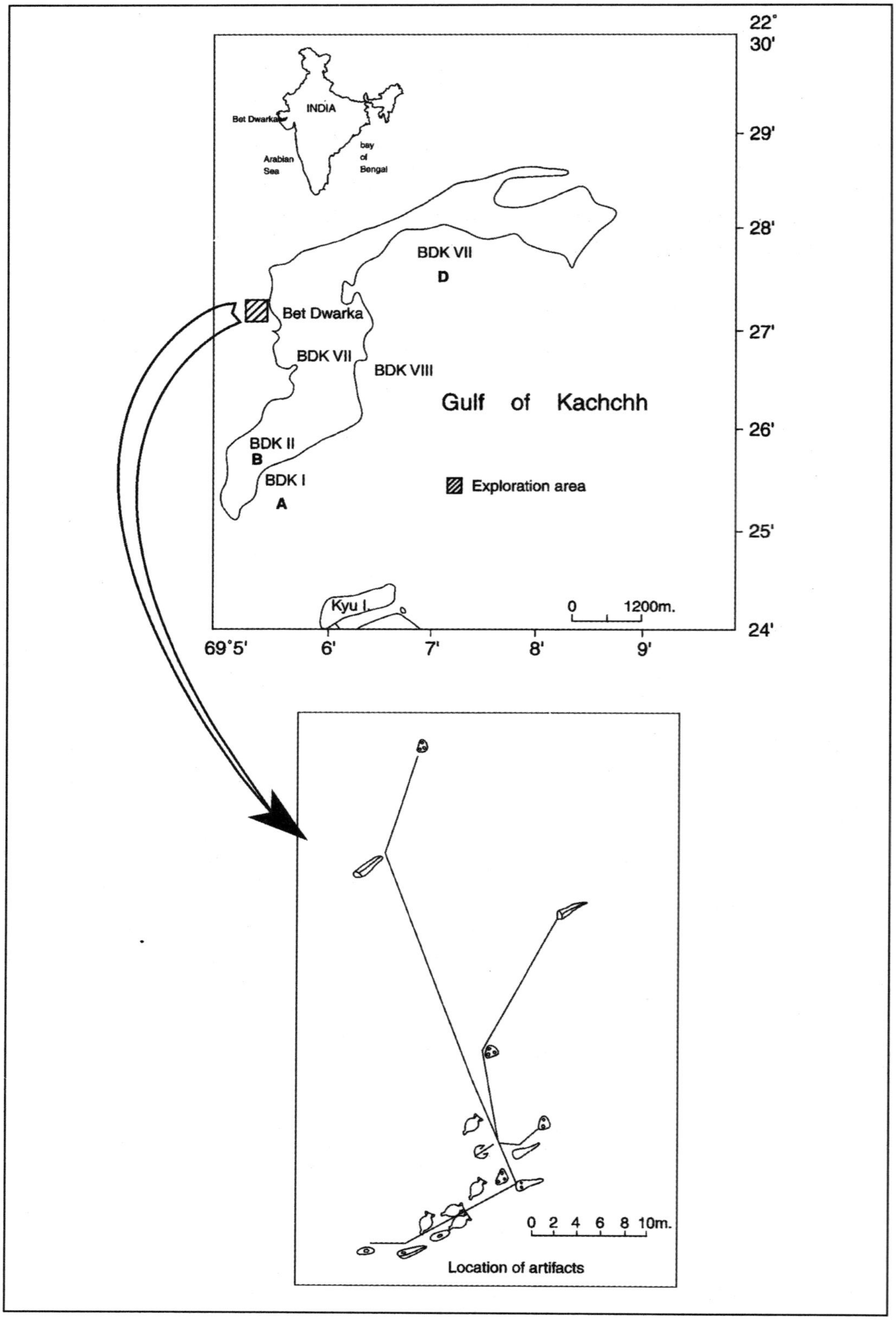

Fig. 48. Underwater distribution of findings off Bet Dwarka.

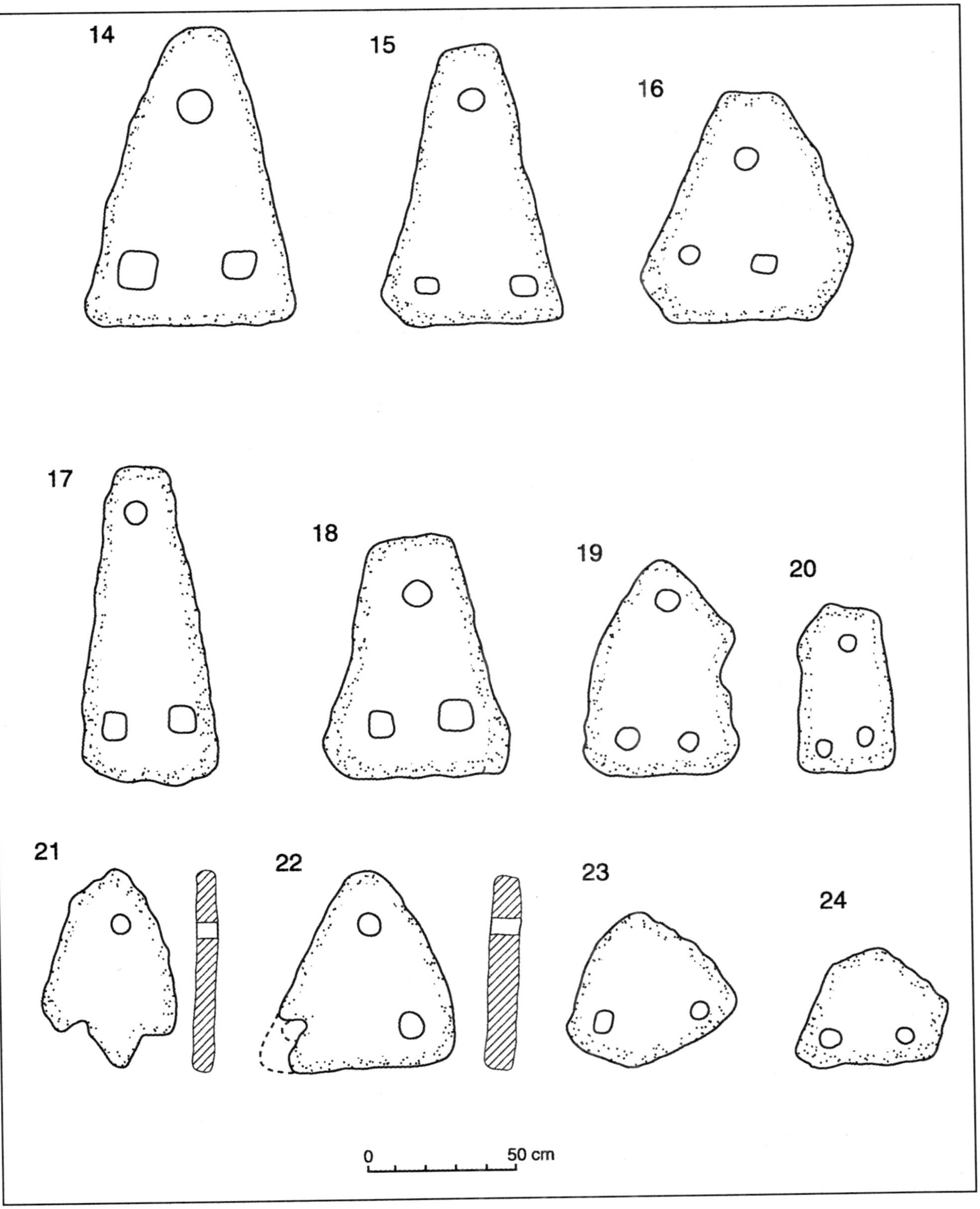

Fig. 49. Composite-type stone anchors found off Bet Dwarka.

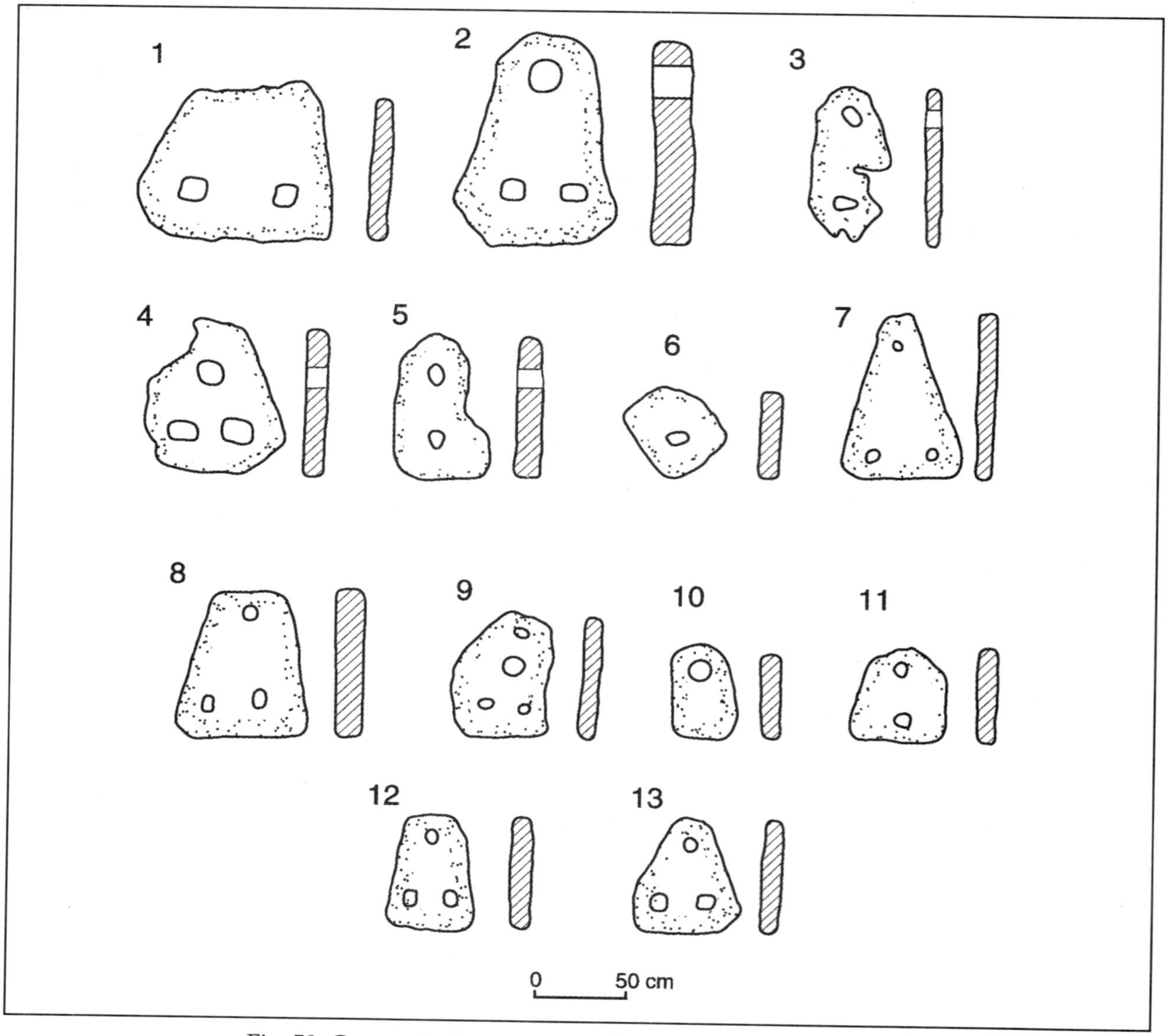

Fig. 50. Composite-type stone anchors found off Bet Dwarka.

obtained in two field seasons, 1997–98 and 2000–2001. In the present report, a detailed description of the stone anchors from Bet Dwarka is given. The possible dates for these anchors are also discussed in order to understand the trends in Indian navigational history.

Explorations were carried out north of the present Bet Dwarka jetty in a water-depth between 5-8 m where the sea-bed comprised of consolidated rocky formation and no noticeable major deposition of sand. Most of the archaeological finds were exposed on the sea-bed and only heavy objects remain *in situ*. In shallower water, between 2-5 m water-depth, the sea-bed consists of a dense growth of seaweeds.

METHODOLOGY

Onshore and inter-tidal zone explorations were carried out at Bet Dwarka and Armada to locate important archaeological objects such as anchors, cannons, unidentified objects, etc that were documented by photography and drawings. The positions of these findings were recorded using a Global Positioning System (GPS).

Based on the results of the onshore survey, diving operations were initiated at a convenient place off Bet Dwarka, near the present jetty in water-depth ranging from 1.5 m-8 m. Each diving team covered an area within a circle of about 50 m radius. A buoy was tied to each location wherever archaeological objects (structures and anchors) were noticed. Each object was inter-connected with ropes and these distances were measured (Fig. 48). Underwater findings were documented by using still camera and drawings.

RESULTS

The surveys were concentrated particularly on the southern coast of the Bet Dwarka island where a settlement of the proto-historic period was noticed. Explorations, however, did not reveal any stone anchors in this area. Twenty stone anchors were noticed in the inter-tidal zone as well as during the offshore survey. The important findings from offshore include a lead anchor, amphorae sherds, and other historical period pottery. Brief descriptions of the stone anchors are given below.

COMPOSITE ANCHORS

Frost (1991) defines composite anchor as an anchor having more than one hole, a wooden 'arms' struck into supplementary holes so as to protrude on either side and ensure that whichever way the stone falls, one end of a stick will hook it into sand or mud. Triangular composite anchors are often carved from a flat, thin stone block, giving a triangular shape with a circular upper hole and two lower holes which may be either rectangular or square. Sometimes, however, composite anchors may have one, two and four holes. In two seasons, explorations discovered 13 composite anchors (Fig. 49-50) near the present Bet Dwarka jetty. One anchor was found in the inter-tidal zone while the remaining 12 anchors are located on the sea-bed in 5-7 m water-depth.

1. Worn-out composite anchor lying to the south of the present jetty (Pl. 55); the anchor is perfectly triangular and has a very rough surface due to the porous nature of the material; the upper hole is broken and the lower two holes are square; the anchor is made from locally-available limestone which is grey in colour.
2. Composite anchor having a very rough and porous surface with a circular upper hole and two square holes at the bottom; the anchor is made out of very porous beach rock; the edges are worn, suggesting it must have been used extensively; the anchor was lying north of the present jetty in 7 m water-depth and about 150 m offshore (Fig. 6).
3. Two-holed stone anchor noticed in a water-depth of 7 m near anchor no. 2; both holes are circular; although it is also made out of beach rock, it is better preserved and is not porous.
4. Composite anchor with all three holes preserved; the anchor has an irregular shape; it has a very rough surface and is made of porous beach rock; the anchor is in a very fragile condition and has worn edges; the anchor was discovered in a water-depth of 6 m.
5. Broken composite anchor with lower two holes preserved; the anchor is made out of the same material as above and is in a very fragile condition; growth of barnacles were noticed; the anchor is lying south of anchors no. 3 and 4, but north of the present jetty in 6 m water-depth.

6. Single-holed, stone anchor made of locally-available beach rock, found near the jetty; it has a very irregular shape and the hole is round.
7. Perfectly shaped, triangular anchor lying on a clay bottom; it has been cut from limestone; the anchor has a circular upper hole and the lower two holes are square; the anchor is of uniform thickness which suggests less erosion, or possibly it was used for a shorter duration; the anchor has a very smooth surface and sharp edges.
8. Composite anchor lying exposed on the rocky and sandy sea-bed; it is also made of limestone; it has a porous surface and is of uneven thickness and is irregular in shape; the anchor has an upper circular hole and the lower two holes are square; it has a rough surface and worn edges.
9. Composite anchor lying exposed on a sandy bottom (Pl. 56); it is made out of limestone; it has one upper circular hole and the lower two are square; the anchor has an additional large circular hole in the centre which could have been used to insert a thick wooden log to hold the anchor from falling into the sea; it has a rough surface and worn edges; the anchor is thicker on its lower side at the base.
10. The anchor is oval-shaped and made of limestone; it was lying exposed on the rocky sea-bed; it has a single upper hole which has got widened, perhaps due to prolonged use; it has a rough surface and worn edges; a large number of pottery and amphorae sherds were also noticed at this site.
11. Composite anchor made of limestone which has been cut in a triangular shape, with its upper side semi-circular; this is the first example in Indian waters which has only one lower square hole and an upper circular hole; it is lying exposed, however, one side trapped below the rocky boulder; marine growth over the anchor was noticed; abundant pottery was noticed in this area; the anchor has a smooth surface and sharp edges.
12. Composite anchor lying partially buried under sediment and a boulder; it has a small upper circular hole and the lower two holes are square; the shape of the upper portion is perfectly semi-circular; the anchor is made of limestone; it has an even thickness, smooth surface and sharp edges.
13. The anchor was lying exposed on the sea-bed and is made out of limestone; as in the other examples, it has an upper circular hole and the lower two holes are square; it has a smooth surface and sharp edges.
14. Triangular anchor lying exposed on the rocky sea-bed; all holes are circular; it is made of limestone; it has a rough surface and irregular thickness; thick marine growth is noticed.
15. Upper portion of the triangular anchor with a circular hole; it is made of limestone; it has a rough surface and blunt edges; half-broken lower holes are noticed; it has uneven thickness and irregular shape; thick marine growth is also observed.
16. Triangular anchor lying exposed on the rocky sea-bed; the length of the anchor is significant in respect of width; it is made of limestone; it has a circular hole; upper hole and lower holes are rectangular; lower holes have been eroded; thick marine growth, and coral growth also observed; it has a rough surface and blunt edges.
17. Broken, small triangular anchor lying exposed on the sea-bed; this is a very thin anchor; it has lower two circular holes in the lower part and the upper one is broken; it is made out of limestone; it has a rough surface and blunt edges.

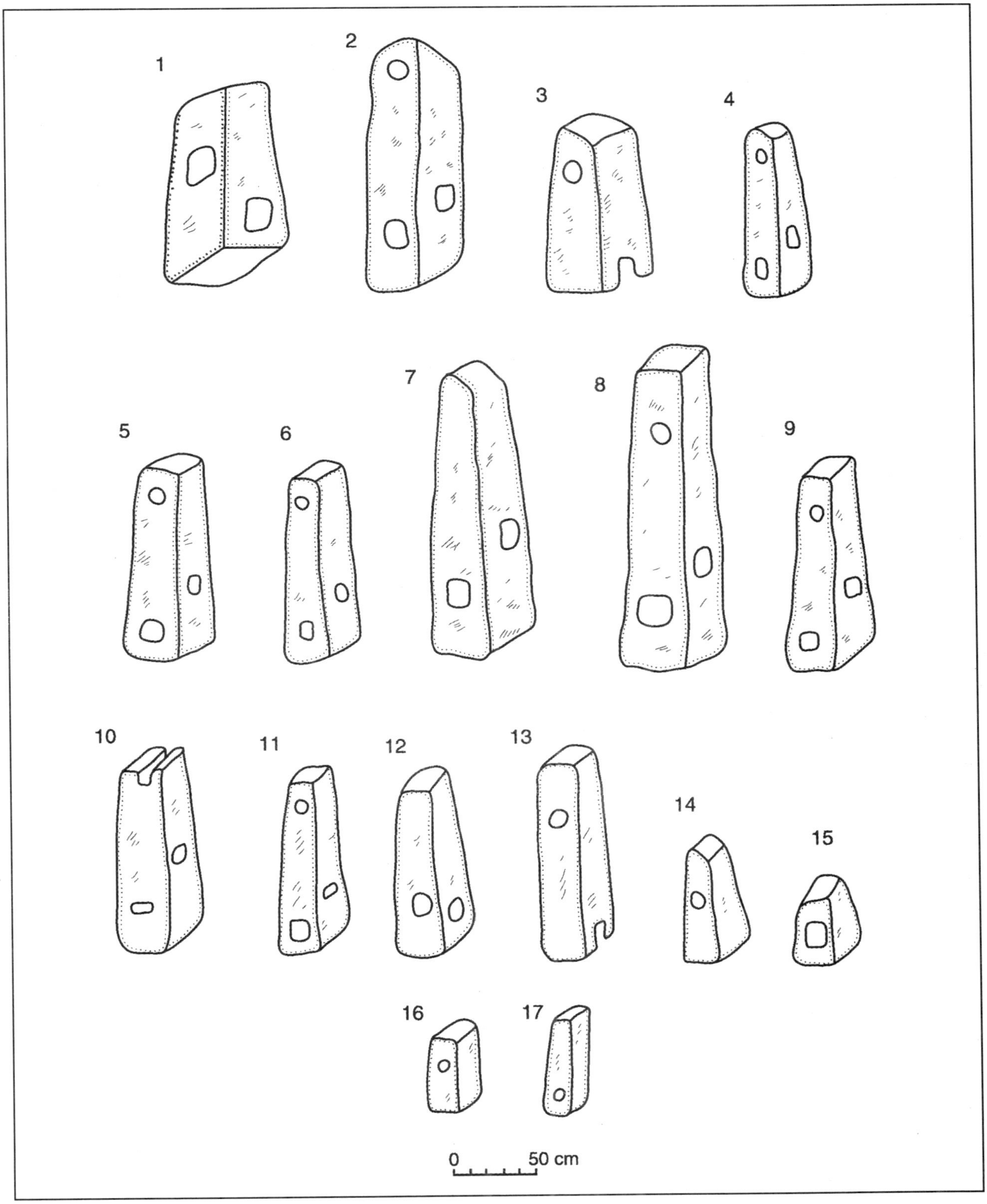

Fig. 51. Grapnel stone anchors from Bet Dwarka waters.

18. Triangular anchor lying exposed on the sea-bed; it is made of limestone; it has a rough surface and blunt edges; holes have been widened; thick growth of vegetation also noticed; it has an even thickness; maximum length is 95 cms.
19. Triangular anchor lying exposed; it is irregular in shape; it is made of limestone; it has a rough surface and blunt edges; upper and lower holes are circular; growth of vegetation also noticed.
20. One of the finest chiselled triangular anchor lying exposed; it is very long and has an even thickness; it has a rough surface and blunt edges; marine growth is also noticed; upper hole is circular and lower holes are square; it is made out of limestone.
21. Triangular anchor lying exposed and made of limestone; holes have been eroded; it has a rough surface and blunt edges; vegetation growth is noticed.
22. Triangular stone anchor lying exposed; it is in irregular shape; one lower hole is broken; other two holes are circular; it is made of limestone; vegetation growth is also noticed; it has a rough surface and irregular shape; blunt edges; coral growth is also noticed.
23. Broken triangular anchor is lying exposed; it is made of limestone; it is irregular in shape; it has a rough surface and blunt edges; one circular and one square hole is noticed; marine growth is also noticed.
24. Triangular stone anchor lying exposed on the sea-bed; it was covered under thick vegetation; it is made of limestone; all holes are circular; this is very well-dressed; it has a smooth surface and sharp edges.
25. Anchor is lying exposed on the sea-bed; it is made of limestone; a layer of marine growth is also observed; this anchor is very different as it has an upper big square hole and the lower two holes are circular; it has a smooth surface and blunt edges and has an irregular shape; however, holes form a triangle in the centre.
26. The anchor is lying exposed and covered with a layer of sand and sea-weed; this has a upper circular hole and the lower two holes are square; it has been cut perfectly and the upper side is semi-circular; similar type of anchor was retrieved the previous year; it has a smooth surface and sharp edges.

GRAPNEL ANCHORS (Table 2)

Grapnel anchors are cut from a long and thick rock with a square section. Often, the anchor has a circular upper hole and the lower two holes on either face are square or rectangular. During the exploration, 17 grapnel anchors were observed (Fig. 51). They were lying exposed on the sea-bed. A detailed description of each anchor is given below.

1. This is a broken grapnel anchor. It is lying north of the present Bet Dwarka jetty in the inter-tidal zone. The lower two holes are preserved. It has a very rough surface and is made out of locally-available conglomerate rock. The anchor was used as a mooring stone on the shore.
2. Grapnel stone anchor was found lying in the inter-tidal zone and buried in mud, on the southern side of the jetty. This is the heaviest anchor found in Bet Dwarka. A circular hole at the top and two square holes at the bottom were noticed. Rope marks within the top hole were also noticed. This is made out of locally-available yellow sandstone and has a smooth surface.

3. Grapnel anchor, lying exposed on the rocky sea-bed and has been cut out of limestone. It has a rough and porous surface. The anchor has a circular upper hole where rope marks were noticed. One of the two rectangular lower holes has been widened, perhaps due to erosion. The surface of the anchor has witnessed severe erosion.
4. Grapnel anchor, lying partially buried in sediment. It has been made out of fine and smooth limestone. A circular upper hole and two rectangular holes on the lower side have been cut perfectly and are intact. It has a smooth surface and sharp edges. This is one of the finest fashioned anchors found in Bet Dwarka waters.
5. Grapnel anchor, lying exposed over the rocky sea bottom. It is made out of limestone. The anchor has a circular upper hole and two rectangular holes on the lower side. It has a smooth surface and sharp edges.
6. Broken grapnel anchor, lying exposed over the rocky sea-bed. It has an upper circular hole and a broken lower hole; the third hole is missing. It is made out of limestone and has a rough surface and blunt edges.
7. Grapnel anchor, lying exposed over the rocky sea-bed (Pl. 57). The anchor does not have an upper circular hole; lower two square holes were noticed. This is one of the heaviest anchors found in Bet Dwarka waters. It is made out of limestone and has a rough surface and blunt edges. Marine growth was noticed over the anchor.
8. Grapnel anchor, lying exposed on the sea-bed. It is densely covered with marine growth. The hole have been eroded and widened. It has three holes. This is the biggest anchor found in the Bet Dwarka waters. It is made of limestone. It has a rough surface and blunt edges.
9. One of the most perfect anchor lying exposed. It has been trapped below a rock slab. It has a rectangular section on both ends. A layer of marine growth is also noticed. Lower holes are square and upper is circular. It has a rough surface and sharp edges. It is made of limestone.
10. Grapnel anchor, lying exposed on the sea-bed. The upper hole is broken. It is made of limestone. It has a square section. It has a rough surface and sharp edges. Thick marine growth is also observed.
11. Grapnel anchor, lying exposed on the rocky sea-bed. It has a circular section. It is well-preserved and made out of limestone. Small scale erosion has been noticed in the lowest hole. It has a rough surface and blunt edges. Thick marine growth is also observed.
12. Broken grapnel anchor, lying exposed. Upper portion is broken and only the lower part with a square hole is surviving. It is made of limestone. It has a rough surface and blunt edges. Holes have been eroded. Marine growth is also noticed.
13. Grapnel anchor, lying exposed on the rocky sea-bed. It is made of limestone. The upper circular hole is absent. It has a rough surface and blunt edges. Two lower holes are square in shape and one of them has been eroded. A thick layer of marine growth is noticed.
14. Broken grapnel anchor, lying exposed. It is covered with a thick layer of marine growth. Holes have been widened. It has a rough surface and blunt edges. It is made of limestone. It has an upper circular hole and the lower one is broken which is square in shape.
15. Broken grapnel anchor, lying partially buried. It is made of limestone. It has only the upper circular hole and the lower holes are absent. It has a rough surface and blunt edges. Sea-weed growth is also noticed.

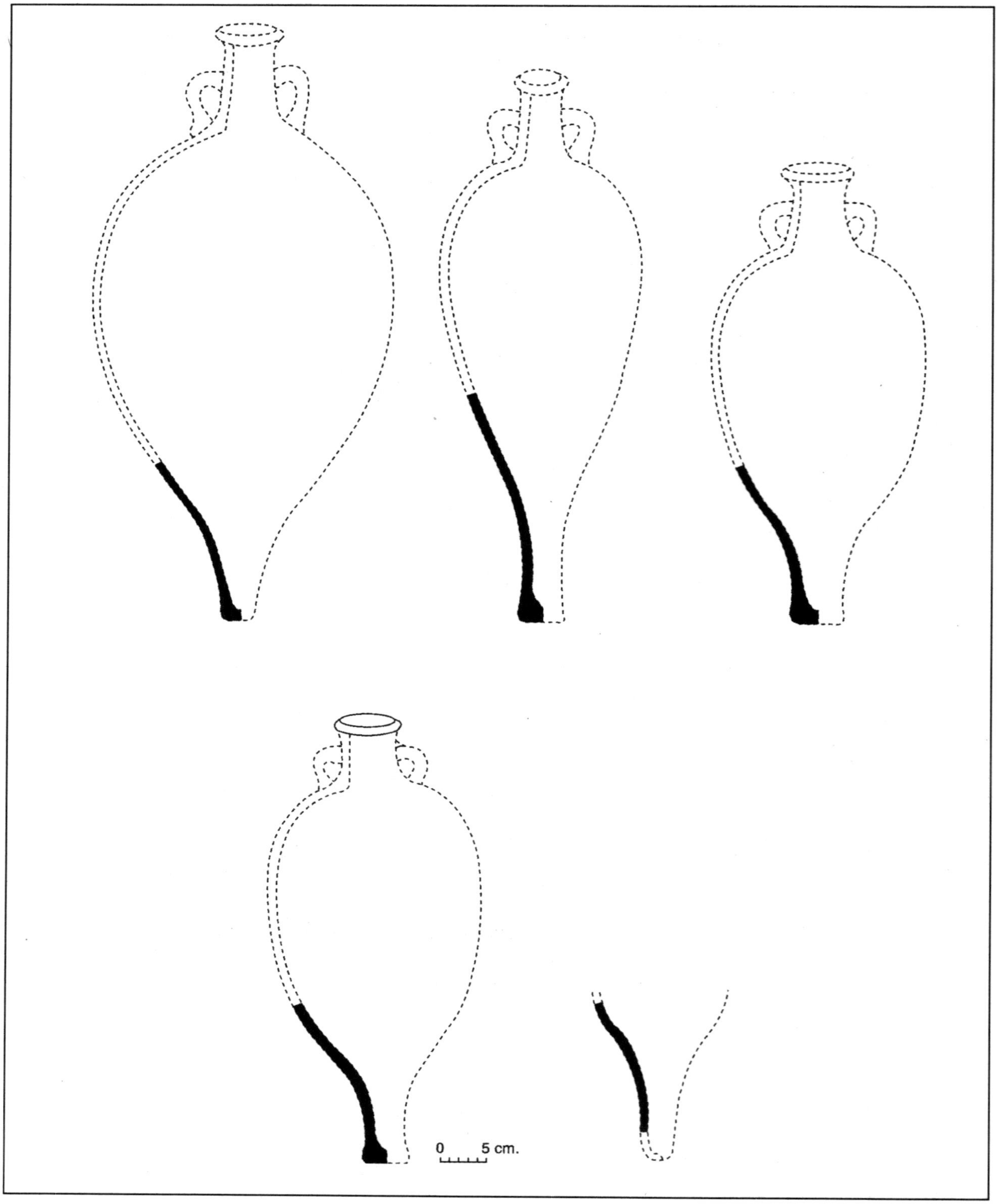

Fig. 52. Amphorae from Bet Dwarka waters.

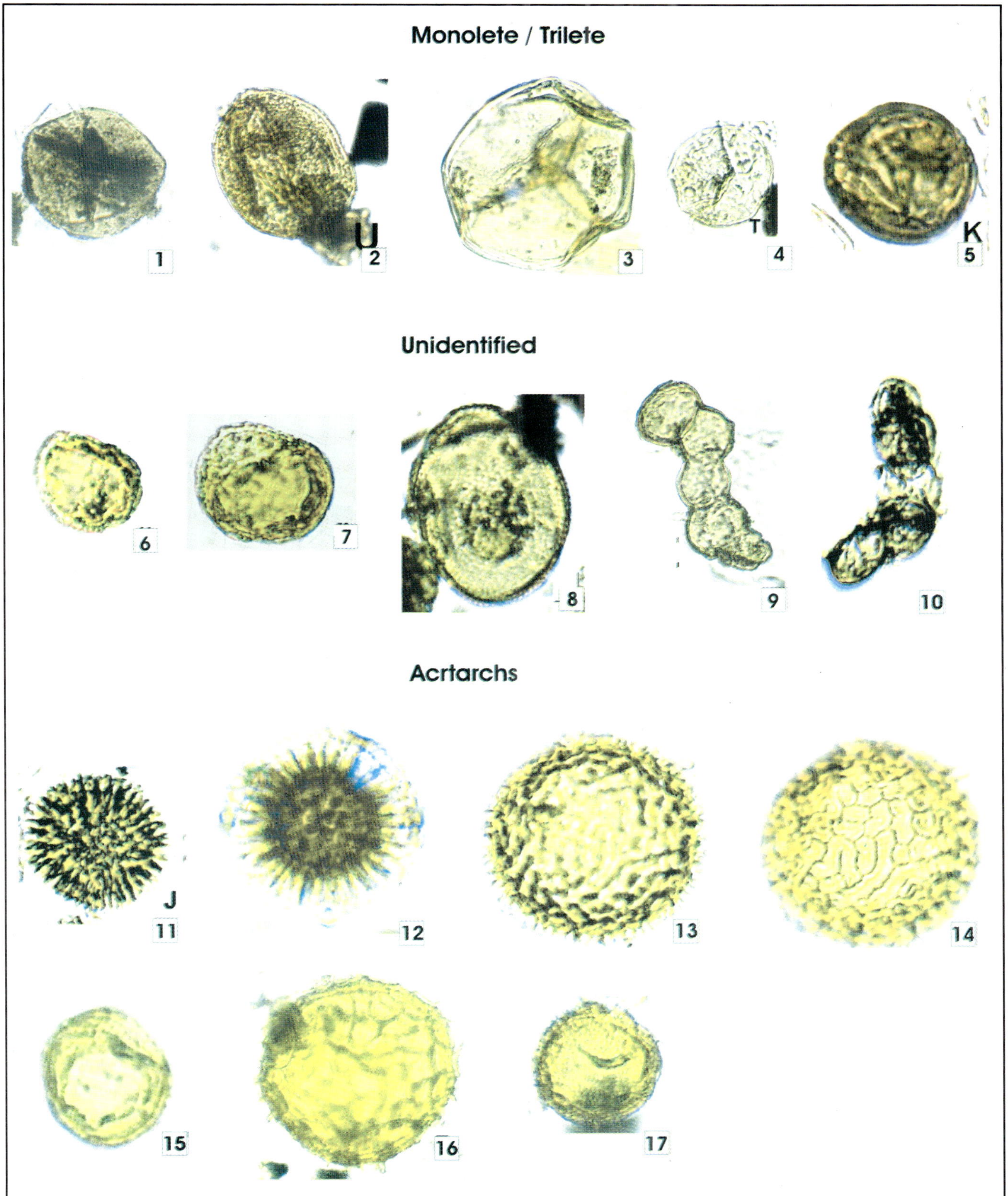

Pl. 45. Photomicrographs of monolete/ trilete, marine acritarchs and unidentified palynomorphs.

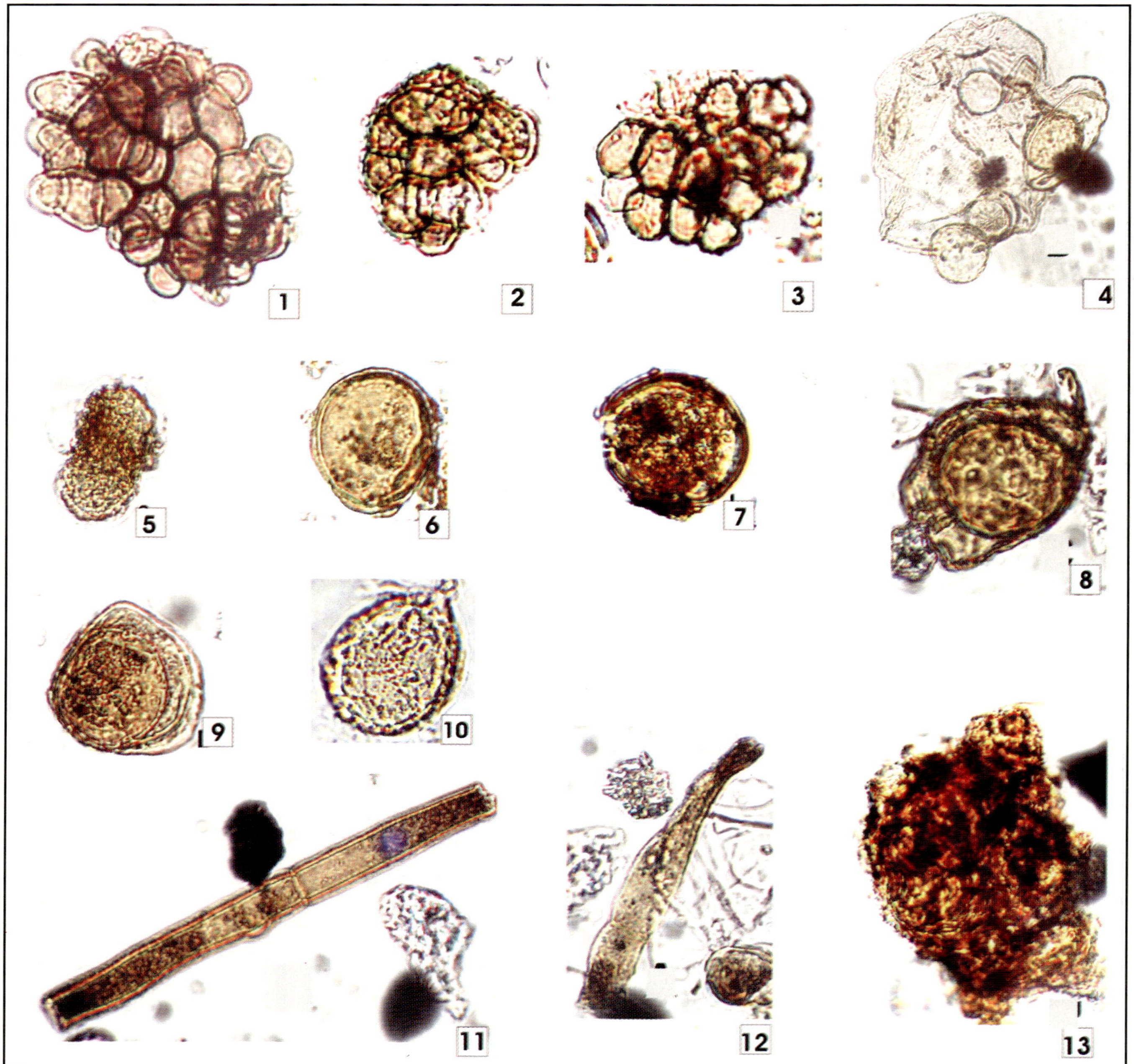

Pl. 46. Wholly marine multicellular/multinucleate vescicles or segments of Siphonocladales in *Dictyospharia* (Benthic green algae) 1-3; Algal fruiting bodies 4-10; Algal filament of *Rhizoclonium* ? 11; *Celyphus rallus* grows in an intermediate mildly saline environment 12; *Oocystis* 13.

Fungal spores

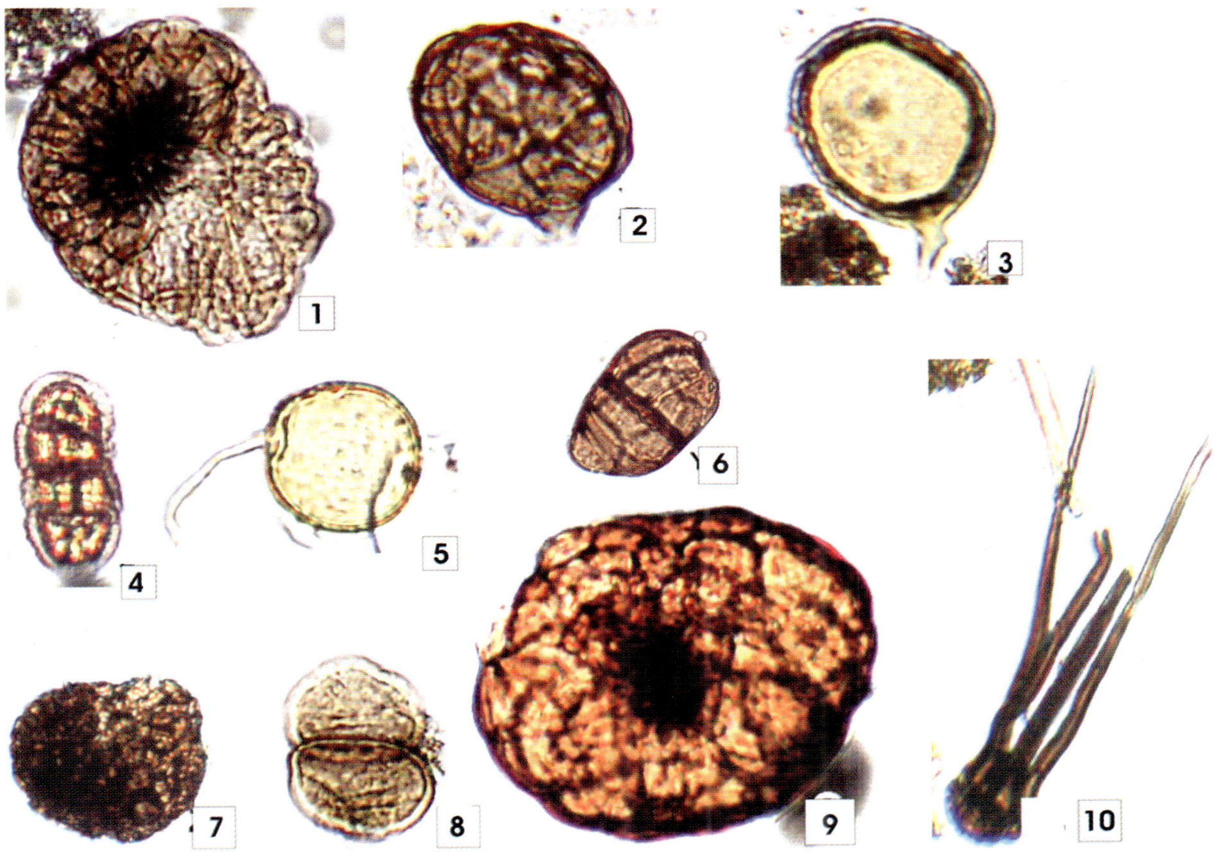

Zooplanktons and parts of animal origin

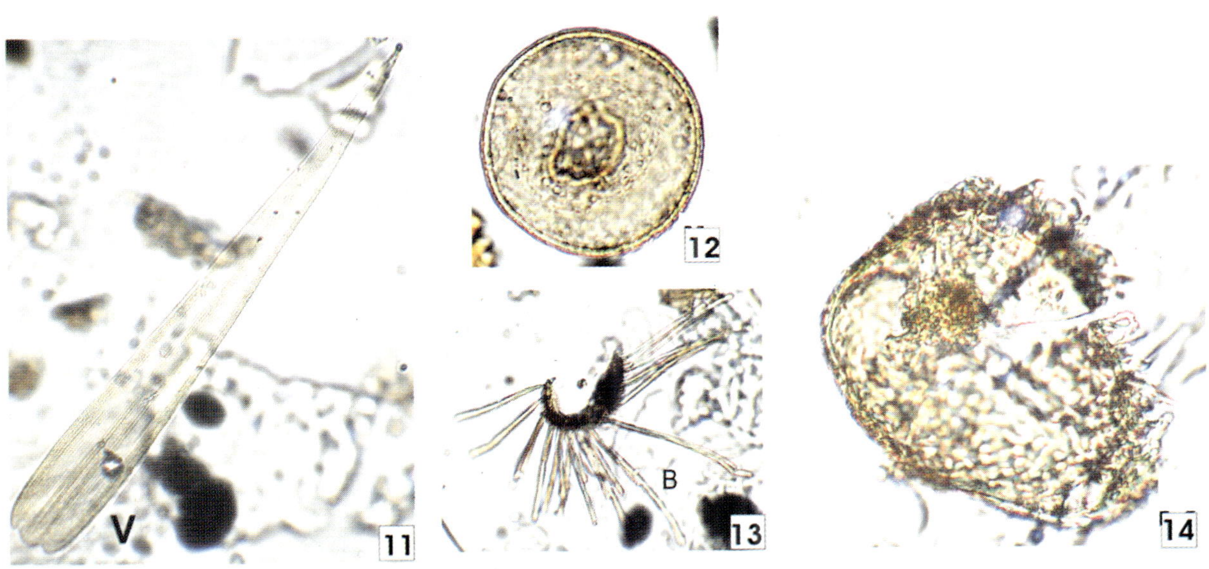

Pl. 47. *Cystopus cadidus* 3; *Gleocapsomorpa* 7; Multicellular thalloid body 9; *Tetraploa* 10; Rest Fungal fruiting body 1, 2, 4-6, 8. Insect wing 11; Protozoan cyst 12; Marine zooplankton 13; Marine chitinous exo-skeleton. Crustacean remain?.

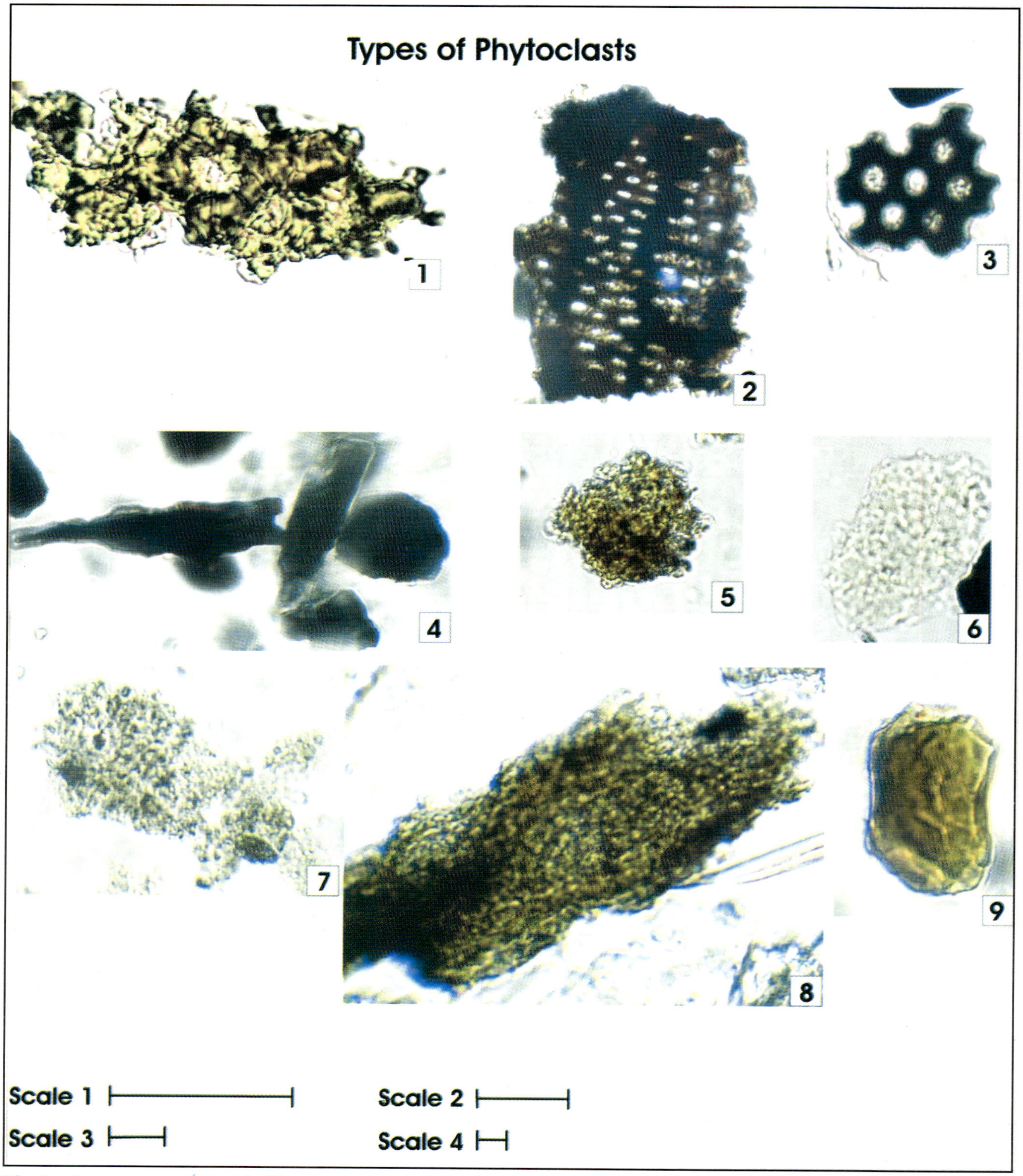

Pl. 48. Photomicrographs of different types of phytoclasts. Upper leaf epidermal surface of *Avicennia* showing salt gland in the centre 1; Biostructured phytoclast (trachieds) 2; Opaque structured phytoclast 3; Lath-shaped opaque black unidentifiable organic debris 4; Outer cellular margin identifiable but inner portion gelified 5; Transparent cellular structure 6; Amorphous organic matter 7; Filamentous identifiable cellular brown phytoclast with irregular margins 8; Resinous particle 9.

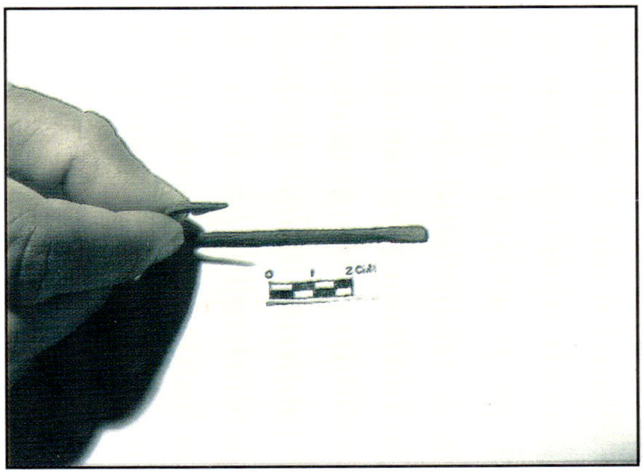

Pl. 49. Copper fishhook from BDK-VI.

Pl. 50 A. Composite plate showing the ancient sand blow on the northern wall, formed over the oldest occupation level at site BDK-II. B. Sketch of the northern trench wall showing level 11 and the overlying sand blow deposit.

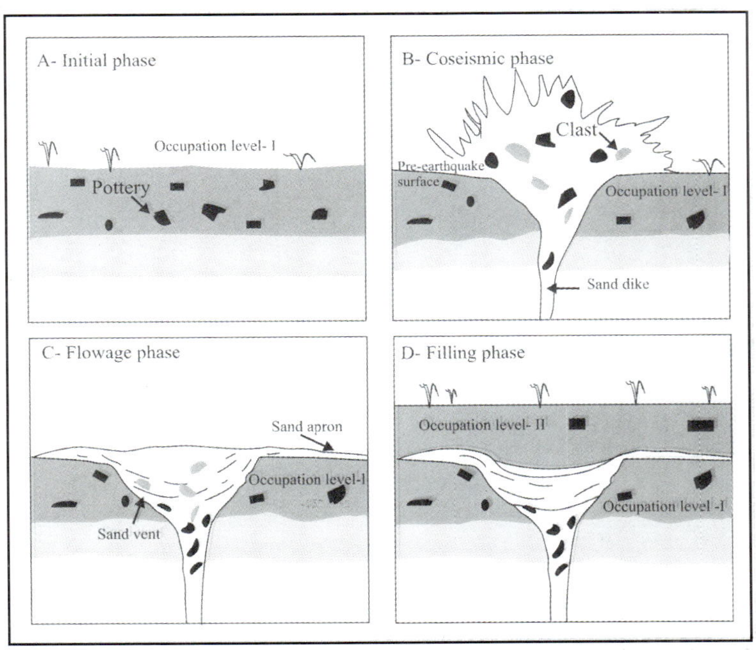

Pl. 52. Schematic model showing stages of earthquake-induced sand blow at Bet Dwarka.

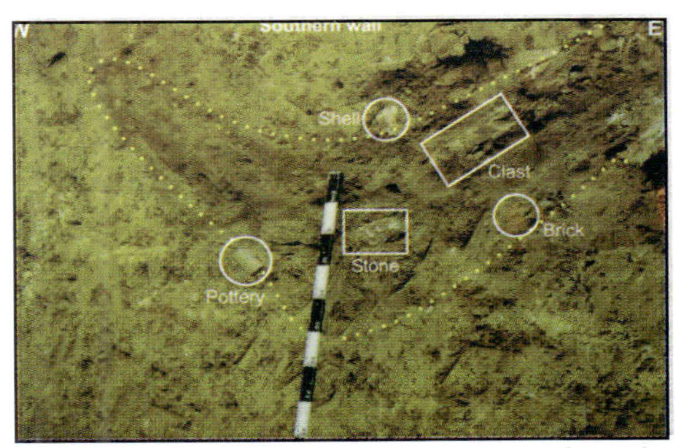

Pl. 51. Sand vent (dashed line) exposed on the southern wall at BDK-II.

Pl. 53. Measurement present shoreline and the oldest habitation at BDK-I.

Pl. 54. Section facing to the sea near BDK-I.

Pl. 55. Composite stone anchor from Bet Dwarka.

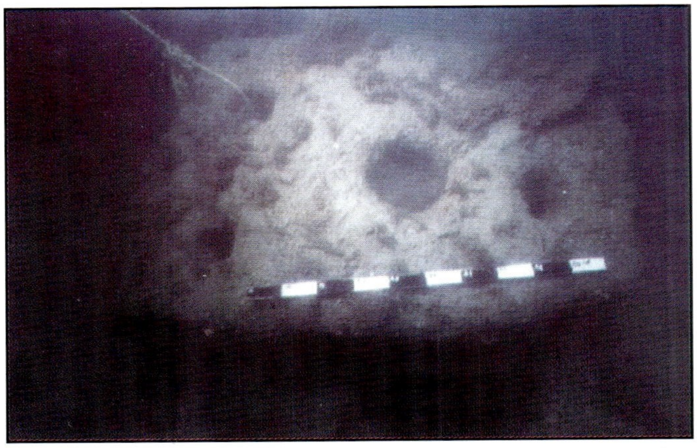

Pl. 56. Composite stone anchor with four holes from Bet Dwarka.

Pl. 57. Grapnel stone anchor lying off Bet Dwarka.

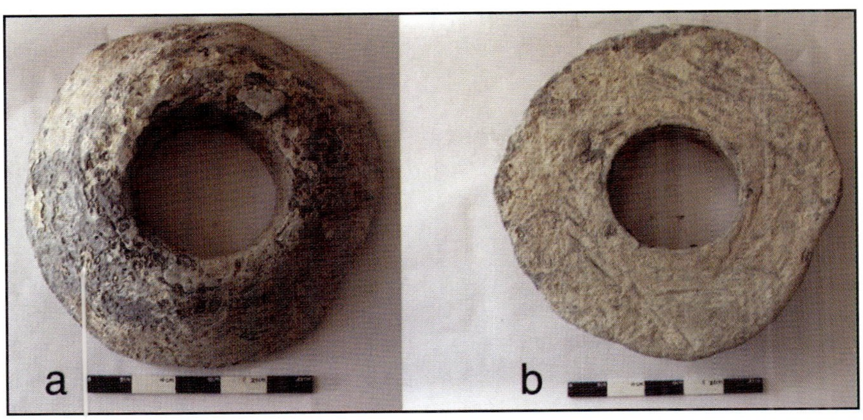

Pl. 58. Circular lead anchor from Bet Dwarka waters.

Pl. 59. Circular lead anchor from Bet Dwarka waters.

Pl. 60. Lead ingot from Bet Dwarka waters.

Pl. 62. Upper portion of an amphora from Bet Dwarka waters.

Pl. 61. Unidentified stone artifact from Bet Dwarka.

16 Broken grapnel anchor, lying exposed. It is made of limestone. Only the upper portion is intact. Upper side section is circular while the lower side is rectangular. It has a rough surface and blunt edges. Marine growth is also noticed.

17 Grapnel anchor has been cut from a thin, long block. This is circular in section. Only one upper hole is noticed. It is lying exposed and is made of limestone. Marine growth is also noticed. This anchor might have belonged to a small boat.

LEAD OBJECTS

Three lead artifacts were discovered during the exploration. A detailed description of each artifact is given below.

Object 1. Discovered in 2000-2001 season and it was lying partially buried in sediment. It has a big axial hole in the centre (Pl. 58). The bottom is flat with a few undulating zig-zag lines. A layer of marine growth is also observed. It tapers on the upper side and the diameter at the top merges with the hole. The diameter of the anchor is 42 cm, height 11 cm and the diameter of the hole is 15 cm. The weight of the anchor is 70.200 kg.

Object 2. This was discovered during field season 2001-2002, and was lying exposed on the sea-bed (Pl. 59). A thick layer of marine growth was observed. The height of the object is 9.5 cm and diameter at bottom is 38 cm. The diameter of the axial hole is 17 cm. This anchor does not have any mark on the bottom. However, on the upper surface a deep groove was observed. The weight of this object is 68.500 kg.

Object 3. Another lead object, circular in shape, was recovered from 7 m water-depth. A layer of marine growth was also noticed. The obverse of this object is rough and thick in the middle and gradually thinning towards the edges (Pl. 60). The reverse is flat and smooth without any marks on it. The diameter is 23 cm and the average height is 3 cm. The weight of the ingot is 8.500 kg.

Based on their shapes and sizes, the first two objects are considered to be the anchors while third one is identified as an ingot.

STONE ARTIFACT

An unidentified circular stone (Pl. 61) with a small axial hole was found near the above lead objects. The lower portion is broader and the bottom is flat. The object is tapering on the upper side with a thin wall. A horizontal slit on the upper side has been noticed, which is narrow on one side and opens on the other side. The upper edge of the axial hole has been widened. This is made of granite stone and a layer of marine growth is noticed over it.

AMPHORA

There are the remains of six amphorae, besides a number of other sherds of amphorae and pots (Fig. 52). They are thick gritty and made of compact clay, and have a coarse fabric and rough surface. This ware was mainly used for exporting wine and olive oil from the Roman Empire. Since olive oil was in lesser demand in India and since sherds have been found with dried resin mixture, it is most probable that majority of Indian examples are wine amphorae. The shape of this vessel is elongated with a pointed base, a narrow cylindrical neck and two handles attached to the rim and the shoulder. The shape could be understood at Nevasa as sherds from different parts of the pots were found there (Ghosh, 1989: 315). Though there are a number of sherds belonging to the body parts of the amphorae found in Bet Dwarka waters, only six amphorae have been described as they have preserved either the upper portion or lower portion.

1. Upper portion of an amphora with an outward-projected nail-headed rim (Pl. 62). One handle is surviving on the shoulder and has a raised neck. The entire pot is covered with a layer of thick marine growth. It is made of well-levigated clay and is well-fired and has a medium fabric. This is very similar to the Roman amphora of the 4th-5th century AD.
2. Lower portion of an amphora with a narrow base of 4 cm diameter. The body part of the vessel starts flaring after a height of 6 cm from the base point. It has a bulbous body and a rough surface. It has a coarse fabric and is well-fired. A layer of marine growth is also observed.
3. Lower portion of an amphora. It has a broader base than the previous one of 5 cm in diameter. Flaring of body portion starts after attaining a height of 5 cm from the base point. It has a smooth surface as compared to the previous one. It has a bulbous body. Internally, a black layer of some liquid material is also noticed. It has a fine fabric and is well-fired.
4. Lower portion of an amphora with a narrow base having 3 cm diameter. Flaring starts after a height of 3 cm from the base point. It has a thin section, rough surface and bulbous body. It has a coarse fabric and is well-fired. A layer of marine growth is also noticed. It is of a smaller size as compared to the previous ones.
5. Lower portion of an amphora. It has a long, narrow and thin base portion. It is of cylindrical type. The diameter of the base is 3.5 cm and flaring of body part starts at a height of 8 cm from the base point. The shape is very different from the above ones. The exterior has a smooth surface and internally it is rough. It is made of coarse fabric and is well-fired. A layer of marine growth is also noticed.
6. Lower portion of an amphora. The base part has been broken. It is very similar to amphora no. 2, however, it has a thin section and a bulbous body. Internally, it has a rough surface and is covered with a layer of marine growth. It has a coarse fabric and is well-fired.

DISCUSSION

The presence of a large number and variety of stone anchors in Bet Dwarka suggests that this was one of the important ports during the historical period. Most of the anchors are made out of limestone which is locally-available in the Okhamandal region. The material of a few composite anchors is porous and fragile, while rock of other composite and grapnel anchors is fine-grained and with a smooth surface; both types of rocks are available in this area.

The earliest dates of composite anchors in the Mediterranean have been assigned to the middle of the 3rd millennium BC (Frost, 1970: 380). In India, the earliest anchors have been reported from Lothal (Rao, 1979) and Kuntasi (Dhavalikar *et al.*, 1996). But these anchors are entirely different in shape and size from those discovered at Bet Dwarka. Therefore, the date of the Bet Dwarka anchors cannot be associated with the Harappan or Late Harappan Phase. A detailed discussion on anchors recovered from the Indian coast is presented below to ascertain the dates of stone anchors.

A number of stone anchors have been reported off Dwarka (Rao, 1990; Sundaresh *et al.*, 1999; Gaur *et al.*, 2001), Somnath (Rao *et al.*, 1992), Vijaydurg (Sila *et al.*,1998), Sindhudurg (Sila & Gaur, 1997) and Tamil Nadu (Jaykumar & Athiyaman, 1999; Athiyaman, 2001) along the

Indian coast. Initially, stone anchors from Dwarka were dated to 12th-14th century BC (Rao, 1987, 1990) on the basis of anchors found from Syria and Cyprus in the Mediterranean Sea. However, similar anchors have been found subsequently from well-known medieval ports at Vijaydurg and also Sindhudurg, along the Indian coast. There is a very strong possibility that the use of composite anchors appeared in India somewhere during the Christian Era, as a few anchors from Dwarka indicate a primitive stage (Sundaresh *et al.*,1999: 235) and as the antiquity of Dwarka commenced from the 1st century BC. However, these anchors were continued till the recent past as a few old fishermen recall the use of composite anchors. The recent discovery from Caesarea Maritima, Israel, suggests the date of composite anchors as 12th-13th century AD (Raban, 2000: 261). The composite anchors no. 10 and 11, and the lead anchor, might be of the early historical period as these types may be associated with Roman traders. However, the remaining anchors may be dated to the Medieval Period between the 8th and 16th century AD.

Grapnel anchors were important features of the Arab trade and several literary references also indicate that the Arab traders used to have several heavy anchors on board (Hourani, 1975). Similar types of anchors have been reported from Islamic ports of East African countries (Raban, 1990) and in the Gulf countries (Whitehouse, 1970) in the context of the 8th to 14th century AD. The dates of grapnel anchors in Bet Dwarka may also fall in the same period as Arab traders were very active during this time along the Indian coast (Hourani, 1975).

Roman Contacts

The discovery of the above findings in Bet Dwarka is significant in view of the maritime history of India in concern. So far, amphorae were considered to be the carriage of liquid material on the boat but the present discoveries confirm the notion. There are at least four sizes of amphorae from Bet Dwarka waters. It is difficult to determine the kind of liquid material transported from Bet Dwarka amphorae, as a thick layer of marine growth was present on them. It is possible that different material was filled in these amphorae as they are of various types. The finds are concentrated in a tidal current channel where, except slag period, the current speed is 3-6 knot, which did not allow the lighter material to settle down. However, the above pottery were found either partially buried in sediment or trapped in-between the rocks. These artifacts are not found towards the shallower side.

Two lead artifacts with an axial hole appear to be anchors. Generally, the anchors have been found in association with Roman shipwrecks in the Mediterranean water and they have been termed as Roman lead anchors (Raban, 1981). However, the lead anchors from Bet Dwarka are not similar to them. Similar types of stone anchors have also been reported from nearby areas of Dwarka and Somnath (Gaur *et al.*, 2002) and as far as Oman (Vosmer, pers. comm., 1999), where they have been termed as ring stone anchors. At present, these lead artifacts are associated with Roman contact only on their association with amphorae, which, however, may be purely a coincidence also. The association and dating of unidentified objects from Bet Dwarka is a difficult and risky task as this place has been used as an anchoring point since historical times and material of different periods can be noticed.

Habitation or a Shipwreck?

As it is stated earlier that findings are concentrated between 5 to 8 m water-depth, and absence of archaeological findings towards the shallower side suggest that these artifacts are not from the habitational site. For instance, a large number of pottery have been collected from the southeastern coast of the island from high water line to 5 m water-depth. Similarly, pottery and other archaeological remains have been traced from inter-tidal zone to 8 m water-depths off Poompuhar (Gaur and Sundaresh, 1998). The sea level history along the Indian coast suggests that so much fluctuation has not taken place during last 2000 years or so. With above evidences, the possibility of a habitational site at this depth is ruled out.

There are no remains of any timber of a wreck, except potsherds related to amphorae, two lead anchors and an ingot. This may be due to the fact that the site is lying in the mouth of the Gulf of Kachchh where tidal currents are severe, which does not allow for settlement of any lighter material and also sediment which preserved organic material and anything lying exposed on the sea-bed will be destroyed by wood borer as they are very active in Indian waters. For example, not a single piece of wood could be traced from a 17th century Portuguese wreck in the Goa waters (Tripati *et al.*, 2001) because the wreck was exposed on the rocky sea-bed. Similarly, in Poompuhar, a partially-exposed shipwreck belonging to the closing decade of the 18th century (Gaur *et al.*, 1997), where metal objects have been surviving and buried portion of wood is intact, was found. All these evidences from Indian waters rule out the possibility of the presence of any hull remains of a shipwreck of the early centuries of the Christian Era. However, archaeological findings support the presence of a shipwreck dating back to the Christian Era.

Similar Findings from other Sites in India

Indian and foreign classical literature have vividly described the active trade relation between India and northern Mediterranean countries during the early centuries of the Christian Era. Warmington (1928) believed that during the first two centuries of the Christian era, the Roman Empire witnessed the establishment and development of a profitable commerce between two great nations – the Mediterranean countries and India. A number of archaeological sites in India have yielded the Roman antiquity including inscriptions, coins and pottery. For the first time, amphorae were recovered from the excavations at Taxila, presently situated in northern Pakistan, which was dated by Sir John Marshall to the first centuries BC-AD. Wheeler believed (1946: 45) that Taxila amphora travelled overland from Western Asia. Another important archaeological coastal site excavated before independence is Arikamedu, which has immense value for the study of Indo-Roman trade. A large number of amphorae sherds, arretine ware, rouletted ware of Mediterranean origin have been discovered from this site. Wheeler (1946: 17) remarked from the findings of Arikamedu:

> numerous sherds both of a red-glazed pottery known to have been made in Italy in the first centuries BC-AD, and of the two-handled jars or amphorae characteristic of the Mediterranean wine trade of the period, together with Roman lamps and glassware, combine to indicate that Arikamedu was one of the regular *Yavana* or Western trading-stations of which both Graeco-Roman and ancient Tamil writer speak.

Vimala Begley (1983), however, suggested an early date for the trade contact between Arikamedu and the Mediterranean world. Later on, Begley (1996) conducted a large-scale excavation between 1989 and 1992 and suggested that some of the pottery found from the excavation was manufactured in Italy. Amphora and other Roman pottery have also been reported from Dwarka and Bet Dwarka (Ansari and Mate, 1966 and Gaur, 1990) in Gujarat, Nevasa (IAR-1954-55: 7), Elephanta (Shinde *et al.*, 2002) in Maharashtra in western India, Tamluka (IAR-1954-55: 20), Chandraketugarh (IAR-1959-60) in West Bengal, Amarawati (1958-59: 5) in Andhra Pradesh, Vasavasamudram

(Nagaswami and Majeed, 1978), Kaveripoompatinam (Soundara Rajan, 1994: 42), Alagankulam (Kasinathan, 1992) and Korkai in the Tamil Nadu coast. The Roman evidences are datable between 3rd century BC and 4th century AD in all these sites.

Shipwrecks with Amphorae in Mediterranean Sea

The identification of a shipwreck in the Mediterranean Sea was generally based on the discovery of amphorae datable to as early as 16th century BC (Bass, 1976). Unlike India, sediment discharge into Mediterranean is negligible which led to the exposure of the most of the cargoes of a ship. However, in shallow waters coral growth have been observed over the remains of the shipwrecks. Several shipwrecks in the Mediterranean Sea contain similar type of amphorae which have been termed as Graeco-Italic type (Frey *et al.*, 1978; Frost *et al.*, 1974; Kapitan, 1979). However, the lead anchor is of a different type when compared with the Roman lead anchors of the Mediterranean. The anchors from Bet Dwarka are circular with an axial hole and taper on the upper side. This is the first time that this type of anchor has been reported from anywhere. Several stone anchors were also reported from this particular place but it is difficult to associate these anchors with the Roman period. However, discovery of these anchors suggest that this place has been an anchoring point since early times.

Dating

It is difficult to assign the date for the lead artifacts in absence of similar findings from other sites. However, the type of amphorae can be relatively dated comparing with other sites along the Indian coast. The excavations at several coastal sites suggest that Romans were active on the Indian coast from the 3rd century BC to 4th century AD. At Nevasa, Roman period settlement has been dated to 1st century BC to 2nd century AD (Sankalia *et al.*, 1960). Similarly, Roman contact at Arikamedu dated to the same period (Wheeler *et al.*, 1946). Recently, Begley (1996) proposed an early date for Arikamedu. Excavations at Dwarka yielded a sherd of amphorae datable to 2nd century AD (Ansari and Mate, 1966). Archaeological, numismatic and inscriptional evidences indicate the time-bracket for Indo-Roman trade between the 3rd century BC and 4th century AD. Recently, Shinde *et al.* (2002) reported a number of amphorae sherds and two bases, similar to Bet Dwarka amphorae bases, dated to 1st-2nd century AD on the basis of their similarity with Dressel 2-4 type bases of the Mediterranean. Similar type of amphorae from *Punic* wreck (Frost *et al.*, 1974), *Capistello* wreck (Frey *et al.*, 1978) and *Porticellow* wreck (Eiseman, 1973) in the Mediterranean Sea have been dated to the 3rd century BC. However, amphorae from Bet Dwarka may be dated to 1st century BC on the basis of active trade relations with the Roman world during this period.

Identification of Baraca/Barake of *Periplus of Erythraean Sea* and Ptolemy

The author of *Periplus of Erythraean Sea* described this area as:

"the Gulf of Baraca, which contains 7 islands, the sea-bed is in some places abrupt, and in others rocky and sharp, so that the anchors lying there are parted, some being quickly cut off, and others chafing on the bottom (Schoff, 1974).

However, Ptolemy mentions Barake as an island in the Gulf of Kanthi which has been identified as the Gulf of Kachchh. Generally, Baraca/Barake has been identified with the present town of Dwarka (McCrindle, 1879).

From the above two references, the following common points emerge:

(1) It was an important coastal town during the Christian Era.

(2) It is a gulf where islands are present.

(3) It is dangerous for navigation.

Archaeologically, the first point is common to present Dwarka and Bet Dwarka but the next two points do not match with the present Dwarka. However, being in the mouth of the Gulf of Kachchh and being an island, Bet Dwarka can be accurately identified with Baraca/ Barake of *Periplus of Erythraean Sea* and Ptolemy, respectively. The hypothesis is also supported by underwater explorations near the present Bet Dwarka jetty, which indicate that boats from Mediterranean countries were anchored at this point during the early centuries of the Christian Era.

CONCLUSION

Bet Dwarka played an important role in maritime activities of the Okhamandal region from the beginning of the 2nd millennium BC. The exploitation of marine resources has been observed from early times. The presence of Roman amphorae suggest that perhaps Roman boats also reached Bet Dwarka waters. The dates of composite stone anchors from Bet Dwarka may be bracketed between the early centuries of the Christian Era and the late Medieval Period. This suggestion is based on the fact that stone anchors have not been reported opposite to proto-historic settlements (1500 years BC) on the southern and western coasts of the island, and the above-mentioned anchors are from opposite to early historic and medieval period sites. However, grapnel type anchors can be safely bracketed between the 8th and 14th century AD, and are often termed an Indo-Arab type. The anchors of various dimensions indicate that boats of different sizes, from different places or countries visited the Okhamandal area in the past.

Table 19. Composite stone anchors discovered from Bet Dwarka waters.

Sl. no.	Year and location	Raw material	Weight (estimated)	Max length	Max width	Thick-ness	Diameter of upper hole	Lower holes
1	1998 IZ	Limestone	134	100	100	10		13X13, 13X13
2	1998 UW	-do-	216	116	76	21	20	10X12, 12X12
3	1998 UW	-do-	23	80	35	7	13	10
4	1998 UW	-do-	80	90	73	12	14	15X15, 15X16
5	1998 UW	-do-	55	70	54	13	10	11
6	1998 UW	-do-	40	66	50	12	11	
7	2000-01 UW	-do-	35	88	58	6	5	6X6, 6X6
8	2000-01 UW	-do-	46	80	65	7	14	6X6, 6X8
9	2000-01 UW	-do-	60	67	50	15	6, 12	5X7, 5X7
10	2000-01 UW	-do-	25	45	25	15	14	
11	2000-01 UW	-do-	49	60	45	13	8	7X7
12	2000-01 UW	-do-	38	61	45	10	6	7X7, 7X7
13	2000-01 UW	-do-	32	60	50	10	8	10X10, 10X10

Table 19 contd.

Sl. no.	Year and location	Raw material	Weight (estimated)	Max length	Max width	Thick-ness	Diameter of upper hole	Lower holes
14	2001-02 UW	-do-	46	60	50	12	5	5, 5
15	2001-02 UW	-do-	31	70	40	8	6	
16	2001-02 UW	-do-	82	110	45	15	7	12X10, 12X10
17	2001-02 UW	-do-	10	40	42	3		3, 3
18	2001-02 UW	-do-	83	95	70	12	12	12X12, 15X20
19	2001-02 UW	-do-	46	78	65	7	7	7, 8X6
20	2001-02 UW	-do-	44	95	62	7	5	6X6, 6X6
21	2001-02 UW	-do-	99	90	60	15	10	8X8, 12X10
22	2001-02 UW	-do-	20	53	50	6	5	6X6
23	2001-02 UW	-do-	24	60	33	8	5	5, 5
24	2001-02 UW	-do-	78	80	75	11	10X10	4, 4
25	2001-02 UW	-do-	42	55	45	13	8	7X7

Table 20. Indo-Arab anchors from Bet Dwarka.

Sl. no.	Year and location	Material	Max length	Max width	Thick-ness	Diameter of upper hole	Lower holes	Estimated weight in kgs
26	1998 IZ	Conglomerate	80	32		-	15X16, 14X16	121
27	1998 IZ	Sandstone	146	36		14	18X18, 18X20	289
28	2001 UW	Limestone	100	25		8	13X14, 8X10	72
29	2001 UW	-do-	90	18		6	10X10, 10X10	48
30	2001 UW	-do-	95	20		6	12X12, 10X10	76
31	2001 UW	-do-	75	20		10	10X10	71
32	2001 UW	-do-	150	30			11X14, 11X15	205
33	2002 UW	-do-	190	45	25	15	20X20, 18X20	283
34	2002 UW	-do-	130	30	28	7	12X12, 12X12	167
35	2002 UW	-do-	115	30	25	7	10X12, 10X10	143
36	2002 UW	-do-	108	25	22	7	11X13, 8X8	93
37	2002 UW	-do-	40	24	20		12X12	30
38	2002 UW	-do-	95	30	22		12X12, 12X12	110
39	2002 UW	-do-	110	25	25	12	12X12	156
40	2002 UW	-do-	65	20	27	6	-	67
41	2002 UW	-do-	50	20	22	6	-	51
42	2002 UW	-do-	65	24	10	4	-	37

Value of sandstone per m3 = 2300 kg.
Value of limestone m3 = 2500 kg.

Annexure G

Conservation of Antiquities

B.G. Naik

Artifacts preservation is one of the most important parts from an archaeological site. Artifacts recovered from anaerobic environments (ie, buried in sediment) are recovered in better condition than artifacts recovered from aerobic environments.

From Bet Dwarka island, the antiquities consisted of iron, copper, stone, terracotta and shells, and chemical treatment was undertaken for the metal objects only, ie, iron and copper. Before the treatment, each object was weighted in the laboratory.

IRON

Four iron objects (two arrow-heads and two nails) were treated with the immersion of objects in 5% dilute caustic soda solution a few times, for the complete removal of any chloride present, followed by thorough washing with distilled water and drying.

COPPER

Coins, fishhook and rings were separately immersed in alkaline solution of Potassium Sodium Tartrate (KNaC4HO6,5H2O) by dissolving 300 gms of Potassium Sodium Tartrate and 100 gms of Sodium Hydroxide in two litre of distilled water. The objects remained for over 12 hours in the solution. All the cupric salts in the object were dissolved in the solution, which turned blue as a result. The same treatment was repeated for a few objects. This was followed by a thorough brushing and washing under running water.

The pink colour deposit of cuprous salts still remained on the object after the above treatment, and the same was removed by immersing the object in 5% solution of sulphuric acid for half an hour. The objects were dried overnight at 40°, then cooled to ambient temperature and weighed to determine their weight and weight loss.

References and Bibliography

Agarwal, D.P., Avasia, R.K. and Guzder, S.J., 1973. 'A multidisciplinary approach to the Quaternary problems in Maharashtra'. *Radiocarbon and Indian Archaeology* (Eds. D.P. Agrawal and A. Ghosh), Bombay, pp. 3-17.

Agrawal, R.C., 1984. 'Aravalli, The major source of copper for the Indus and Indus-related Cultures'; in: *Frontiers of the Indus Civilization* (Eds. B.B. Lal and S.P. Gupta), pp. 157-162, Delhi: Books and Books.

Ansari, Z.D. and Mate, S.M., 1966. *Excavations at Dwarka,* Deccan College Postgraduate and Research Institute, Pune, p. 103.

Amick, D. and Gelinas, R., 1991. 'The search for evidence of large prehistoric earthquakes along the Atlantic coast', *Science,* 251, 655-658.

Athiyaman, N. 2001. 'Stone Anchors from East Coast of India a Precursor for Marine Archaeology of Tamilnadu'; in: *Historical Archaeology, Epigraphy, Numismatics and Archives*; Proceedings of 61st Session of Indian History Congress.

Banerjee, P.K., 2000. 'Holocene and late pleistocene relative sea level fluctuations along the east coast of India', *Marine Geology,* 167: 243-260.

Bass, G.F., 1967. 'Cape Gelidonya: a Bronze Age Shipwreck', *Transaction of American Phil. Society,* 57.8.

——, 1976. 'Sheytan Desesi: Preliminary Report', *IJNA,* 5.4:293-303.

——, 1986. 'Bronze Age Shipwreck at Ul Burun (Kas): 1984 campaign', *AJA,* 90.3: 269-96.

Begley, V., 1983. 'Arikamedu Reconsidered', *AJA,* 87.4: 461-481.

——, 1996. *The Ancient Port at Arikamedu*, Pondicherry.

Bendick, R., Bilham, R., Fielding, E., Gaur, V.K., Hough, S.E., Kier, G., Kulkarni, M.N., Martin, S., Mueller, K. and Mukul, M., 2001. 'The 26 January 2001 "Republic Day" Earthquake, India', *Seismological Research Letters*, Vol. 72, No.3, pp. 328-335.

Bhan, K.K. and Kenoyer, J.M., 1984. 'Nageswar: a Mature Shell Working Site on the Gulf of Kutch (Gujarat)', *Journal of Oriental Institute of Baroda*, 34: 67-80.

Bhatt, N. and Patel, M.P., 1998. 'Bioclastic shore deposits: indicators of Late Quaternary high sea in Saurashtra, Western India', *JGSI,* 52: 537-42.

Bhatt, N., 2000. 'Lithostratigraphy of the Neogene-Quaternary Deposits of Dwarka-Okha Area, Gujarat', *JGSI,* 55: 139-148.

Biswas, S.K., 1982. 'Rift basins in western margin of India and their hydrocarbon prospects with special reference to Kutch basin', *Am. Assoc. Pet. Geol. Bull.,* 66, 1497-1513.

Bruckner, H., 1989. 'Late Quaternary shorelines in India', *Late Quaternary Sea-Level Correlation and Applications,* (Eds. D.B. Scott, P.A. Pirazzoli and C.A. Honig), Dordrecht, pp.169-194.

Chandra, M., 1977. *Trade and trade routes in ancient India,* Abhinav Publications, New Delhi.

Chatterjee, S.P., 1962. 'Fluctuation of sea-level around coasts of India during Quaternary Period', *Zeitschrift fur Geomorphologic,* Suppl. 3, Berlin, 48-56.

Chittick, N., 1980, 'Stone anchor shanks in Western Indian Ocean', *IJNA,* 9.1: 73-6.

Cleuziou, S., 1992. 'The Oman Peninsula and the Indus Civilization: A Reassessment', *ME,* XVII (2): 93-103.

de Boer, J.Z., Hale, J.R. and Chanton, J., 2001. 'New evidence for the geological origins of the ancient Delphic oracle' (Greece), *Geology,* 29, pp. 707-710.

Dhavalikar, M.K., Raval, M.R. and Y.M. Chitalwala, 1996. *Kuntasi-A Harappan Emporium on West Coast,* Pune.

Duffield, W., 2001. 'At least Noah had some warning', *EOS,* 82, 305, 309.

Durante, S., 1979. 'Marine shells from Balakot, Shahr-I-Sokhta and Tepe Yayha: their Significance for Trade and Technology in Ancient Indo-Iran', *South Asian Archaeology,* 1977 (ed. M. Taddei), Istituto Universitario Orientale, Naples, pp. 317-342.

Dyer-Williams, K. and Haynes, M., 1996. 'Use of archaeology to date liquefaction features and seismic events in the New Madrid seismic zone, central United States', *Geoarchaeology: An International Journal,* 11, 451-480.

Eiseman, C.J., 1973. 'Amphoras from the Porticellow shipwreck' (Calabria), *IJNA,* 2.1: 13-24.

Ellison, J.C., 1989. 'Pollen analysis of mangrove sediments as sea level indicator: assessment from Tongatapu, Tonga', *Palaeogeography, Palaeoclimatology and Palaeoecology,* 74: 327-341.

Epigraphia Indica, 1981. Archaeological Survey of India, New Delhi, Vol. VII: 47-74 and Vol. VIII: 59-96.

Erdtman, G., 1943. *An Introduction to Pollen Analysis,* Chronica Botanica Co., Waltham Mass, U.S.

Fairbridge, R.W., 1960. 'The changing level of the sea', *Scientific American,* 202.5: 70-79.

Farooqui, A. and Vaz, G. G., 2000. 'Holocene sea-level and climate fluctuations: Pulicat lagoon – A case study', *CS,* 79(10) 1484-1488.

Fedden, F., 1884. 'Geology of Kathiawar peninsula in Guzerat', *Mem. Geol. Survey of India,* V. 21-22: 78-125.

Flemming, N.C., 1972. *Cities in the Sea,* Doubleday, New York.

——, 1984. 'Survival of submerged lithic and Bronze Age artifact sites: A Review of Case Histories', *Quaternary Coastline and Marine Archaeology,* (Eds. P.M. Masters and N.C. Flemming), London: Academic Press Inc., pp. 135-173.

Frankfort, D., 1933. *Tell Asmar, Khafage and Khosabad,* Chicago.

Frey, D., Hentschel, F.D., and Keith, D.M., 1978. 'Deep water archaeology, the Capistello wreck excavation Lipari, Aeolion Island', *IJNA,* 7.4: 279-300.

Frost, H., Culicon, W. and Curtis, J.E., 1974. 'The Punic wreck in Sicily: Second season of excavation', *IJNA,* 3.1: 35-54.

Frost, H., 1970. 'Bronze Age Stone Anchors from the Eastern Mediterranean', *MM,* 56.4: 377-94.

——, 1979. Egypt and stone achors: some recent discoveries, *MM,* 65.2: 137-161.

——, 1991. 'Anchors', *Ras Shamra-Qugarit, VI.* ERC, Paris.

Gaur, A.S., 1990. 'Ceramic Industries of Dwarka', *JMA,* 1: 110-113.

Gaur, A.S., Sundaresh, Gudigar, P. and Tripati, S., 1994. 'Protohistoric Ceramics of Dwarka and Bet Dwarka', *RURIMA* (Ed. S.R. Rao), NIO, Goa, pp. 165-71.

——, 1997. 'An 18th century shipwreck off Poompuhar Tamil Nadu coast' (India), *IJNA*, 26.2: 118-126.

Gaur, A.S. and Sundaresh, 1998. 'Underwater Exploration off Poompuhar and possible causes of its Submergence', *Puratattva*, 28: 84-90.

Gaur, A.S. and Vora, K.H., 1999. 'Ancient Shorelines of Gujarat during Indus Civilization', (Late Mid-Holocene Period), a study based on archaeological evidences, *CS*, 77.1: 180-5.

Gaur, A.S., 2000. *Harappan Maritime Legacies of Gujarat*, Asian Publication Services, New Delhi.

Gaur, A.S., Sundaresh, Gudigar, P. Sila Tripati, Vora, K.H. and Bandodkar, S.N., 2000. 'Recent underwater explorations at Dwarka and surroundings in Okhamandal region', Gujarat, *ME*, 25.1: 67–74.

Gaur, A.S., Sundaresh, Tripati, S., Gudigar, P., Vora, K.H., and Bandodkar, 2001. 'A group of 20 stone anchors from the waters of Dwarka, on the Gujarat Coast', India, *IJNA*, 30.1: 95–108.

Gaur, A.S., Sundaresh, Sila Tripati, and Bandodkar, S.N., 2002. 'Ring stones from Gujarat Coast, West Coast of India', *MM*, 88.4: 390-404.

Gaur, A.S. and Sundaresh, 2003. 'Onshore excavation at Bet Dwarka Island, in the Gulf of Kachchh, Gujarat', *ME*, XXVIII (1): 57-66.

Gaur, A.S., Sundaresh and Sila Tripati, 2004. 'Dwarka: an ancient harbour', *CS*, 86.9: 1256-60.

Gaur, A.S., Sundaresh, and Sila Tripati, 2004. 'Grapnel anchors from Saurashtra: Remnants of Indo-Arab Trade route in Indian Ocean', *MM*, 90.2: 134-151.

Gaur, A.S. and Sundaresh, 2004. 'A late Bronze Age Copper Fish-hook from Bet Dwarka, Gujarat: An evidence on the advance fishing technology', *CS*, 86.4: 512-514.

Ghate, S., 1988. 'Sea level fluctuations of North Konkan with special reference to Sopara', *CS*, 57.24: 1317-20.

Ghose, A., 1989. *An Encyclopaedia of Indian Archaeology*, Delhi, pp. 348-50.

Gokani, P., 1988. 'Marine Archaeology Entering a New Era of Ancient History with Special Reference to Dwarka of Beloved Lord Krishna', *MAIOC*, (Ed. S.R. Rao), NIO, Goa, pp. 17-18.

Gopal, L., 1970. 'Indian Shipping in Early Medieval Period', in: *India's contribution to world thought and culture*; Vivekanand Commemoration Volume, (Ed. Lokeshchandra), Madras, pp. 108-122.

Grossmann, E. and Kingsley, S.A., 1996. 'A three-hole stone anchor with wood remain from Crusadar Arsuf (Apollonia) Israel', *IJNA*, 25.1: 49-54.

Gupta, S.K., 1972. 'Chronology of raised beaches and inland coral reefs of the Saurashtra coast', *Journal of Geology*, 80: 357-61.

Gupta, S.K. and Amin, B.S., 1974. 'Io/U ages of corals from Saurashtra coast', *Marine Geology*, 16: M79-M83.

Gupta, S.K., 1977. 'Quaternary sea-level changes on the Saurashtra coast', *Ecology and Archaeology of Western India* (Eds. D.P. Agrawal and B.M. Pande).

Hashimi, N.H. and Nair, R.R., 1988. 'Dynamic tidal barrier of Gulf of Kutch and its relevance to the submergence of the ancient Dwarka', *MAIOC* (Ed. S.R. Rao), NIO, Goa, pp. 56-57.

Hashimi, N.H., Rao, S.R. and Gaur, A.S., 1994. 'Use of X-Ray Diffractometry in identifying mineral suite in Protohistoric pottery: A case study from Bet Dwarka', *(Abstract)*, Fourth Marine Archaeology Conference on Indian Ocean Countries, p. 15.

Hegde, K.T.M., Bhan, K.K., Sonawane, V.H., Krishnan, K. and Shah, D.R., 1990. *Excavation at Nageswar-Gujarat*, M.S. University, Baroda.

Hora, S.L., 1954. 'Angling in ancient India', *Ancient India* No. 10-11, Archaeological Survey of India, New Delhi.

Hornell, J., 1913. 'The chank bangle industry: its antiquity and present conditions', *Memoirs of the Asiatic Society of Bengal*, III: 407-448.

——, 1916. 'The Indian varieties and races of the Genus Turinel', *Memoirs of the Indian Museum*, VI: 111-122.

——, 1942. 'The chank shell cult of India', *Antiquity*, 16: 113-33.

——, 1951. *Indian Molluscs*, Bombay Natural History Society, Bombay.

Hourani, G.F., 1975, *Arab Seafaring in the Indian Ocean and Early Medieval Times*, New York.

Indian Archaeology - A Review, 1954-55. Archaeological Survey of India, New Delhi.

——, 1958-59. Archaeological Survey of India, New Delhi.

——, 1959-60. Archaeological Survey of India, New Delhi.

——, 1969-70. Annual Bulletin of Archaeological Survey of India, New Delhi.

——, 1971-72. Archaeological Survey of India, New Delhi, p.12.

——, 1975-76. Archaeological Survey of India, New Delhi, p. 13.

IAR, *Indian Archaeology -A Review*, 1979-80. Archaeological Survey of India, New Delhi.

Jain, R.L., 1990. 'Tertiary rocks of Gujarat', *Rec. Geol. Surv. India*, 123/7: 36-38.

——, 1997. 'A study of Miocene Mollusca from Jamnagar district, Gujarat', Ph.D. Thesis, M.L. Sukhadia University , Udaypur (Unpublished).

Jaykumar, P. and Athiyaman, N., 1999. 'Stone Anchors of Tamilnadu Coast', Paper presented in Second International Conference on Marine Archaeology, Thane, Mumbai on 8-10 January, 1999.

Joglekar, P.P., Thomas, P.K., Matsushima, Y. and Pawankar, S.J., 1994. 'Osteological Differences between the forelimb bones of Ox (*Bos indicus*), Buffalo (*Bubalus bubalis*) and Nilgai (*Boselaphus tragocamelus*)', *Journal of Bombay Veterinary College*, 5 (1-2): 17-20.

Joglekar, P.P., 1991. *A Biometric approach to the faunal remains of western India with special reference to Kaothe and Walki*, Unpublished Ph.D. dissertation, Pune; University of Poona.

——, 1993-94. 'A Preliminary Report on the Faunal Remains from Padri-Gohil, a Small Harappan Site in South Gujarat', *Puratattava*, 24: 32-35.

——, 1996-97. 'Faunal Remains from Padri: a Second Preliminary Report', *BDCPRI*, 56-57: 55-68.

——, 2000-2001. 'Application of Mathematics and Statistics in Archaeozoological Research: a Review', *BDCPRI*, 60-61: 109-136.

Joshi, J.P., 1990. *Excavation at Surkotada 1971-72 and exploration in Kutch*; MASI No. 87, Archaeological Survey of India, New Delhi.

Joshi, J.P. and Bisht, R.S., 1994. 'India and the Indus Civilization', National Museum, New Delhi.

Joshi, U.S., 1946. *Puranoma Gujarat (Gujarati)*, Gujarat Vidyasabha, Ahmedabad.

Kapitan, G., 1979. 'Laoteria from the sea', *IJNA*, 8.2: 97-100.

——, 1994. 'Stone-shank anchors of the Arab-Indian trade period – were they mooring anchors?' *BAIMA*, 18.2: 1–6.

Kasinathan, N., 1992. 'Alagankulam: A preliminary report', Department of Archaeology, Govt. of Tamil Nadu, Madras.

——, 1997. 'Antiquity of sea voyage in Tamilnadu', Paper presented in Ist International Conference on Marine Archaeology of Indian Ocean Countries, held at Chennai in September, 1997.

Kenny, L.B., 1993. 'Archaeology and Krsna's Dvaraka', *The Journal of the Asiatic Society of Bombay*, Vol. 64-66: 95-100.

Kenoyer, J.M., 1983. *Shell working industries of the Indus Civilization: an archaeological and ethnographic perspective*; Unpublished Ph.D. dissertation, Department of South and Southeast Asian Studies, Berkeley: University of California.

——, 1984. 'Shell working Industries of the Indus Civilization: a Summary', *Palaeorient*, 10(1): 49-63.

——, 1984. 'Shell Industries at Mohenjo-Daro, Pakistan', in: *Interim Reports Vol. I* (Eds. M. Jansen and G. Urbans), Istituto Italiano Per IL Medio ed Esteemooriente, Roma, 1984, pp. 99-115.

——, 1985. 'Shell working at Mohenjo-daro, Pakistan'. *South Asian Archaeology*, 1983 (Eds. J. Schotsmans and M. Taddei, Naples, pp. 297-344.

Kramer, S.N., 1964. 'The Indus Civilization and Dilmun: The Sumerian Paradise Land Expedition', 6.3:

Kraft, J.C., Belknap, D.F. and Kayan, I., 1984. 'Potentials of discovery of human occupation sites on the continental shelves and nearshore zone'; in: *Quaternary Coastline and Marine Archaeology*, (Eds. P.M. Masters and N.C. Flemming), London: Academic Press Inc., pp. 87-120.

Lowe, D.R., 1975. 'Water escape structures in coarse-grained sediments', *Sedimentology*, 22, 157-204.

Lucchi, F.R., 1995. 'Sedimentological indicators of paleoseismicity'; In: *Perspectives in paleoseismology*, Special Publication No. 6., Assoc. Eng. Geologists, Sudbury, MA, USA, pp. 7-17.

Mackay, E.J.H., 1976. *Further excavations at Mohenjo-daro (1927-31)*, Indological Book Corporation, New Delhi, pp. 582-597.

Mackay, E., 1976. *Chanhu-Daro Excavation 1935-36*, Bharatiya Publishing House, Varanasi, pp. 231-233.

Mahadevan, S. and Nayar, K.N., 1974. 'Ecological of pearl oyster and chank beds. The commercial molluses of India', *ICAR Bull. of the Central Marine Fisheries Research Inst.*, (Eds. R.N. Nair and K.S. Rao), no. 25: 106-121, Cochin.

Mahabharata, Mausalparva, 7.41-42: (Hindi Translation) Geeta Press, Gorakhpur.

Majumdar, N.G., 1934. *Explorations in Sind*, Memoir of Archaeological Survey of India, No. 48.

Marshall, J., 1931. *Mohenjo-Daro and the Indus Civilization*, London: Arthur Probsthain, London, Reprinted in 1973 by Indological Book House, New Delhi.

Mathur, U.B., Verma, K.K. and Mehra, S., 1988. 'Tertiary-Qaternary stratigraphy of Porbandar area, southern Saurashtra, Gujarat', *Special Publ., 11(II)*, Geological Survey of India, pp. 333-345.

Max Muller, F. (Ed.), 1894. *The Sacred Books of the East: The Questions of King Milinda* (translated by T.W. Rhys Davids), Part II, Vol. 36. Reprinted in 1988, Motilal Banarasidass, New Delhi, p. 299.

McCalpin, J.P. (Ed.), 1966, *Paleoseismology*, Academic Press, London, p. 588.

McCrindle, J.W., 1879. *The commerce and navigation of the Erythraean Sea*, Reprinted in 1987 by Eastern Book House, Patna.

——, 1885. 'Ancient India described by Ptolemy', (ed.) R.C. Jain, reprinted in 1985, New Delhi, p. 36.

Menon, P.K.B., Datta Gupta, A.K. and Dasgupta, D., 1961. 'The marine fauna of Gulf of Kachchh Part II-Gastropods', *Journal of the Bombay Natural History Society*, 58.2: 475-494.

Merh S.S., 1992. 'Quaternary sea level changes along Indian Coast', *Proc. Indian Natl. Sci. Academy*, A58, 461-472.

——, 1987. 'Quaternary sea level changes: the present status vis-a-vis records along coasts of India, *IJES*, 14.3-4: 235-51.

Moreland, W.H., 1939. 'The ships of the Arabian Sea about A.D. 1500', *Journal of the Royal Asiatic Society*, 63-74.

Morner, N.A., 1999. 'Sea level and climate: rapid regressions at local warm phases', *Quaternary International*, 60: 75-82.

Nagaswamy, R. and Abdul Majeed, A., 1978. *Vasavasamudram*, State Department of Archaeology, Government of Tamil Nadu, Madras.

Naidu, P.D., 1996. 'Onset of an arid climate at 3.5 Ka in the tropics: Evidence from monsoon upwelling records', *CS*, 71.9: 715-18.

Nair, R.R., 1971. 'Beach rock and associated carbonate sediments on the Fifty Fathom Flat, a submarine terrace on the outer continental shelf off Bombay', *Proc. Ind. Acad. Sci.*, 73: 148-155.

——, 1974. 'Holocene sea-level on the western continental shelf of India', *Proc. Ind. Acad. Sci.*, 79: 197-203.

Nayar, K.N. and Mahadevan, S., 1973. 'Chank resources of India', *Proc. Symp. on Living Resources of the Seas around India*, Central Marine Fisheries Research Institute, Cochin, Special Publications, pp. 672-686.

Obermeier, S.F., Gohn, G.S., Weems, R.E., Gelinas, R.L., and Rubin, M., 1985. 'Geologic evidence for recurrent moderate to large earthquakes near Charleston, South Carolina', *Science*, 227, 408-411.

Obermeier, S.F., 1995. 'Using liquefaction-induced features for paleoseismic analysis', *U.S. Geological Survey Open-File Report*, 94-663. 1-56.

Oldham, R.D., 1926. 'The Cutch (Kachchh) earthquakes of 16th June 1819 with a revision of the great earthquake of 12th June 1897', *Mem. Geol. Survey of India*, Vol. XLVI, part 2, Calcutta, p. 77.

Pandey, D.K., Mathur, U.B., Singh, R. and Bahadur, T., 2003. 'Late Pleistocene Coral-Algal Sediments of Chaya Formation of Mithapur Area, Jamnagar, Gujarat', *JGSI*, 61: 195-201.

Pargiter, F.E., 1904. *The Markandeya Purana* (English Translation), Calcutta: The Asiatic Society.

——, 1922. *Ancient Indian Historical Tradition*, Delhi: Motilal Banarasi Dass.

Patel M.P., 1991. 'Depositional environment of the inland miliolite occurrences of Saurashtra and Kutch', *Proc. of the Quat. Landscape of Indian Subcontinent*, Baroda, 197-118.

Pathak, M.C., Kotnala, K.L., Prabaharan, N. and Sivakholundu, K.M., 1988. 'Disastrous Effects of Transgressing Sea Over Coastal Area – A Case Study of Dwarka and Bet Dwarka', *MAIOC* (Ed. S.R. Roa), Goa: NIO, pp. 58-62.

Pawankar, S.J. and Thomas, P.K., 2001. 'Osteological Differences between Blackbuck (*Antolope cervicapra*), Goat (*Capra hircus*) and Sheep (*Ovis aries*)', *ME*, 26 (1): 109-126.

Pillai, R.S., 1989. *Cilappatikaram*, Tamil University, Thanjavur.

Pinter, N., 1996. *Excercises in Active Tectonics*, Prentice Hall, NJ, U.S.A., p. 166.

Pusalkar, A.D., 1943. 'Historicity of Krishna', *The Glory that was Gurjaradesa* (K.M. Munshi Ed.), pp. 111-127, Bombay: Bharatiya Vidya Bhavan.

——, 1945. 'Dwarka'; in: *B.C. Law Volume 1* (Eds. D.R. Bhandarkar, K.A. Nilkantha Shastri, B.M. Barua, B.K. Ghosh and P.K. Gode), pp. 218-224.

Raban, A., 1984. 'Submerged prehistoric sites off the Mediterranean Coast of Israel'; *Quaternary Coastline and Marine Archaeology* (Eds. P.M. Masters and N.C. Flemming), London: Academic Press Inc., pp. 215-232.

——, 1981. 'Recent maritime archaeological research in Israel', *IJNA*, 10.4: 287-308.

——, 1990. 'Medieval anchors from the Red Sea', *IJNA*, 19: 299-306

——, 2000. 'Three-hole composite stone anchors from a medieval context at Caesarea Maritima, Israel', *IJNA*, 29.2: 260–272.

Raikes, R.L., 1964. 'The End of the Ancient Cities of the Indus', *AA*, 66.2: 284-99.

Rajaguru, S.N. and Guzder, S.J., 1973. 'A Review of research on Quaternary Sea Level changes and archaeological sites in India', *BDCPRI*, XXXIII: 193-208.

Rajamanickam, G.V., 1992. 'Marine Archaeological Exploration Activities from the Centre of Tamil University, Tamilnadu', *Seminar on Marine Archaeology*, (Ed.) N. Kasinathan, Madras: 34-44.

Rajendran, C.P. and Rajendran, K., 2001. 'Characteristics of deformation and past seismicity associated with the 1819 Kutch earthquake, northwestern India', *Bull. Seismol. Soc. Am.*, 91, 407-426.

——, 2002. 'Historical constraints on previous seismic activity and morphologic changes near the source zone of the 1819 Rann of Kachchh earthquake: Further light on the penultimate event', *Seismological Research Letters*, 73.4:470-479.

Rajendran, C.P. and Talwani, P., 1993. 'Paleoseismic indicators near Bluffton, South Carolina: An appraisal of their tectonic implications', *Geology*, 21, 987-990.

Rajendran, K., Rajendran, C.P., Thakkar, M., and Tuttle, M., 2001. 'The 2001 Kutch (Bhuj) earthquake: Coseismic surface features and their significance', *CS*, 80: 1397-1405.

Rajendran, C.P., Kusala R., Vora, K.H. and Gaur, A.S., 2003. 'Odds of a seismic source near Dwarka, NW Gujarat: An evaluation based on proxies', *CS*, 84.5: 695-701.

Ramchandran, C.E., 1974. *Ahananuru in its historical setting*, University of Madras, Madras.

Rao, K.M. and Rao, T.C.S., 1994. 'Holocene Sea Levels of Visakhapatnam Shelf, East Coast of India', *JGSI*, 44: 685-89.

Rao, S.R., 1962-63. 'Excavation at Rangpur and other explorations in Gujarat', *Ancient India*, 18-19: 5-207.

——, 1973. *Lothal and the Indus Civilization*, London.

——, 1979. *Lothal – A Harappan Port Town*, Memoir of Archaeological Survey of India, New Delhi.

——, 1984. 'Submergence of Dwarka is a Fact', *Jnan Jyothi* (Ed. S.R. Rao), Bangalore, pp. 16-26.

——, 1985. *Lothal – A Harappan Port Town (1955-62)*, MASI-78, New Delhi, pp. 614-624.

——, 1985. 'Marine Archaeological Explorations of Dwarka, Northwest Coast of India', *IJMS*, Vol. 16

——, 1987. *Progress and Prospects of Marine Archaeology in India*, NIO, Goa.

——, 1988. 'Excavation of Submerged Ports – Dwarka a Case Study', *MAIOC* (Ed. S.R. Rao), NIO, Goa, pp. 47-53.

——, 1988. 'Marine Archaeological Research in India', *40 years of Research – A CSIR Overview* (Ed. Rajagopal, N.R.), New Delhi, pp. 231-53.

——, 1990. 'Excavation of the legendary city of Dwarka in the Arabian Sea', *JMA*, 1: 59-98.

Rao, S.R., Tripati, S. and Gaur, A.S., 1992. 'A Preliminary Exploration of Prabhasa-Somnath', *JMA*, 3: 13-16.

Rao, S.R. and Gaur, A.S., 1992. 'Excavation at Bet Dwarka', *JMA*, 3: 42-47.

Rao, S.R., 1992. 'Further excavations off Dwarka and Bet Dwarka', *RAMA* (Ed. S.R. Rao), NIO, Goa, pp. 51-59.

Rao, S.R., Tripati, S., Gaur, A.S., Gudigar, P., Sundaresh and Vora, K.H., 1994. 'Underwater Archaeological Exploration of Dwarka and Somnath – Results of 1992 Survey and Problems to Attend', *RURIMA* (Ed. S.R. Rao), NIO, Goa, pp. 113-119.

Rao, S.R., 1999. *The Lost City of Dwarka*, Aditya Prakasan, New Delhi.

Rao, V.P., Rajagopalan, G., Vora, K.H. and Almeida, F., 2003. 'Late Quaternary sea level and environmental changes from relic carbonate deposits of the western margin of India', *Proc. Indian Acad. Sci. (Earth Planet. Sci.)*, 112, no.1; 1-25.

Ratnagar, S., 1981. *Encounters: the Westernally Trade of the Harappan Civilization*, Delhi.

Ratnagar, S., 2001. *Understanding Harappa-Civilization in the Greater Indus Valley*, Tulika, New Delhi, p. 165.

Sahni, M.R., 1956. 'Bio-geological evidence bearing on the decline of the Indus Valley Civilization', *Journal of the Paleontological Society of India*, 1: 101-7.

Sakhawala, M.V. and Shringarpure, D.M., 1990. 'Age of Dwarka beds and subsequent strata at Bet Shankhodhar, Gulf of Katch, Gujarat State', *Mem. Geological Society of India*, no. 16: 111-116.

Sankalia, H.D., Deo, S.B., Ansari, Z.A. and Ehrhardi, S., 1960. *From History to Prehistory at Nevasa (1954-60)*, Poona.

Sankalia, H.D., 1966. 'Dwarka in Literature and Archaeology', *Excavations at Dwarka* (Ansari and Mate), Poona.

——, 1974. *Prehistory and Protohistory of India and Pakistan*, Bombay.

Sarkar, H., 1953. 'Fish-hooks from the Indus valley', *Journal of Asiatic Society, Science*, XIX: 133-39.

Saucier, R.T., 1991. 'Geoarchaeological evidence of strong prehistoric earthquakes in the New Madrid (Missouri) seismic zone', *Geology*, 19, 296-298.

Schmid, E., 1972. *Atlas of Animal Bones*, Amsterdam: Elsevier.

Schoff, W.H., 1974. *The Periplus of the Erythraean Sea, Travel and Trade in the Indian Ocean*, Delhi.

Seed, H.B. and Idriss, I.M., 1983. 'Evaluation of liquefaction potential using field performance data', *Jour. Geotech. Eng.*, 109, 458-482.

Sharma, G.R., 1969. *Excavations at Kausambi 1949-1950*, MASI No. 74, New Delhi.

Shastree, K.K., 1988. 'Where Was Dwarka ?' *MAIOC* (S.R. Rao, Ed), NIO, Goa, p. 25.

Shastri, H.N., 1936. *Annual Report of the Department of Archaeology*, Baroda.

Shinde, V.S. and Thomus, E., 1993. 'A Unique Harappan Copper Fishhook from Padri, Gujarat', *ME*, XVIII: 145-147.

Shinde, V., Gupta, S. and Rajgor, D., 2002. 'An Archaeological Reconnaissance of the Konkan Coast from Bharuch to Janjira', *ME*, XXVII (1): 73-82.

Sila, Tripati and Gaur, A.S., 1997. 'Stone Anchors from Sindhudurg-west coast of India', *IJNA*, 26.1: 51-57.

Sila, Tripati, Saxena, M.K., Sundaresh, Gudigar, P. and Bandodker, S.N., 1998. 'Marine archaeological exploration and excavation of Vijaydurg – a naval base of the Maratha Period, Maharashtra, on the west coast of India', *IJNA*, 27.1: 51-57.

Sila, Tripati, Gaur, A.S., Sundaresh, Gudigar, P. and Bandodker, 1998. 'Historical Stone Anchors from Vijaydurg, Maharashtra, West Coast of India', *BAIMA*, 22(1&2): 1-8.

Sila, Tripati., Gaur, A.S., Sundaresh and S.N. Bandodkar, 2001. 'Shipwreck exploration in Sunchi reef in Goa waters, west coast of India', *WA*, 32.3: 357-69.

Sims, J.D. and Garvin, C.D., 1995. 'Recurrent liquefaction induced by the 1989 Loma Prieta earthquake and 1990-1991 aftershocks: Implications for paleoseismicity studies', *Bull. Seismol. Soc. Am.*, 85, 51-65.

Singh, G., 1971. 'The Indus Valley Culture, Archaeology and Physical Anthropology', *Oceania*, 6.2: 177-189.

Somayajulu, B.L.K., Boecker, W.S. and Goddard, J., 1985. 'Dating indian corals by U-Th decay series method', *Quat. Res.*, V. 24: 235-39.

Sordinas, A., 1984. 'Quaternary shorelines in the region of Corfu and adjacent islets, Western Greece', *Quaternary Coastline and Marine Archaeology* (Eds. P.M. Masters and N.C. Flemming), London: Academic Press Inc., pp. 335-344.

Soundara Rajan, K.V., 1994. *Kaveripattinam Excavations 1963-73: A port city on the Tamilnadu Coast*, Archaeological Survey of India, New Delhi.

Souter, C., 1998. 'Stone anchors near Black Fort, Galle, Sri Lanka', *IJNA*, 27.4: 331-342.

Sridharan, K., 1982. *Maritime history of India*, Publication Division, Government of India, New Delhi.

Srinivasan, S., 1984. "Prabhasa or Prabhasa Mahatmya" in Aspects of Indian History & Culture, (Eds.) C.E. Ramachandran and K.V. Raman, New Delhi.

Srivastava, K.M., 1985. 'Bahrain-Indus Valley Connection', *Khaluj Times*, 23 August 1985.

Stanley, D.J., 2001. 'Dating modern deltas: Progress, Problems, and Prognostics', *Ann. Rev. Earth Planet. Sci.*, 29, 257-294.

Stiros, S. and Jones, R.E. (ed.), 1996. *Archaeoseismology*, British School at Athens, p. 268.

Stuiver, M., Reimer, P.J., Bard, E., Beck, J.W., Burr, G.S., Hughen, K.A., Kromer, B., McCormac, F.G., V.D. Plicht, J., and Spurk, M., 1998. *Radiocarbon*, 40 (3), 1041-1083.

Subbarao, 1958. *Personality of India. A study in the development of material culture of India and Pakistan*, M.S. University, Archaeology Series 3, Baroda.

Sundaresh, Gaur, A.S. and Nair, R.R., 1997. 'Our Threatened Archaeological Heritage: A Case Study from Tamil Nadu Coast', *CS*, 73 (7): 593-98.

Sundaresh and Gaur, A.S., 1998. 'Archaeology of Bet Dwarka', *ME,* XXII (2): 77-86.

Sundaresh, Gaur, A.S., Gudigar, P., Sila Tripati, Vora, K.H. and Bandodkar, S.N., 1999. 'Stone anchors from Okhamandal area, Gujarat coast India', *IJNA*, 28.3: 229-252.

Sundaresh, Gaur, A.S., Sila Tripati, Gudigar, P. and Bandodkar, S.N., 2002. 'Stone anchors from Bet Dwarka island, Gujarat Coast', *BAIMA*, 26: 43-50.

Talwani, P. and Schaeffer, W.T., 2001. 'Recurrence rates of large earthquakes in the South Carolina coastal plain based on paleoliquefaction data', *Jour. Geophys. Res.*, 106, 6621-6642.

Talwani, P. and Gangopadhyay, A., 2001. 'Tectonic framework of the Kachchh earthquake of 26 January 2001', *Seism. Res. Lett.*, 72, 336-345.

Technical Report, 1985. *Oceanographic Studies off Sutrapada*, NIO, R.C. Bombay, pp. 7-8.

Technical Report, 1992. *Marine Archaeological Exploration off Dwarka and Somnath Waters,* NIO, Goa, pp. 6-7.

Technical Report, 2000. *Marine Archaeological Explorations off Dwarka, Bet Dwarka and Somnath, Phase-II,* NIO, Goa.

Technical Report, 2001. *Marine Archaeological Explorations off Dwarka, Bet Dwarka and Somnath, Phase-II,* NIO, Goa.

Taylor, P., 1976. *Marine Archaeology,* London, p. 192.

Thapar, B.K., 1991. 'Recent archaeological discoveries', *Problem and Prospects in Cultural Heritage of Indian Village* (B. Durrans and T.R. Blurton, Eds.), pp. 1-9, London: British Museum Occasional Papers, No. 47.

Thomas, P.K. and Joglekar, P.P., 1995. 'Faunal Studies in Archaeology', *Quaternary Environments and Geoarchaeology of India* (S. Wadia, R. Korisettar and V.S. Kale, Eds.), pp. 486-514, Bangalore: Geological Society of India.

Tripathi, A., 1996. 'Dvaraka in Literature and Archaeology, *ME,* XXI (2): 49-58.

Tuttle, M.P., Law, T., Seeber, L. and Jacob, K., 1990. 'Liquefaction and ground failure induced by the 1988 Saguenay, Quebec earthquake', *Canadian Geotechnical Journal,* 27, 580-589.

Tyson, R.V., 1995. 'Sedimentary Organic Matter, Organicfacies and Palynofacies', Published by Chapman and Hall, 615.

Vats, M.S., 1975. *Excavations at Harappa,* Bhartiya Publishing House, Varanasi, pp. 107, 332.

Vaz, G.G. and Banerjee, 1997. 'Middle and late Holocene sea level changes in and around Pulicat Lagoon, Bay of Bengal, India', *Marine Geology*, 138: 261-271.

Vishnu Puran, 5.23.13: (Hindi Translation), Geeta Press, Gorakhapur.

Vora, K.H., Naik, D.K., Ganeshan, P. and Moraes, C.N., 1991. 'Offshore Extension of Gomati River, Dwarka', *JMA,* Vol. 2: 32-38.

Vora, K.H., Gaur, A.S., David Price and Sundaresh, 2002. 'Cultural Sequence of Bet Dwarka Island Based on Thermoluminescence Dating', *CS,* 82.11: 1351-56.

Warmington, E.H., 1928. *The Commerce between Roman Empire and India,* Cambridge.

Watelin, L. Ch., 1934. *Excavations at Kish,* IV, Paris, pp. 25-26.

Wheeler, R.E.M., Ghosh, A. and Deva K., 1946. 'Arikamedu: an Indo-Roman Trading Station on the East Coast of India', *AI,* no. 2: 17-124.

Whitehouse, D., 1970. 'Excavation at Siraf', Third Interim Report, Iran, VIII: 1-17.

Woodcock, G., 1966. *The Greeks in India*, London.

Wreschner, E.E., 1984. 'The submerged neolithic village "Newe Yam" on the Israel Mediterranean Coast', *Quaternary Coastline and Marine Archaeology* (Eds. P.M. Masters and N.C. Flemming), London: Academic Press Inc., pp. 325-334.

Index